Copyright: *Bolton Evening News*

THE FORGOTTEN FIFTEEN

How Bury triumphed
in British football's worst year

JAMES BENTLEY

SilverWood

Published in 2015 by SilverWood Books

SilverWood Books Ltd
14 Small Street, Bristol, BS1 1DE, United Kingdom
www.silverwoodbooks.co.uk

ISBN 978-1-78132-424-0 (hardback)
ISBN 978-1-78132-425-7 (ebook)

British Library Cataloguing in Publication Data
A CIP catalogue record for this book is available from the British Library

Set in Sabon by SilverWood Books
Printed by Latimer Trend on responsibly sourced paper

For my dad Graham,
who first took me to Gigg Lane in 1988,
and my mum Bridget,
who's had to put up with twice the silliness ever since.

This book is also dedicated to the memory
of Keith Freeman. Friend of the Fifteen
and Bury fans everywhere.

Information

For ease of reference, all clubs and stadiums are referred to as they were named in the 1980s. For instance, Wimbledon are the club which played at Plough Lane and Scunthorpe play at the Old Show Ground.

The Football League Structure and its mid-80s equivalent are as follows:

1985 name	2015 name
Division One	FA Premier League
Division Two	Football League Championship
Division Three	Football League One
Division Four	Football League Two

Articles, television programmes and other outlets that are quoted are done so in single quotes, 'like this'.

Interviews conducted especially for this publication are quoted in double quotes, "like this".

Foreword by Alastair Campbell

Why on earth is a Burnley fan writing the foreword for a book about Bury?

Until I learned about the nature of this project, I'd have thought that this was a very reasonable question to ask too. But I've been asked to introduce the story of Bury's promotion from the Fourth Division in 1985 because it's a tale with a claret and blue strand running right through it.

I knew that Martin Dobson had left Turf Moor for the player-manager's job at Gigg Lane over the Easter of 1984, but at the time I was much more preoccupied with my own team slipping further down the league ladder. As reigning Football League champions when I first went to watch them aged five in the early 1960s, twenty-five years later we had to win our last match of the season to stay in it. Burnley fans know the story of that survival inside out – and we know that 1984/85 was the season we slipped into the basement for the first time as Bury climbed above us into the third tier.

Dobson has always been one of my favourite Burnley players, unquestionably the most elegant footballer I've ever had the privilege of watching. He's one of the few constants in my ever-changing 'best ever' team, and although I knew that Bury was one of the teams replacing us following our relegation, I didn't know the circumstances under which his squad had achieved promotion. Now, I do, which is why I am pleased to write the foreword to this account of an important season in Bury's history which will help ensure Dobbo gets the recognition he deserves.

Frank Casper is another hero of my teenage years, and the partnership which he and Dobson showed on the field as players was put to formidable use in management at Bury when Frank became Dobbo's assistant. We might have been diving towards near-oblivion at Burnley, but the principles which had brought about our First Division title win in 1960 were being put to good use at Gigg Lane. It's hardly surprising given that a member of that title-winning squad, Ray Pointer, was also on board at Gigg Lane coaching Bury's youth team.

Another ever-present in my team of all-time Burnley favourites is Leighton James. He too is an important part of this story, as the signing of his old teammate was Dobbo's first masterstroke that would lead to Bury's success. But what was also remarkable was how the foundations on which the new player-manager was building already had 'Made in Burnley' stamped upon them, with the solid dependency of Terry Pashley at the back and the midfield engine room of inspirational captain Joe Jakub, who'd both begun their careers with us, already on Bury's playing staff. Kevin Young, who came through our youth system and so knew all about what's come to be known as 'the Burnley way', would emerge as another important signing before the promotion season began.

To go with Dobbo's elegance was his intelligence, which is how he came to get the best of a squad that included future Claret Winston White, who was as dazzling a presence on the right wing as Leighton James was on the left. We'd been casting envious glances at a goalscorer in the mould of Craig Madden for years, and together with Wayne Entwistle, who'd also play for us in the future, Bury had goals. They could also keep them out thanks to 'keeper David Brown's command of his area, the towering John Bramhall and shrewd signings by the new manager, like Andy Hill and Trevor Ross.

After Burnley's fall to the foot of the league from the top in those twenty-five years, we clambered our way back into the top flight in both 2009 and 2014. It's an example that it can be done. Stories like ours, and Bury's from 1985, are why people love football.

It's also why football plays such an important role in the community in small but proud towns. Burnley is the smallest town to have a team which has won the championship at the highest level of English football and we continue to boast the highest ratio of population to attendance at matches. Bury have won the FA Cup twice, the first time being in the inaugural final of the 20th century, and the second, three years later versus Derby County, by a record 6–0 winning margin which will almost certainly never be surpassed. Our clubs are a central point of the community, and a big part of securing the future for clubs like Bury, living so close to some of the biggest footballing brands in the world, is to make sure that the importance of their past is understood.

The 1985 promotion is an overlooked but important part of that past, and it is a story which deserves to be told once more.

Alastair Campbell
London, December 2014

Prologue

On 1 May 2010, the BBC's *Football Focus* programme came live from the Valley Parade stadium in Bradford. Two of the empty stands at the ground looked colossal on the small screen, which served as a shuddering reminder of what can happen to clubs if they live the Premier League dream but the money runs out. The Bantams had been relegated from the top flight only nine years before, but, after slipping into the bottom tier in 2007, had been plying their trade against the likes of Aldershot, Rochdale and Barnet. It was a far cry from those heady days at the turn of the millennium when Liverpool, Arsenal and Manchester United came to town.

Ordinarily, the decision to broadcast BBC1's weekly Saturday lunchtime football fix from a stadium that hosted basement level football would be an odd one. But this afternoon it made perfect sense. It marked Bradford's last home game of the season, an occasion when the club's supporters come together to mourn the deaths of fifty-six spectators who perished in a fire at the ground on 11 May 1985. This afternoon, twenty-five years on, was the closest home game to the anniversary of the appalling tragedy.

After the programme had ended and the corporation's cameras were being packed away in Yorkshire, Bury were preparing to host Torquay United at Gigg Lane in the penultimate game of their bottom tier season. It had been a campaign of mixed fortunes so far for the Shakers; after missing out on promotion by a single goal the previous season, they had struggled to find consistency as they dealt with the hangover and some excellent performances had rubbed shoulders with some absolute dross. A play-off place was still a possibility but a win against the Devonians was imperative.

Also on the agenda on the same afternoon was the culmination of Bury's one hundred and twenty-fifth anniversary celebrations. Much had been made of this milestone in the preceding nine months, with the club wearing a home shirt in the colours that the Shakers had worn before they were even known as the Shakers for one last season, together with a new crest designed to go on the chocolate and blue halved tops. A mark of the inconsistency that had dogged Bury all season had come the week before though, when, on the exact date 125 years after the club was formed in The White Horse pub, Bury collapsed to a passion-free 2–0 defeat at Lincoln's Sincil Bank.

To mark the club's birthday on the afternoon of the Torquay game, Bury had invited a clutch of former players back to Gigg Lane where they would be introduced on the pitch at half-time. There appeared to be little rhyme or reason in the selection process that each ex-footballer fulfilled; it merely seemed to be that if you had played for Bury in the past, the club claimed that it would be great to have you along. Sixteen former players took the applause from a sparse crowd in what proved to be the high point of the afternoon, as Bury disintegrated in the second half and shipped two further goals without reply, having gone in at the break already 1–0 down.

After the final whistle, I did what I do after every game: I went to the social club for a pint and some post-match analysis. Though it had undoubtedly seen better days before its 2014 makeover, the club remained a favourite place for me. Its threadbare carpet and peeling wallpaper weren't so important when considering it was the match day watering hole for fans who have been going to Bury games for years and who are always expert yarn-tellers.

Aside from the company, one of the things I liked most about the club was the photographs that lined the walls of the Tommy Marshall Lounge (named after the former groundsman and 'Opened by Major G.B. Horridge, 23 December 1982' as the brass plaque always reminded me). I loved the fashions on show in the picture of fans queuing for tickets for the 1980 FA Cup 5th round tie at

Liverpool. I loved the adulation being showered on Craig Madden in the picture of him wheeling away from a packed Cemetery End after another goal towards his record total for the club. I loved the snap of the 1968 team, in glorious plain white shirts muddied brown, after their elevation to the second tier.

As the grumbling at that afternoon's defeat continued around me, there was one photo on the wall which I paid particularly close attention to. Pulled sharply into focus by the BBC1 programme earlier that afternoon, I took in the details of the picture showing the Bury squad that was promoted from Division Four in 1985 and was photographed celebrating in the dressing room. I knew their names, but apart from this picture, which I saw every other week, and occasional mentions of a paper-thin squad from the old guard of supporters and a few snatched lines in fanzines ('Leighton James could hit a forty-yard pass and still find a white shirt') I didn't know a thing about the squad or the season.

I moved my face closer to the glass of the frame to get an almost forensic understanding of who was in the picture. Promotion was only achieved once in the 1980s, the decade in which I was born, and these were the men who had accomplished the mission three years before I started watching Bury.

Perching on the front row are Craig Madden and Andy Hill, their long hair drenched in sweat. Hill looks barely old enough to shave, yet he's raising a green champagne (or, more likely, Pomagne) bottle to his lips. The squad's captain, Joe Jakub, stands tall over the back row with a beaming smile underneath his bristling, brilliant moustache. Trevor Ross is crouching next to Hill and Madden, the camera catching him with his eyes closed in the melee of the dressing room sing-song, making it look like he's undergoing a religious experience in a Pentecostal church.

Assistant manager Frank Casper is wearing the replica shirt for that season, a natty white-with-royal-blue-pinstripe number with the improbable phrase *Spray Breaker* emblazoned across his torso.

Kissing the badge hadn't yet become a clichéd goal celebration in 1985, but you couldn't do that with this shirt anyway as there wasn't a badge to kiss. Replacing the seventies-infused V-shaped badge, but before the town of Bury's proud crest and its accompanying *Vincit Omnia Industria* returned to the left breast, is a simple *BFC* in calligraphy.

Kevin Young stands smiling in the middle of the frame with a scuff of mud on his cheek. Next to him, John Bramhall scratches his right eye. Two men, Gary Buckley and John Kerr, are incongruously wearing smart shirts and ties in among the liniment and sweat of the dressing room environment. Kerr is looking admiringly at Wilf McGuinness, the man who was famously the last pre-Munich 'Busby Babe' and who took over from his mentor in the Old Trafford hot seat for an ill-fated nineteen months in 1969 going into 1970. Now in situ as Bury's physio in the mid-eighties, McGuinness's bald head is free from the wig he'd sometimes wear for solely comic effect.

Wayne Entwistle, the Bury-born lad who had perhaps the best season of his career in 1984/85 in his second spell at Gigg Lane, isn't smiling, but you get the impression he's chuffed with a job well done. Ray Pointer, the coach who was also in his second spell at Bury after starring in the first XI in the 1960s, has a broad smile and hair so thick it would have been the envy of Scott Walker twenty years previously.

Winston White is one of three men who dominate the picture, not least because his is the only black face in it. He's another one holding a bottle with torn foil around its neck, but it's his proto-Usain Bolt stance that really sticks out. Chairman Terry Robinson, at the end of his first full season in the position, also draws attention. He looks every inch like a used car dealer in his long overcoat and has a smile which belies the headaches that this season, and the repercussions of the Bradford fire in particular, will land on him.

Only one man is looking straight at the camera. Player-manager Martin Dobson isn't grinning, but he has the studious look of a quietly satisfied man who's done what he said he would. He's holding a china cup that looks like it would be carrying tea on any other day except today, when its contents are almost certainly white, fizzy and alcoholic.

Just one of these men – Wayne Entwistle – was introduced to the crowd an hour-and-a-half before I was standing in the social club and looking at the picture. Why was this? Why was the remarkable squad not getting the attention it deserved in this twenty-fifth year since they did something special? Football teams are, by their very nature, ethereal: they're brought together to perform and often disbanded just as quickly as injuries, financial constraints and age take their toll. But surely such a small squad, featuring some big names, must have had a core spirit and mentality which bound them tightly together?

Taken in the year that it was, the picture also appealed to the social historian in me because I've always found the 1980s a fascinating decade to look back on. It's a ten-year span that seemed to contain death and destruction at every turn. Even today, thinking of the decade of Culture Club and Wham! brings to mind memories of disasters instantly recalled by the simple trigger of the name where they took place: Zeebrugge, Kings Cross, Clapham Junction, Lockerbie, Piper Alpha, Hungerford and so many more tragedies claimed dozens of lives. Looking at the decade retrospectively, distress never seems far away.

While George Orwell claimed that 1984 was to be the representation of a dystopian future, it always seemed to me that his prediction was twelve months early. He may have been spot on if he was concerned with the miners' strike and the IRA's audacious attempt to assassinate the Prime Minister at the Grand Hotel in Brighton, but for the football fan there's only one apocalyptic year when the game's very future seemed threatened.

Although filmed in 1983, two years before British football's worst year, the video for 'Kicker Conspiracy' by The Fall demonstrates what an appalling state football grounds were in at the time. Made at

Burnley's Turf Moor, it shows lead singer Mark E. Smith marauding through a crumbling, empty stadium that had barely changed since the Clarets' glory days of the 1960s. The press box, in which Smith sits to lip-sync some of the acidic lyrics, hardly looks any different to the rest of the Bob Lord Stand apart from a few rotting, woodworm-ridden desks. His words are those of a man who fell out of love with the game some time ago, as he spits references to 'J. Hill's satanic reign', flair being punished and 'under marble [Bert] Millichip, the FA broods.'

Spectator safety and comfort hadn't been considered in the twenty-three years that had followed Burnley's championship win and the video showed this in abundance. Metal fences topped with barbed wire penned fans into stands and gave the impression of East Berlin in 1965 rather than East Lancashire in what was supposedly a progressive decade. When Neil Kinnock said in the run-up to the 1983 general election 'If Margaret Thatcher wins on Thursday, I warn you not to be ordinary, I warn you not to be young, I warn you not to fall ill, I warn you not to be old,' he may as well have added a note advising people to swerve being a football fan too. The public perception of the game at the time was, in the words of a *Sunday Times* editorial quoted in the June 2015 edition of *When Saturday Comes*, 'a slum sport watched in slum stadiums by slum people'.

Safety matters at these dilapidated grounds came to a some-what inevitable head in the disaster at Bradford, but the archaic amphitheatres up and down the country and across Europe also gave hundreds of hooligans ready-made and readily available missiles at Kenilworth Road in Luton, Stamford Bridge in London, St Andrews in Birmingham and, most significantly of all, Heysel Stadium in Brussels.

Away from football, and even in terms of popular culture the mid-part of the decade seems decidedly grim. Despite the joie de vivre of July 13, when it was '12 noon in London, 7am in Philadelphia' and around the world it was time for *Live Aid*, darkness always seemed to lurk in the shadows. The *Only Fools and Horses* Christmas special from the year is a case in point as it falls oddly flat for the programme that was to become the traditional Yuletide rib-tickler. Titled 'To Hull and Back', it's instantly different to other adventures from Nelson Mandela House because it doesn't feature a laughter track. Shot on grainy film, the story is also much more sinister than the usual wheeling and dealing hooky gear off the back of a lorry as it concerns diamond smuggling and police corruption.

Saturday teatime entertainment was getting in on the act too, with Noel Edmonds's *Late, Late Breakfast Show* putting ordinary members of the public in grave danger for the sake of laughs. A horrific live smash at Santa Pod raceway in 1983 should have seen the end of viewer participation, but it didn't. The 1986 death of Michael Lush, thankfully in an untelevised rehearsal for a stunt due to take place the following weekend, finally led to the show being axed.

Elsewhere, pop music from 1984 and 1985 has an undercurrent of menace, but also an intellectualism, that's rarely been present since. The third and fourth biggest-selling singles of 1984 were by Frankie Goes To Hollywood. In the latter, they tapped into the burgeoning fear of nuclear war in the decade with the chilling 'Two Tribes', which sampled the voiceover from the government's hopelessly ineffective *Protect and Survive* messages. These public service broadcasts made retrospectively laughable claims that a door standing against a wall could withstand a blast, its subsequent fallout and the unforgiving nuclear winter that would follow.

Holly Johnson and his band-mates may have upset celebrity Bury fan Mike Read with their lyrics to 'Relax', the third-most important platter that mattered in 1984, but they understood the futility of superpowers launching warheads at each other ('A point is all that you can score'). The wailing air raid sirens and the actor Patrick Allen's words ('You and your family must take cover') that were sampled in 'Two Tribes' still have the capacity to send a shiver down the spine today.

Making their chart bow just three years after riots in the Toxteth district had threatened the future of their home city of Liverpool, Frankie stood as defiant show-offs who wouldn't be pigeon-holed by their location and their social standing as decided by the London-centric music media. Their top ten hit from 1985, 'Welcome to the Pleasuredome', was astonishingly based on and quoted the poem 'Kubla Khan' by the romantic poet Samuel Taylor Coleridge and bristled with the self-belief of their exciting subterranean culture.

The biggest-selling single of 1984 had none of the bombastic production of Trevor Horn's work with Frankie, but it was written following a news report on a story of human desperation and suffering that was infinitely more unsettling than anything happening in this country when taking a broader, worldlier view. It was, of course, 'Do They Know It's Christmas?' and it was sung by almost anybody who was anybody from inside the covers of *Smash Hits*. Along with a synthesiser enthusiast from Blackpool who rarely committed his voice to vinyl, the former deputy editor of the very same magazine made his chart debut at around this time too. Nothing in the sanitised, minutely choreographed charts of today, not even hip-hop, can compete with the opening line from the first of their many hit singles, 'West End Girls' by the Pet Shop Boys, as sung in Neil Tennant's clipped tones: 'Sometimes you're better off dead/There's a gun in your hand and it's pointing at your head'.

Possibly humming that very same song as I stepped back from the photo in the social club and thought about all things mid-eighties, I felt determined to learn more about the 1984/85 team and their season. I didn't actually know at that time just how many players Bury had used across the season, but subsequently found that just fifteen players started the forty-six games, with one more making a substitute appearance in the very last game of the season. I knew then that these fifteen men had a story and that story was ready to be told.

1982–1984

It would go on to become one of the most iconic football images of the 1980s. Luton Town manager David Pleat, in a beige suit, skips across Manchester City's Maine Road turf on the last day of the 1982/83 season and heads straight for Brian Horton. He tightly embraces his skipper, who would go on to manage the hosts of that afternoon's game a decade later.

Pleat's Luton team started the match in the relegation zone of the First Division below City. Raddy Antic – whose own managerial career would take him to Real Madrid rather than Moss Side – scored the only goal of the game four minutes from time to give his club a late, late reprieve and send the Blues tumbling into the Second Division instead. 'And that's it! Luton Town have survived!' shrieks John Motson at the final whistle as Pleat begins his merry dance. None of the cameras are focusing on John Benson in the City dugout, who took over after John Bond resigned in the February. For the second season in three, *Match of the Day* will be broadcast on the Sunday night rather than the Saturday this weekend, and instantly this nail-biter of a game is promoted to tomorrow night's top slot.

Meanwhile, about twelve miles away from Maine Road as the crow flies, one of the featured games in commercial TV's Saturday night round-up is heading for a glum conclusion. Martin

Tyler, the future voice of the Premier League on Sky TV who would commentate on City's 2012 Premier League win, is perched in a makeshift commentary box on the South Stand side of Gigg Lane for Bury's clash with already-promoted Wimbledon.

It had been a good campaign so far for Bury, who hadn't been out of the top four all season before the previous Tuesday night. A victory for Scunthorpe in a game in hand shunted the Shakers into fifth, and just as Motson had described Manchester City-Luton as 'do or die' as the teams ran out, so the same description could have been applied here. To stand any chance at all of promotion to the third tier, Bury had to beat the Dons and hope that Scunthorpe didn't win in their game against Chester.

Granada TV's cameras had been following Bury manager Jim Iley's preparations for the game all week. Denis Law, who is often erroneously credited with relegating Manchester City's cross-town rivals with that back-heel in 1974, was at the ground in his capacity as a reporter for their programme *Kick-Off*. Daniel Yates was eight years old that day and Bury's mascot.

"My dad walked me earlier than usual through the cemetery to the ground," he now remembers. "I had to buy a brand new pair of football boots, my first pair I think, because I didn't have any at the time. I remember waiting for a while in an old snooker room [later used as the Sponsors' Lounge and Directors' Area] with some VIPs who were older than me, then Denis Law turned up and I remember walking around the empty ground with him for a while and seeing the television crew."

The cameras weren't the only strangers allowed into the inner sanctum of the changing room before the match began. Daniel was allowed to get changed in there too. "I remember walking on to the pitch through the tunnel, leading all the players out and feeling the roar from the crowd. It's something you don't ever forget. Later on in my life, as a young footballer for a local team and my school team, I've run out on to Deepdale and Bloomfield Road, but nothing compares to the atmosphere I felt that day at Gigg Lane. I feel very privileged to have done that on such an important occasion," he continues.

After the traditional pre-match knockabout with the players, Daniel took his seat in the Main Stand for the match. Jim Iley was, of course, in the home dugout where he was accompanied by physio Wilf McGuinness. But with them was another member of Granada Television's team, whose brief was to get reactions to the crucial encounter as it happened.

Years before he became ITV's face of Sunday afternoon top-flight football, Elton Welsby was making good headway in his TV sports broadcasting career at a regional level after switching from radio. "I've reported on a lot of games involving a lot of North West clubs. I've forgotten most of them, but I've never forgotten this one," Welsby now recalls.

It's hardly surprising that the match is imprinted on Welsby's memory. Highlights broadcast by southern broadcaster TVS have been uploaded to YouTube, and watching them now, it's clear that Bury look nervy from the start. When Wimbledon take the lead, Iley tells Welsby that conceding is 'a shocker' and that Bury 'don't need that at this stage of the game, no way'. As the home side struggles to find its feet, it's no surprise that Wimbledon are soon two goals to the good after future Bury coach Wally Downes's strike from the edge of the area.

The Shakers are given a chance to get back into the game just before half-time. Craig Madden wins a dubious penalty when the referee adjudges a handball to have taken place inside the area. Number four Tommy Gore steps up and smashes the ball to the goalkeeper's right, but it's at the perfect height for him and the ball flicks off his hand and over the crossbar. Five years before he became the first 'keeper to save a penalty in an FA Cup final, Dave Beasant broke Bury hearts in the same way he would go on to break Liverpool's at Wembley.

In the second half, the weather takes an appropriately grey

turn, and by the time sub Stuart Parker pulls a goal back for Bury with a scruffy shot from distance, the players are drenched from drizzle. It's a glimmer of hope that's snuffed out in the dying moments of the game, when Paul Fishenden loops the ball over advancing Bury goalkeeper David Brown in the Manchester Road End goal to make it 3–1 to the visitors.

The slow-motion replay of this goal, taken from a camera positioned at the opposite Cemetery End of the ground, is tremendously evocative. It shows part of the 6,000-plus crowd shuffling across the face of the huge home terrace behind advertising hoardings with still-resonant names, getting soaked. They're resigned to the game being up even before this speculative shot hits the back of the net with such little force that it makes the net bulge only gently. One can only imagine the grumbling that went on in the social club that evening by patrons who would have been in the same place after the Torquay game twenty-seven years later. It's a grumbling that will soon be replaced by a dull ache when the realisation emerges through the Sunday morning hangover that the game actually did happen, it wasn't a dream and that Bury will be playing next season in the bottom division again.

So-near-yet-so-far disappointment is a regular feeling for Bury fans, which is why this Wimbledon game is not really anything special in that regard. It is elevated to the top tier of awful footballing memories of supporters who witnessed it, however, by an incident that happened in the dugout. It's also probably the incident that makes Elton Welsby remember the game so clearly.

Despite Bury's game kicking off fifteen minutes after Scunthorpe's – as Bury's 3.15pm starts back then always did in relation to the rest of the Football League, allegedly to allow as much time as possible for drinking in the social club before the enforced closure time of 3pm – Iley received incorrect information that the Iron were not winning against Chester at Sealand Road. The manager leapt from the dugout and began doing a celebratory dance through the rain down the touchline, before shaking hands with his opposite number Dave Bassett.

22

"It was pandemonium in the stand," says Elton. "My producer was in the outside broadcast unit, shouting, 'What the f***'s he doing?' down my earpiece at me. Wilf McGuinness told me to get out there and pull him back down to earth," he laughs.

By the time it was discovered that the Chester goal was a fabrication, it was too late. There was to be no way back for the Bury team and they missed out on promotion by two points. "Jim had an infectious love for Bury, he loved his time there. He loved his teams playing on that brilliant Gigg Lane pitch, but he also knew the opposition loved playing on it too. He asked me after the game 'Did I look a berk?' and I reassured him that he didn't. He looked broken. I didn't have the heart to say anything," Welsby concludes.

In this age of smartphones, mobile Internet, social media and instant access to information as it happens, it seems inconceivable that such an error of judgement could be made. But it was, and with it came the cementing of Jim Iley's reputation in the annals of the club. His achievements in getting his side to a position where they were a game away from promotion have been largely forgotten. The jig in front of the Main Stand hasn't been.

Before arriving at Gigg Lane in the 1980 close season, Iley had had a successful playing career as he made over 550 Football League appearances for Sheffield United, Tottenham Hotspur, Nottingham Forest, Newcastle United and Peterborough United. Then, on moving into management, he took the reins at the Posh (where he acted as player-manager) and then Barnsley before crossing into Lancashire and joining Blackburn Rovers.

The memories of supporters who saw his Rovers teams aren't particularly flattering, such as those from Gordon Snape who was a regular when Iley arrived in 1978. "I recall those times at Ewood being a bit of an ordeal. We had had Jim Smith as manager for nearly three years. He was well-liked and was being successful before he defected to Birmingham. That was followed by a very frustrating spell when the team just couldn't keep up the achievements that we had under Smith, with John Pickering and then Jim Iley in charge. We rapidly went back down to Division Three again before Howard Kendall steadied the ship and brought us back up.

"The fading memory of Jim Iley for Blackburn fans is rather negative. It's a feeling that he was out of his depth at the time. Maybe he was just unlucky and I'm doing him an injustice, but football fans are not renowned for their patience," he says.

It's a view shared by Michael Taylor, the chairman of Downtown Manchester in Business and lifelong Rovers fan, who stood as the Labour candidate in Hazel Grove for the 2015 general election. "For Blackburn Rovers supporters in the early part of the 2010s, shouting for the manager to be sacked was a Pavlovian response. 'Kean out, Kean out' was heard at every home game. But Steve Kean only inherited the title once held by Jim Iley of the most unpopular Rovers manager in living memory. I was only a kid when he managed, but I still remember the disgruntlement and unhappiness at his style of play and miserable demeanour. Rovers legend Simon Garner said that he was 'a very dour, very down-to-earth Yorkshireman with absolutely no sense of humour. Compared to Iley, Howard Wilkinson was like Ken Dodd'," Taylor says.

Simon Garner would also level accusations of bizarre training practices at Iley that were echoed by former Bury players and also Roy McDonough. The former Colchester striker wrote in his blustering autobiography *Red Card Roy* that the warm-up on the training pitch when he played under Iley at Exeter, such as it was, was a game of hide-and-seek. In an interview with the BBC's *Late Kick Off North West* in 2012, Neville Southall confirmed that murky mornings at Lower Gigg followed a similar pattern. 'We were all standing in the middle of the pitch and he said 'Last one out of sight'. We had to climb over fences and go behind a bush and hide. There was no warm-up, just last one out of sight or touching all four goalposts as quickly as possible,' he remembers.

Popular Scouse striker Steve Johnson made his final appearance for Bury after five years at the club in the Wimbledon game. Jim Iley's last instruction to him as he left the dressing room that afternoon was caught on Granada's cameras: a jabbed thumbs-up accompanied by an intent stare and the simple word 'Johnno!'

"He was a nice fella, but training wasn't the best. We just ran and ran, sometimes we didn't even kick a ball which is all I wanted to do," Johnson now says over a coffee in a Bury town centre cafe. He also quashes rumours, albeit with a smile, that when Southall signed for Bury in 1980, Iley eventually banned him from training with the rest of the squad because the outfield players got despondent at the new 'keeper stopping everything which was thrown at him.

Craig Madden takes a similar view to Johnson about his former gaffer. "I felt quite sorry for Jim. I don't want to be disrespectful to him because I quite liked him. The game had possibly moved on a bit and he didn't have the necessary current thinking on it even though he was a great player himself," he says.

Like every other player who turned out for the Shakers that afternoon against the Dons, Steve Johnson groans at the mention of it. "The Wimbledon game? Pass. It was a horrible, horrible feeling after we'd been in the top four all season and only dropped out in the midweek before the game. Jim got the news from an apprentice that Scunthorpe weren't winning and we were up, but of course it was wrong. It was a horrible feeling that we took into the summer, even me personally after I moved to Rochdale. We blew it," he sighs.

It's an opinion that Bury's goalkeeper that afternoon, David Brown, agrees with. "We were nervous, obviously, but Wimbledon were already promoted. We thought they'd be thinking of the beach. We only lost narrowly to them at Plough Lane that season, 2–1, so we had a degree of confidence and we took the game in our stride, but we froze and a few decisions went against us. Unfortunately they weren't thinking of the golf course and they beat us easily," he says.

As well as being a significant afternoon in the careers of the Bury squad, the match was also a significant afternoon for Martin

Tyler. That seat on a rickety piece of scaffolding in the South Stand was the last position from which he commentated on a game as a member of Granada's staff based at Quay Street in Manchester. "I moved to ITV's central 'pool' of commentators after that game and got farmed out around the country rather than just concentrating on the North West," he now remembers.

"I felt sorry for Jim Iley. He was extremely helpful in the run up to the match and he'd had a good career playing the game too, so he understood it. Everything just went wrong for his Bury team that afternoon. Wimbledon weren't a bad side – they'd won the league after all – but on the day Jim's side wasn't good enough to beat Dave Bassett's. I remember when Wimbledon went two up, Elton asked Dave what the difference was between the two sides. In his typical North London style, Dave just said 'Two goals, mate.' He didn't want the intrusion, but Jim tried to work with us.

"It was a day of unmet expectation. Craig Madden had a difficult day and maybe if Bury had scored that penalty then it could have been different. I could see how upset the players were after the final whistle, but when the news of Manchester City's relegation broke I was told to get one of their players back to Quay Street for an interview. So rather than talking to John Breckin in the dressing room at Bury, my last action as a Granada employee was to get Paul Power into the studio for that night's show," Tyler remembers.

The inevitable hangover of such a spirit-crushing, snatched sense of success followed through for Bury into the following season. Despite starting the season well, confidence plummeted and never really recovered after an autumn night at Upton Park in East London, when Bury travelled to West Ham in the second leg of a second round League Cup tie. After a narrow 2–1 defeat in the first leg at Gigg Lane, hopes were high that an upset in the chilly late-October air might not be totally off the agenda.

Craig Madden certainly thought so. "I wasn't playing that night because I had a hamstring injury after I'd scored in the first leg. I remember taking my seat in the dugout and turning to Wilf and saying 'I've got a really good feeling that we could get something tonight.' I turned back and we were 1–0 down!" he laughs.

"I broke my thumb the day before the game," explains David Brown. "Clubs like Bury didn't have another goalkeeper in those days because of the cost. Money was tight so they tended to employ one goalkeeper and had an amateur as a reserve.

"I had to play and the history books will show that we lost 10–0. It was devastating for both me and the rest of the team," he says with a note of hurt still traceable in his voice. "Some top division clubs have a plan against lower division sides in cup competitions. West Ham just said 'We're better than you and we're going to show it' which is what they did with Tony Cottee getting his four goals," he says.

West Ham did indeed show their class that night. A star-studded team ran Bury, in their yellow change strip, ragged. A kind soul has uploaded all ten goals to YouTube and the difference in class of players such as Sir Trevor Brooking and Alan Devonshire is blatantly, almost offensively, apparent in a similar way to Leeds United's showboating versus Southampton in 1972. Watching it online as a Bury fan over thirty years later, you almost want to harry the side off the pitch to protect them from the metropolitan bullies.

Terry Pashley had joined Bury in the summer before the game and started at left back. "Paul Gardiner was on the other side and was given an awful time by Brooking and Devonshire. I was thankful that I was on the left because I just had a very young Paul Allen to deal with who didn't do much. They were so good, though, I even applauded their fifth goal," he says.

As was frequently the case, it fell to Wilf McGuinness to ease the broken hearts that the match caused. In an anecdote that takes pride of place in his after-dinner routine, Wilf reportedly told the players 'At least we were consistent, lads. Five goals in the first half, five in the second.'

Following the national ridicule that a 10–0 defeat brings with it, Bury's 1983/84 season ambled numbly along with little sense of purpose. Promotion became mathematically impossible weeks before the final day of the season, negating any repeat heartache of the previous campaign. Paul Hilton, who played at the back in the catastrophic loss at Upton Park, bizarrely joined the Hammers for £85,000 in February 1984. Iley would tell the *Bury Times*, with a certain degree of prophecy, that 'it could well turn out that this transfer will cost me my job.'

Two weeks after Hilton signed for the Hammers, the boss was sacked after one win in nine dismal games. "I think Iley did a good job when you look at the resources he had," remembers Bury fan Malcolm Parr today. "He got us within two points of promotion but unfortunately it ended badly and publicly for him and I don't think the fans ever really forgave him for it. Looking back, I think he'd taken the club as far as he could on the budget available to him and I think a change was needed. The result at West Ham had made us a national laughing stock too, but I've met Jim in the time since he was manager at Bury and he's a true footballing man who, as well as being very knowledgeable, is very nice too," he continues.

Wilf McGuinness took temporary charge of the squad and won his first game against Hartlepool 3–0. The youngster he introduced to the squad, Chris Cutler, grabbed his first league goal in the game, but former Manchester United manager McGuinness made it clear that he didn't want this particular hot seat and stepped aside a month later to join the new player-manager's backroom staff. That player-manager was Burnley's Martin Dobson, who had most recently been playing under John Bond, who by then had been appointed to the top job at Turf Moor and was setting about leaving his indelible mark on the club.

"I came in March 1984 and it was the ideal time. I felt that John Bond wanted me to go, and the timing was right as Bury were struggling. I took over with about eight or nine games to go so it gave me the chance to assess the squad and to see where I wanted to make changes," Dobson now recalls.

"We all knew Martin, he was an ex-England international, of course," says David Brown. "I only had to do one thing: keep the ball out of the net. So from my point of view things didn't really change when he took over from Jim Iley. Some people say you need pressure, but Jim never put me under any and neither did Martin. He wanted to play the game a bit more than Jim and I wanted to give him a bit more because of his reputation, but if I played well I was in the team," he says.

With automatic relegation from the Football League to the Conference still three years away, Dobson could afford to be experimental with his selections that followed his appointment. His Burnley fluency had replaced Iley's former Blackburn brusqueness and Bury were about to reap the benefits. It would take patience though, which was something that very few of Bury's townsfolk seemed to have, as on 5 May 1984 only 1,096 of them felt the urge to attend a 2–1 defeat at home to Northampton Town.

The 1983/84 season drew to a whimpering close with a 2–1 win over Swindon Town on 12 May. Only 1,214 people, just 118 more than were at the Northampton game, saw Bury limp to a final position of 15th in the basement.

It's hard to believe just what would happen in the next twelve months.

Summer 1984

The summer of 1984 was notable for two themes which were written through those hazy, crazy days like the name of a seaside town through a stick of rock: politics and sport.

As Martin Dobson was starting to collect his thoughts and organise his squad for his first full season in charge of Bury, the country was in the grip of industrial action the like of which hadn't been seen since the previous decade. Men who tunnelled under the ground for coal had downed tools in 1972 and 1974, but whenever the phrase 'miners' strike' is used nowadays, it's always in reference to the dispute between Margaret Thatcher and the National Union of Miners (NUM) secretary Arthur Scargill that ran from March 1984 into 1985.

The national strike was called for by Scargill as rifts developed between miners who wanted to strike and those who wanted to keep working. Those rifts still haven't healed years later. And when a cut doesn't heal, you're left with a word which represents the volatility of feeling between the two groups and which is still used as a term of abuse today: scab.

The pervading image of the strike thirty years later is undoubtedly what became known as the Battle of Orgreave. The coking plant in South Yorkshire was to be the location of a mass picket by thousands of striking miners on 18 June, watched over by a similar number of South Yorkshire Police. Stones were thrown and baton charges were led. "It was like something from the civil war," remembered a former miner called Chris Skidmore in an interview on the BBC News website from 2013.

Ninety-three arrests were made and ninety-five picketers were charged with a variety of offences after the disturbance, but all charges were dropped three years later and a number of lawsuits brought against the constabulary. In June 2015, it was confirmed by the Independent Police Complaints Commission that South Yorkshire Police were not to be investigated over their role in the violent clashes due to 'the passage of time'.

Meanwhile, politics and sport were married with each other in the summer of 1984 at the Olympic Games in Los Angeles. In return for the American boycott of the Moscow games four years previously due to the Soviet-led invasion of Afghanistan, the Soviet Union and thirteen other Eastern Bloc countries weren't present for an opening ceremony that included hover jet packs and dozens of pianists in top hats and tails playing George Gershwin's *Rhapsody in Blue* on grand pianos.

One of the UK's brightest medal hopes at the games was the most controversial. South African runner Zola Budd's British father had been encouraged to apply for her UK citizenship by the *Daily Mail* and the application was completed in short order, despite protests from anti-apartheid groups who claimed that Budd was receiving preferential treatment. On 11 August Zola lined up against her main rival for the 3,000m gold medal, the American runner Mary Decker. It was the athlete on home turf who set the early pace, though just after the halfway point Budd made a break for the lead. The two collided as Budd's foot brushed Decker's thigh. Decker lost her balance and tumbled forward into the runners and on to the infield of the track.

Out of the race, Mary Decker lay on the grass next to the track, sobbing in both the pain of her hip injury and frustration at missing out on a medal in her home games. Budd later led the race at various points, but eventually finished seventh as boos towards her echoed around the stadium in the muggy early evening heat. 'I had to finish the race,' she wrote just days later in the same newspaper that had supported her bid for citizenship. 'What I couldn't endure, however, was the thought of facing all those people on the rostrum. It sounds easy to say, but I knew once the race had started that I was good enough to win a silver or bronze medal. Deep inside me, though, was now a dread of standing on a rostrum, and I began running slower and slower. People passed me and I didn't care – everything had collapsed and I just wanted out,' she added in the piece, which was quoted in *The Guardian* in the lead-up to the 2012 London Olympics.

In football, England's national team weren't having a great time of it as the mid-point of the decade approached. Kevin Keegan's glaring miss against hosts Spain in the second stage of the 1982 World Cup had triggered a downward spiral that culminated in the Three Lions being absent for the 1984 European Championships in France. Despite a campaign in which future Bury striker Luther Blissett scored a hat-trick in a 9–0 demolition of Luxembourg, England finished second in the qualifying group and played a series of friendlies while group champions Denmark were making their way to the finals. There would be no repeat of the hooliganism which blighted England's appearance at Euro 80 in Italy, when tear gas was used to disperse fighting in a first round match against Belgium.

Instead of crossing the Channel in the summer, England instead crossed the Atlantic. A 0–0 draw in Chile brought the curtain down on a three-game tour in a match which was preceded by a 2–0 defeat in Uruguay. But it's the first game of the series that's always remembered.

To commemorate their seventy-fifth anniversary, the Brazilian FA requested a match with England, the founders of the modern game, at the Maracanã stadium. Lancaster Gate duly obliged and Bobby Robson's men showed the comparative new kids on the block how it was done with a stunning 2–0 win. Mark Hateley scored the second goal that's barely recalled, coming as it did after John Barnes's jinking, slaloming run through the home defence and past the home goalkeeper that left him with nothing more to do than slot the ball into the empty net. Barnes's future reputation, and its accompanying heavy burden of expectation, was sealed.

Under the wooden Main Stand at Gigg Lane, unchanged since it was built sixty years previously in 1924 to house flat-capped fans for Bury's return to the top flight, Martin Dobson was plotting. The finish of fifteenth in the preceding Fourth Division campaign was disappointing, but the boss had had plenty of time to analyse the areas he wanted to strengthen after joining the previous Easter.

"When I went to Bury, I knew there'd be players out there from the catchment area of Manchester United, Manchester City and clubs like that," he says today. "I looked for players with ability who were being released and basically in the same position as I was when I left Bolton having not made a first team appearance."

It's undoubtedly the job of the local press to drum up support for the local team, but even the most enthusiastic sports hack would have raised an eyebrow at the headline of John Dyson's story on the back page of the *Bury Times* from 27 July. Following on from the sluggish end to the previous season, to claim that Bury were 'ALL SYSTEMS GO FOR PROMOTION' must have seemed like optimism in the extreme.

But in precisely the same manner as how he comes across in the picture of the promotion squad that used to hang in the social club, Dobson shows how he is driven by an immovable self-belief in the accompanying article. He is described as being 'Quietly confident... as he puts the final touches to his preparation for his first full season at the Gigg Lane helm.' The piece goes on to state that 'Promotion, naturally, is Dobson's number one aim...and the Shakers chief has assembled a new-look squad with the accent on youth during the summer break.'

The man himself is quoted as saying 'I can't guarantee promotion but that's certainly what this club is looking for this season. You've got to think you're good enough to do anything in this league and I'm very confident that the players will do well.'

Today, Dobson remembers the close season well. "I gave the chairman a list of the players that I wanted to keep. There were only seven or eight names on there and I think I panicked him a bit. There was David Brown, the goalkeeper, Terry Pashley and John Bramhall at the back, Joe Jakub in midfield, Winston White on the right and Wayne Entwistle and Craig Madden up front. Chris Cutler was also in there," he says.

In the same newspaper article back in 1984, the manager also asks fans to show patience towards his squad as he searches for the right mix of established players to go with the new faces. 'It won't just happen overnight and we must all pull together from the start. I felt it was important to change a few faces at the end of last season and there's now a more youthful look. The place is bubbling at the moment and the players have worked hard during training' reads his summing-up.

The young players brought in were named as Andy Hill, who arrived on a free transfer from Manchester United ("An exciting signing, as any player arriving from United would be," remembers supporter Malcolm Parr), and Kevin Young who, like the boss, had been released by John Bond at Burnley. After leaving Manchester City before their relegation in May 1983, Bond had pitched up in East Lancashire and set about dismantling the club's notable youth system as the Clarets began their spiral into the basement. It was a journey which would end with the 1960 Football League champions being one game away from the drop into non-league at the end of the 1986/87 season.

More signings, in particular two astonishing transfers reported by the paper in the space of four days, would follow before the season kicked off. But in the meantime, following on from the club's shareholders voting to raise the share capital from £15,000 to £150,000, there was the annual Lancashire Cup to look forward to. At the AGM at which the share capital motion was passed and Ray Jacks and John Smith joined the board, the latter only leaving in the 2010s, Dobson told the assembled shareholders of his 'futuristic approach' to the coming season and its focus on youth.

One player who wouldn't be playing a part would be YTS lad Callum O'Shea, who failed to break into the first team during his time at Gigg Lane. In a sidebar with the headline 'SHAKERS' EVE OF SEASON INJURY PILE-UP' the reader is informed that he won't be starting the pre-season tournament as he is 'recovering from a domestic accident which left him needing thirty-one stitches in a neck wound'. Sinisterly, no more is said about the injury.

To pick up the two copies of the *Bury Times* published on 10 and 14 August as a Shakers fan must have been like a dream. In the first issue of the paper, it was confirmed that Dobson had turned to his former Everton teammate Trevor Ross to add some bite to the midfield. In the second, the gaffer's teammate from Burnley, Leighton James, is named as the second high-profile player to sign on the dotted line for the revolution.

On Ross, who was only twenty-seven when he made the move, John Dyson reports that Dobson had given him 'the opportunity to erase a 12-month nightmare in Greece [at AEK Athens] and resurrect his career in the Fourth Division' and goes on to describe him as 'a hard tackling and aggressive midfielder who complemented Dobson's elegant style in their halcyon days at Goodison Park'. Dobson says in the article that 'Aggression is one of his best qualities and that's something we need, but he is also a fine striker of the ball, a good athlete and a hard worker.'

Despite his reputation as a big name player which went before him, Ross does not see himself in the same light that perhaps Bury fans did when they turned to the back page of the paper on that Friday in August. "Even today when people say 'You've played with such-and-such-a-body' I just think I've done what I've done. I never looked at myself any differently to any other player at Bury when I was there. I never took it upon me to think I was bigger than anyone else. We were equal, all of us," he now remembers.

Ross made his first start in a Bury shirt the day after the newspaper was published, in a 3–2 defeat at Blackburn Rovers in the first game of the Lancashire Manx Cup. Having gone in for the half-time break 3–0 down, the new man got what Dyson described as a 'thumping volley' on his debut before Wayne Entwistle met a cross from the right by Winston White to make it 3–2. Martin Dobson tells the newspaperman that he was 'very upset by the manner of the performance. [The team] let me down badly and it opened my eyes to one or two things'.

The report of the match in the following Tuesday's *Bury Times* is squeezed to the periphery of the page, however, by the news of who would be on the opposite wing to White for the season. 'LEIGHTON GETS DOBSON'S VOTE' runs the splash, with an accompanying picture of Bury's two *galacticos* with their manager and assistant manager.

'Barely seventy-two hours after snapping up the signature of former Everton colleague Trevor Ross, Bury player-manager Martin Dobson has lured an ex-Burnley team-mate into the Gigg Lane fold… Leighton James' reads the tantalising first paragraph. The report goes on to explain how the Welshman was playing in the First Division for Sunderland just weeks before and that he has signed a one year deal with the Shakers. 'Controversy seems to have followed James around…but Bury's player-boss stressed that in his view the player's ability on the field outweighed his outspoken nature,' it continues.

Dobson is quoted as saying 'I remember him well as an outstanding young player at Burnley who won a lot of matches for us and was a great asset to the team. He is a quality player and I believe that if you bring quality to a club, other players will respond to it.'

If the Leighton James that Dobson remembered was the

sprinting winger with flowing strawberry blond hair, still in his honeymoon period with the game and tearing up and down in front of the Longside at Turf Moor, the 1984 version was somewhat different. "I was on the verge of retiring when Martin phoned me and asked me to speak to him, which I did," Leighton now remembers.

To get him to commit to playing at Hartlepool and Halifax rather than Newcastle and Nottingham Forest that he'd only just been visiting with the Rokerites, Dobson presumably had quite a hard sell on his hands to a man ready to hang up his boots. But in presumably the same way that he enthused to the local newspaper about his new signing, Dobson sold the club to Leighton too. "Martin told me his aims and ambitions and I signed," James now says simply.

Like Trevor Ross in his debut in the first game of the Lancashire Manx Cup, Leighton made an immediate impact in his first appearance for Bury in the second game of the tournament, away at Preston North End's Deepdale, the home of the 1888/89 Invincibles. 'LEIGHTON POINTS THE WAY AHEAD' is the headline for the report of a 0–0 described as uninspiring but which featured the 'heartening aspect of the second half contributions made by James'. With Leighton playing in a central midfield role rather than on the left wing, it must have seemed like the flame from that Burnley honeymoon period had been rekindled as 'his constant demand to be given the ball enabled him to dictate proceedings and give Bury a slight edge'.

Despite the rave review for Taffy's debut, the preview for Bury's final game of the season's curtain-raising tournament is understated to the point of negativity. Ahead of the match against the old enemy from up Bolton Road, supporters are described in the *Bury Times* of Friday 17 August as being 'disillusioned', presumably on the basis of the previous season's dismal finish and the defeat and draw in the cup competition so far. In the article, Dobson tells the fans that he understands their concerns before matches at Gigg Lane, as this one would be: 'We need to show the fans that we mean business in our home games. They will respond if the players work hard and commit themselves to the club and that's what I'm looking for against Bolton.'

Less than twenty-four hours before the Bolton game kicked off, Bury faced a strong West Ham side in a friendly, also at home. Rather than it being an act of contrition for the shoeing doled out at Upton Park less than twelve months previously, it was instead a part of the deal which took Paul Hilton from the centre of Bury's defence to the East End of the capital. The visitors, who had finished four places clear of the top-flight relegation zone in the preceding season, kept their class under a tighter rein than in the last encounter between the two sides and ran out 3–1 winners with two goals from Paul Goddard and one from Hilton himself. Craig Madden got Bury's consolation with a thirty-yard volley, but that wasn't the event which made the headline. 'KICK OF SHAME' highlighted the red card handed to Steve Whitton for his possible foolishness in lashing out and booting hard man Trevor Ross in the shin.

The next day, Bury bowed out of the Lancashire Manx Cup after a 4–3 defeat to the Wanderers in front of 1,947 presumably-ardent fans, just 32,553 fewer than Gigg Lane's record crowd in an FA Cup third round tie against the same opponents in January 1960. Wayne Entwistle, Paul Williams and Craig Madden all got on the scoresheet, but the defence was described as 'vulnerable' in the paper in another report squeezed on to the edge of the *Midweeker*'s back page.

The main sports story on Tuesday 21 August is that 'KEY MEN [ARE] IN BATTLE TO GET FIT'. Ahead of the season starting that coming Saturday, Dobson claims not to have been worried by only one win in seven pre-season games. 'I've been generally pleased with our performances and the major concern is the injury pile-up. If we can get four or five players fit as soon as possible we'll be alright. We have several things to sort out from a defensive point of view but on the positive side there are encouraging signs in that we are creating chances and scoring a few goals,' he is quoted as saying.

The players named as being on the treatment table are David Brown, John Bramhall, Trevor Ross, Terry Pashley and Kevin Young. Whatever it was that physio Wilf McGuinness did in the three days between the publication of that midweek *Bury Times* and its Friday big brother worked wonders, as on the eve of the season and under the banner rallying call of 'READY TO JOIN BATTLE', Dobson's fully fit squad is scrutinised.

David Brown's recovery from a foot injury is noted after the North Easterner relinquished his pre-season place between the sticks to new signing from Burnley – and brother of future Manchester United assistant manager Mike – Marcus Phelan. The defence is assumed as being made up of Andy Hill, Terry Pashley, John Bramhall and Dobson himself, while forward berths are handed to Winston White, Wayne Entwistle and Craig Madden. The fiercest competition in the fourteen man squad is in midfield, where Joe Jakub, Gary Buckley, Trevor Ross, Leighton James and Kevin Young vied for the remaining starting places. 'We're aiming for success this season and we'll give it our best shot' are Dobson's parting words.

Also at this late stage, the local newspaper reported how Bury would wear a sponsor's name on their strip for the first time for the duration of the season that would begin the next day. Having received £5,000 for the privilege, Bury would display the title of director Ray Jacks's company's new name in road safety spread across the midriffs of its kit, printed on to Spall Sports' finest polyester.

And so it was that on Saturday 27 August, British football's most troubled season began with Bury taking to the field at Feethams in Darlington, with everyone in attendance at one of the loveliest grounds in the Football League asking '*Spray Breaker*? What does that mean?'

August 1984

As revolutionary football seasons go, it was very nearly a non-starter. Despite all that they would achieve – the contemporary plaudits, the retrospective misty-eyed nostalgia at their style of play, the ultimate prize of promotion – Bury's 1984/85 squad were just ten seconds away from a morale-sapping defeat on the opening day of the season. Craig Madden's snatched equaliser, in front of just 1,441 hardy souls in Darlington's loveable old Tin Shed that backed on to the cricket field, meant that the Shakers at least emerged from the opener with something, however much they might not have deserved it. Described once more in the match report of the *Bury Times* dated 28 August as 'defensively vulnerable', it seems Bury had little on show that would have improved the disillusioned mood that the same paper had accused fans of feeling eleven days previously.

Perhaps as expected, Leighton James was the only Bury highlight, as the press reported he stood head and shoulders above the rest of his teammates. John Dyson apparently had his crystal ball with him in the press box on that balmy afternoon in County Durham though, as he wrote '[James] took on Darlington single handed with constructive approach play and forceful attacking which augurs well for the future once he and his teammates develop greater understanding.'

After starting the game in the first XI himself, player-manager Martin Dobson's post-match analysis was appreciative of his players' efforts but conceding that the defence was at fault for the hosts' goal. His summing up accepts that his side was responsible for making a mistake, but that generally their standard of football was good, and that though Bury had attacked well, he wasn't too pleased with the second half performance.

The report also highlights how Andy Hill hit the bar from a Leighton James corner after just six minutes. Considering that he was making his Football League debut that afternoon, the first of 264 league appearances for Bury, it could have been a Roy of the Rovers-style first bow for the nineteen-year-old Yorkshireman.

Andy was still playing for Bury five years after the promotion, by which time I was a confirmed fan myself. A bluff, no-nonsense type, he was always a favourite of my younger self because of his dependability and stoicism. When I was interviewing former players for the match day programme, though, it always rankled that I was never able to find Hill and commit his memories to a 500 word feature for the magazine.

Andy Hill's 1984/85 season pen picture. (Copyright: Bury Football Club)

It was through a friend of his son Scott that I eventually found Andy. Infuriatingly, when thinking of all those times I wondered where he was, it turned out that he was literally up the road from me in Ramsbottom. On a warm summer's Sunday afternoon in 2012, we met up in the Masons Arms on Bolton Road West where Andy remembered his time at Gigg Lane under Martin Dobson, Sam Ellis and lastly Mike Walsh over a couple of pints.

"I'd been given a free transfer by Manchester United and there were four clubs who were really keen on me: Norwich, Derby, Halifax and Bury. I asked my dad for a bit of advice on where to go. I didn't really want to go to Norwich or Derby because I felt that if I went there then I'd just be in the same position that I was in at United, in the reserves, when I wanted to announce myself to the league.

"So basically, I cut it down to Bury and Halifax and I went and spoke to both of them. I think it was Mick Jones who was manager at Halifax at the time and he didn't really impress me. Luckily, I then went to speak to Martin and as soon as I spoke to him I knew what he was about and that he was my kind of person. There are no guarantees in football but he told me that he thought I was good enough for his first team. I never got that assurance from Mick Jones and I felt that Martin rated me so I signed. Gigg Lane was a better ground than the Shay too," he laughs.

Six years after Hill signed on the dotted line, it was physio Wilf McGuinness's testimonial year at Gigg Lane. In the brochure produced to mark the occasion, Hill had a page in his capacity as Bury's skipper. He writes about his excitement at scribbling his signature on the professional contract placed before him in Dobson's office before he went looking for the man who used to manage his former club. Bury's latest recruit finds the physio, not unreasonably, in the treatment room. Perhaps maybe a touch unreasonably, he was pouring himself a drink. 'After spitting the mouthful of whisky back into the glass through the gap in his teeth,' Hill writes, 'he said "Hello Andy, Wilf McGuinness. Glad you've decided to join us."

Andy goes on to write that it was Wilf who recommended the young defender to Dobson. 'Wilf [told me]…he had seen me play for Manchester United reserves. Imagine me, recommended by someone who had actually managed players like Charlton, Best and Law to name but a few. I felt so proud.'

"I didn't feel as though I'd 'ended up' at Bury after playing for United," he now says. "I was on a high because I was doing what I'd always wanted to. The doldrums just didn't exist, it didn't enter my head.

"In fact, I'd stepped up a level. Unless one of them was coming back from injury and was playing in the reserves, I rarely saw the senior pros at United, but I was with them right from the start at Bury. It was a bit of an eye-opener because when you're not with lads your own age you've got to stand on your own two feet, but I think being at United prepared me for that too," he adds.

"In the dressing room that we had, with the likes of Trevor Ross and Leighton James, it was sink or swim. Eric Harrison, who brought the Nevilles and Beckham and Butt and Scholes through at United, brought me up at Old Trafford and it stood me in good stead. Plus, you look at the team I was in there with lads like Norman Whiteside and Mark Hughes and Graeme Hogg: we all had good careers. That whole 'Class of 92' thing wasn't an accident, it wasn't the first time that Eric produced that calibre of player," he says.

While the training regime under Dobson was undoubtedly different than that of his predecessor Jim Iley, it was another similarity from his first club that enabled Andy to settle in straightaway. "I wouldn't say that Martin, Frank Casper and Ray Pointer did things in what you'd call 'the Burnley way,'" he says. "We had the reputation of playing passing football which they brought in, but it was what I was used to.

"I was doing well at United as an eighteen-year-old and was in the England Youth team, ahead of a lot of other people. I went to Lilleshall with them and did two weeks' training. I got back and Ron Atkinson [then Manchester United manager] asked what I'd been doing. I told him it was all work on this word 'pomo', all about the Position of Maximum Opportunity.

"He said 'What the bloody hell's that?' so I told him it was about me being a full-back and when you're near the halfway line, getting the ball into the penalty area as a 'pomo'. He said 'You're not going there again. I'm having none of my players playing that way,' so with the way that Martin wanted to play, the ethos was already bred into me," he says.

Bury's reputation as a sophisticated passing side that emerged as the season went on wasn't always quite so clear cut. With players like Trevor Ross, the side had a streak to it that could put both feet in where necessary.

"Even Leighton had an edge to him, though he was obviously known more for his silky skills. He was one of those people that, if you got on with him, he was great, but if you didn't, there was no middle ground with him. He was very straightforward and very focused on what he did," Andy says.

"I played forty-three games in the season and I played the majority of them behind him, which helped me along. I knew that if I gave him the ball then he wasn't going to give it away. I could go past him with confidence because he wasn't going to give it away and I was going to get it back. In your first season in the league, that's a massive boost.

"I learned so much from his talking. He was great, probably the catalyst of the side to be honest. Anybody could give him the ball and he'd hang on to it while you were given the time to make your runs. That's probably what Wayne and Charlie [Craig Madden] would say about him too, his delivery was quality.

"I remember the day Trevor Ross signed as well. Most of the players in the squad weren't journeymen, but they'd been at that kind of level for all of their careers. Then all of a sudden Trevor walks through the door and we're getting a First Division player who'd played for Arsenal and Everton. You knew things were changing a bit.

"I've worked in youth development for ten years now and that's actually one of the reasons that it's harder for our kids to make the breakthrough. They don't have the experience that somebody coming from the top like Leighton James or Trevor Ross might have and the good habits that they'll bring with them. They're playing players who have played at pretty much the same level for all of their careers. There were others in the squad who'd played at a higher level too, like Wayne Entwistle at Sunderland and Leeds, which was good for us," he says.

Despite his youth, Andy settled in well at Gigg Lane and made friends among the younger lads and also the senior pros. "We'd have tournaments on the snooker table, which was still in the Sponsors' Lounge, after training. No one really wanted to go home, we all stuck together. There was a drinking culture throughout football in those days so we liked a pint after training too. Me and Gary Buckley would go for a drink at Keith Freeman's place on Bell Lane, but we'd train hard as well. I always remember running with Terry Pashley in the pre-season. I think a lot of the older lads didn't like going back to training. I was only eighteen obviously and he'd be saying to me 'Slow down, slow down, you're like a bloody Rolls Royce,'" he laughs.

"I didn't play for Jim Iley obviously, but I think that Martin brought his own professionalism to the club. Him and Frank Casper were inspiring to work with. Frank had stopped playing by then of course, but you could still see the quality in his left foot during training," he says.

It's tempting to think of Bury's assistant manager back in 1984 taking his sons to the club in school holidays to learn more about what was to become the family business. One of the Casper Juniors, Christopher, would go on to play for Manchester United and Reading before injury ended his career at the indecently early age of twenty-four. A move into coaching would follow at the University of Bath's side, Team Bath, before he returned to Gigg Lane as an employee on the coaching staff himself rather than the son of one. And it was thanks to Andy Hill that he got the role.

"I was appointed youth team manager at Bury after my old Bury teammate from the late-eighties Andy Feeley left the same position," Hill remembers. "The club decided to disband the youth team while I was over in America coaching and they told me over the phone. To cut a long story short, I came back and the team was reinstated after board meetings that went on until 1am, but I resigned in principle at what they'd tried to do. From that, Chris got the job [after which he was eventually appointed as Bury manager in 2005]. Maybe if I'd stayed I could have been Bury manager," he laughs.

Chris Casper wasn't the only youngster going to work with his father at Gigg Lane in the mid-to-late 1980s. The sadly-missed Neville Neville joined the club's commercial department at a similar time and turned to Andy for advice on how his sons should progress in the game. "After I'd become captain at Bury, Nev asked me what Gary and Phil should do when United came in for them, because I'd been there too. He said 'I think I should keep them here, what do you think?' but I told him that if they had a chance to go to United then they should take it. I said that they shouldn't give it up and that if they didn't make it then they could always get into the professional game in the same way I did," he says.

Following on from his debut season, Andy went on to be one of the most dependable squad members for the next five years. It was a time when the players had a greater kinship with the fans too, as he remembers. "After every game, Martin would make us go into the social club and mix with the fans, regardless of the result. It's the only club where I've ever done that. It didn't matter how we'd played or anything, he just wanted us to show our faces. And we did, and that's how we got to know people like Keith Freeman and what made Bury such a friendly club," he says.

Perennial money troubles returned to haunt Bury in 1990 and Hill was one of the first players to depart. "Without wanting to be disrespectful, I'd probably stayed at Bury a little bit longer than I wanted to," he now says. "I got caught up in a situation that didn't really benefit me. I said when I first moved there that I wanted to move up the ladder, and although we got promoted in that first season, we stood still for a while. Because a benefactor like Hugh Eaves arrived, we didn't need to sell anyone.

"Martin was very clever with the players he brought in, though, and the club owes him a debt of gratitude for them. All of the younger players he brought in were saleable assets. I remember

Terry Robinson once being asked who his favourite player was and him saying David Lee, because he knew he would be the one he'd get the most money for.

"I'd had a great six years and I enjoyed my time, but as soon as the money troubles were announced I was out. I did an interview with *Granada Reports* when the announcement was made and I said something like 'Obviously it's a worrying time for us, we've got mortgages to pay and families to feed.' It wasn't like how it is today. You had to put food on the table like the ordinary working man. We weren't badly paid at Bury, certainly not, but I remember it was a bit of a culture shock when I moved to the First Division that the difference in salaries wasn't that great," he says.

The club that Andy moved to was the sky blue cross-city rival of his first club. Initially on loan, the £200,000 fee that followed went a long way to keeping the wolf from the door in the autumn of 1990 that followed a profligate summer which, internationally, was dominated by England's progression to the World Cup semi-final. Domestically, Martin Dobson's successor Sam Ellis spent more than £400,000 on Colin Greenall, Roger Stanislaus, Ronnie Mauge and £175,000 club record signing John McGinlay.

"I think that if Martin had had that kind of money to spend then the club would have been more successful. He would have bought a different kind of player to the ones that Sam bought. Sam tried making his mark and bringing about a bit of a change in our character from Dobbo's team with players like Tony Cunningham," Andy now says.

After making ninety-seven appearances for Manchester City, Andy saw out the rest of his professional career with Port Vale, still in the second tier of the English game, before retiring in 1998. Various coaching roles followed, such as the aforementioned roles with Bury and in the USA, before he arrived at Bacup Borough and their player development process. Andy is now unable to work, which he revealed on his @Hill08Andy Twitter account in March 2015 as he wrote:

'Thanks to all my well wishes I have severe congenital spinal stenosis which has resulted in deep depression but I will keep strong'.

Back in our interview, the memories of his first season in the starting line-up of a Football League team, which culminated in a player of the season trophy, remain clear.

"It was probably one of my happiest times in football, to be fair," he now reflects. "I probably didn't appreciate what the achievement was because I was so young. It's pleasing to think that I was part of a successful team with good players and good senior players too. For me to be voted as player of the season by the fans in my first season at the club was something special really, even with my Bryan Robson haircut of the time," he concludes in the half-light of the snug in the Masons.

A pub divided, the walls host squad pictures, scarves and replica street signs devoted to both sides of the Mancunian football divide that Hill straddled. There's nothing about Bury on the wall, though, or the full-back who now lives nearby and was making his name in 1985.

In the same edition of the *Bury Times* that featured the report of the Darlington game, a preview for the first round, first leg of the League Cup tie versus Port Vale, to be played that night in Staffordshire, appears. Now sponsored by the Milk Marketing Board, the competition that Bury reached the semi-final of in 1962 is billed as a 'big incentive' in the banner headline.

Memories of the ten goals shipped without reply at Upton Park the previous season are still raw in the introduction to the article. 'Now, with at least four new faces in the first team squad, the Shakers will be anxious to establish themselves in the money-spinning competition,' it continues, before outlining just how much cash Liverpool span from their victory over Everton in the Merseyside derby that constituted the 1984 final. While Bury received £2,000 remuneration for that spirit-crushing night in East London, the

Reds received a princely £64,000 for going all the way, based on the 'double-up' method of receiving twice the previous round's payment for progressing through its stages.

The local press view Vale as tough opposition with something to prove to their fans after being relegated from the Third Division last season, while Dobson agrees that the game will be a 'big test' for his men.

As it was, the fight proved just that little bit too much in the first tie of the double header. Despite what the *Bury Times* saw as a strong Shakers defence, it was the pace of Robbie Earle, who scored the only goal of the game after fourteen minutes, which made the difference at Vale Park. As the first half progressed, the paper reports, Bury's cause wasn't helped by an inability to counter attack 'on a night when the defensive qualities of Joe Jakub and Trevor Ross in midfield proved far more valuable than the attacking potential of Leighton James.'

The second half appeared brighter for Bury as the hosts started to lose their imagination when it came to breaking down the visitors' defence, which featured a bossing performance by the player-manager at its heart. Despite getting more and more into the game, Bury's play in the closing stages is described as being eerily reminiscent of that at Darlington just days earlier, but without the late equaliser which would have added some spicy potential before the return leg at Gigg Lane the following week.

Slowly, very slowly, but surely, it was coming together. All that Bury needed was a win.

September 1984

Alongside the usual anodyne answers that their pre-match meal was beans on toast and that their favourite singer was Lionel Richie, one of the things that player profiles in match programmes from the mid-1980s would often teach us is that footballers were a superstitious bunch. It's unclear whether Martin Dobson fell into this category, but if he got out of bed on 1 September and said 'White rabbits!' then it was certainly a good luck charm ahead of that afternoon's game against Halifax Town at Gigg Lane.

In his programme notes before the first home game of the season, Dobson urges caution and reiterates points made in the local press that he can't guarantee success. He declares himself pleased with the pre-season build-up, however, and also plants the subliminal seed that Bury are lucky to have some players at their disposal who could very easily be playing at a higher level as he writes: 'I've warned the new players that playing in Division Four isn't like playing in Division One. Players must motivate themselves in the dressing room, but if all our fans can get behind the team at every available opportunity it will help the players considerably.'

One of those new players took on board his gaffer's words with gusto. 'JAMES SPARKS BURY SUPER SHOW' is the banner headline from the back page of the *Bury Times Midweeker* that features the

50

match report three days later. The introduction from John Dyson takes on a similar effusive tone: 'It was football with a capital 'F' when Bury opened their [home] Football League programme on Saturday,' he gushes.

'They turned the clock back to pre-1966 and all that by fielding two wingers and played the sort of game that those with greying locks remember with affection and that those of lesser years will, hopefully, come to accept as the norm, a marvellously entertaining alternative to the Friday night *Match of the Day* sludge served up by Chelsea and Everton,' he continues.

As the headline suggests, it was one of those wingers who showed his class in the Shakers' first home game of the season, with his scintillating home debut on the left wing earning Leighton James high praise. 'Skill, pace, the ability to cross dangerously from the tightest of situations, shooting power, passing ability and enthusiasm. Yes, James had all that and has set himself a very high standard for the rest of the season. But then so have his teammates' is the assessment in an emboldened standalone paragraph.

Up against future Bury player and later manager Alan Knill, making only his second ever league start having joined the visitors from Southampton that summer, and also future assistant manager Billy Ayre, Bury's three goals without reply came from Trevor Ross, John Bramhall and Kevin Young. Ross's is described as being a fierce shot which evaded all eleven opposition players lined up shoulder-to-shoulder in the goalmouth after the ball was knocked to him from an indirect free kick six yards out. Given how hard Bury's new signing could strike a ball, it's a fair deal that the mind's eye will conjure up images of ducking, scattering and cowering in the face of an Exocet.

Bramhall's first of a quartet of league goals for the season came as a result of a Craig Madden chip to the back post that had the 'permanently warm' hands of visiting goalkeeper Paddy Roche grasping at thin air. Completing the scoring, a second new signing, Kevin Young, hit what sounds like a beautiful effort from twenty-five yards out that scorched the turf and went in off the post. If all was going to plan in attack, it was the beginning of business as usual in defence too, as Dyson describes how David Brown had shrugged off his pre-season injury to be his 'usual, competent self' to deny a host of chances for the visitors.

Even after taking into account relative travelling times for two sets of away fans, the crowd for this game was markedly higher than that for the preceding competitive game at Gigg Lane as excitement about Bury's new squad presumably spread. Those 1,214 fans who saw a lukewarm 2–1 win over Swindon Town in May 1984, which included a goal by Eric Potts, were joined by an additional 500 to see the wizardry of Leighton James and Winston White. While in all probability more would have travelled across the Pennines from the West Riding than up from Wiltshire, the buzz was gathering momentum.

As well as their eating and easy-listening habits, player profile pieces in programmes also told us what our favourite players drove. That way, you could say with a degree of certainty that if you thought you saw Gary Buckley driving a Ford Escort down Manchester Road, whether it would have been him or not. Adjacent to the match report from the Halifax game, we learn, perhaps with a tinge of disappointment, that Trevor Ross and Leighton James each drove nothing fancier than a Fiat Uno in the mid-eighties.

The football club's associate director Patrick Corrigan, who ran the Blackford Bridge showroom which specialised in the Italian model, is described as stepping in to offer a vehicle each to the star men as a way of securing their services for the season. Both footballers are pictured receiving their keys from a beaming Terry Robinson and a pensive-looking Mr Corrigan, who gets his sales pitch in well with his attributed quote: 'The Fiat Uno was voted *Car of the Year* by European motoring correspondents and I can only hope that either Leighton or Trevor will go on to be Bury's Player of the Year. They certainly made good starts,' he says, a fixed grin imaginable on his face.

Even after the good fortune that maybe followed a pinch and a punch on the first of the month, Martin Dobson kept a tight rein on his emotions as he previewed the second leg of the League Cup first round tie against Port Vale that would be played on the same night that the paper was published. Speaking after the Halifax win, he told Dyson: 'This is completely different opposition. We start a goal down and it won't be easy but there's everything to play for. I was very pleased with the all-round display and attitude, but it would be foolish to get too carried away at this early stage. There is still a long way to go and we start from scratch tonight.'

It proved to be a prescient comment as, despite a 2–1 win, Bury crashed out of the competition by virtue of their opponents scoring an away goal to add to their 1–0 win from the first leg at Vale Park. Playing on the Milk Marketing Board being sponsors of the competition, the *Bury Times* sub-editing team ran with the headline 'LOTTA BOTTLE BUT NO EXTRA PINT' to sum up the brave but ultimately futile effort. There was to be no thumping from a top-flight team at the second stage of this season's competition, but that's not to say some cash from a big tie wouldn't have been appreciated. It always would be at Bury, of course, even to this day, but on this night a power cut and, one can only imagine, several dozen quips of "Anyone got 50p for the meter?" meant that there would have been a kernel of dark truth to some of the jokes.

The match report highlights how Bury's bottle showed itself in the last half hour of normal time and the period of extra time that was needed. Special praise was once again doled out to Winston White and Leighton James, though Joe Jakub was also reported to be a persistent driving force. Andy Hill received fulsome praise as he began to nurture his understanding with James: the report raves about his settling into the unaccustomed left back position, which allowed him to make countless overlapping raids. Such darting runs took their toll on the youngster as cramp was reported to have taken hold in the dying seconds.

It was a cross from James which led to Bury's first goal of the evening, a Craig Madden header which brought Bury level on the night after Port Vale had doubled their aggregate lead in the early stages. Sensing that the tie might not be beyond them, Bury launched 'a frenzied bombardment' before John Bramhall was allowed a free run at a Winston White corner kick which culminated in him heading home.

Despite Andy Hill's best efforts with a rasping shot which hit the crossbar with just six minutes of normal time remaining, the Shakers were out: 'If there can be any consolation in defeat, then perhaps Bury's efforts in two highly entertaining home encounters with Halifax and their Milk Cup conquerors will be rewarded by an increased show of public support through the turnstiles in months to come,' concludes the report. Statistics bore out the fact that this was already happening, as factories and playgrounds across the town started to hear more about Dobson's exciting brand of football. An extra 500 people on top of those who saw the Halifax game decided to give this game the following Tuesday a try.

"We were 2–0 down on aggregate at one point and we got back into the tie largely through Winston White's wing play," remembers Bury fan Malcolm Parr. "We really ought to have won even though they got the away goal to beat us, but we were a revelation in the way we now played which was a joy to watch, showing a lot of attitude with it."

Bury's new-found tenacity was highlighted the following Saturday. In a game dominated by the sending off of genial Wearsider Kevin Young, the Shakers returned up the M56 from Chester City's Sealand Road with all three points following a 3–2 win.

The *Bury Times* from 11 September describes how the 'elegant' Young was fined and censured by Dobson for his misdemeanour. The player-manager comes across almost as a Victorian father figure in the story which dominates the back page. He sounds like a strict disciplinarian, albeit one who had a soft centre when the welfare of one of his clan was called into question: 'I have no sympathy with players who retaliate and strike opponents,' said Dobson of Young's head-butt on Peter Sayer. 'Kevin put us in a position which could have cost us the game. He knows it was an indiscretion on his part and he's really disappointed. We feel he was the victim of a bad tackle, but I don't condone what he did. Retaliation is pointless,' said the boss with one eye on karma.

It was Joe Jakub who was the star for Bury in the first away win of the season, scoring the Shakers' first goal that afternoon and also their last. The former sounds like a beauty from John Dyson's description, in which Joe hit 'a superbly flighted chip from the left corner of the penalty area [which] found the far corner of the net'. After some Cestrian pressure, Bury struck a psychological blow by going 2–0 up on the stroke of half-time when 'the constant menace' Winston White chipped a cross from the right which was headed home by Craig Madden.

Young's dismissal ten minutes into the second half roused the Chester team which contained future Bury (and England and Arsenal) defender Lee Dixon. It was his hopeful punt into the Bury area which led to a melee in which they grabbed their first, but Jakub restored Bury's two-goal cushion with eleven minutes to go after he put the final angled drive to a move involving Dobson, White and Ross. Chester's second consolation, from Owen Brown who beat his namesake David with a downward header, wouldn't matter in the final analysis.

Sealand Road was a ground that Joe Jakub would get to know well. After leaving Bury for AZ Alkmaar in Holland in 1986, it was Chester where he made his return to the Football League two years later. I already had a phone number for Joe after I initially found him in 2007 for a match day programme interview. After I contacted him again and outlined the new, long-form story that I wanted to tell in which he was included, he agreed to meet me.

We met under the Grosvenor Street clock, and as Saturday shoppers

relaxed with a refreshing lunchtime drink in between purchases, it was in the Queens Head in Chester city centre where he remembered his time at Bury and the promotion season that followed the heartache of being part of the team that blew out to Wimbledon in 1983.

"I always remember the promotion because as a player you always remember the good times," he now recalls over a pint. "We had great players like Kevin Young and Leighton James, so were worth it. It didn't really come as a surprise that with lads like them and Frank Casper as the assistant manager we played well," he says.

It's obvious why these former Burnley stars are the first two players that Joe – born Yanek Jakub in Falkirk in 1956 and still sounding very much north of the border – brought to mind. As one of the former Burnley brethren himself, he was a crucial cog with the knowledge that came from being schooled at Turf Moor. When Joe travelled down from Scotland to begin his football career in East Lancashire aged just sixteen, his future player-manager was an established first teamer.

"A manager usually has respect straightaway, but I knew Martin from when I signed for Burnley in 1973. He was the captain when they won the Second Division championship that year and he had my respect from being a teenager. He might look serious in the photo in the dressing room after promotion, but that wasn't the case at all. He had a great sense of humour. Looking at that picture and the people in it again, I can say that Leighton is probably the best player I've ever played with and Craig Madden's probably the best striker.

"I came to Bury just after Burnley had been relegated to the Third Division in 1980. I'd played forty games for them in the top two divisions, and I went to Bury who were ninety-second in the Football League. We had the near miss against Wimbledon under Jim Iley, obviously, and it took us a while to get over it, which led to Martin coming in. When he did, though, he brought in players from a higher level, and when you do that it doesn't take you long before you start climbing the leagues.

"I think that you just get into a groove of winning, and that's what Martin did with us. Even if you don't play well, you can still grind out wins and you're breeding a winning mentality," Joe adds.

Bury's paper-thin squad in 1984/85 suited the desire that Joe and his fellow players had for the game. "I couldn't last in today's game with squad rotations. I just wanted to play Saturday, Tuesday, Saturday, Tuesday. We had an immaculate pitch that was a joy to play on, and although we weren't known as a hard or dirty side, we had lads like Wayne Entwistle who would run through walls for you and was extremely brave, going in where other players wouldn't. We could look after ourselves. We had our reputation as a passing side because of Martin's belief in playing an attractive game and that showed itself in training when all we did was ball work," he says, bringing to mind an instant difference between Dobson and Steve Johnson's memory of training hosted by Jim Iley, which consisted of chasing a ball that had been booted from the halfway line by the former gaffer.

Just twelve months after the promotion was achieved in a season in which he was named in the PFA's divisional team of the year,

Joe in action against Southend United as Craig Madden looks on.
(Copyright: *Bolton Evening News*)

Joe was on his way from Gigg Lane. "It was a brilliant season because promotions are obviously the highlight of your career. I really enjoyed my time at Bury. It's a great club, and I was happy to stay. But I was given the opportunity to go to Holland and play for Alkmaar against the likes of Marco van Basten. You'd take it, wouldn't you?" he asks, not unreasonably.

"I came back to the Football League in the 1988/89 season when I played for Graham Barrow at Chester, and then I rejoined Frank Casper when he was manager at Burnley in the summer of 1989. Burnley were in the Fourth Division at the time and we won the championship in 1992, so the season after when I played in the third tier meant I'd played in all four divisions for them after my first time there," he says.

Another spell at Chester, who had by now relocated to the Deva Stadium, followed before Joe called time on his playing days after a short period at Wigan Athletic which brought his league tally to more than 650 games. "I moved into coaching after I'd done some work with the youth team when I went back to Chester. I joined the set-up at Stockport where I worked with Dave Jones, and when he went to Southampton he took me with him. I had two years where I worked with players like Wayne Bridge and Garry Monk," he reveals.

On this Saturday afternoon during the close season, Joe's new-found employment duties covering games for the Press Association weren't an issue. As he sits in the press box at the Racecourse Ground in Wrexham or at the Deva Stadium, it's intriguing to think how he must view today's games compared to those from thirty years ago when he led the Bury team out each week. A softly-spoken man who is rightly proud of his achievements, the smile that's painted broadly on his face amid the dressing room celebrations was more than justified.

Despite the creeping rise in attendances from the end of the Jim Iley era onwards, the perennial Bury problem of low crowds was highlighted in the local paper the day before Colchester United came to Gigg Lane. The back page's scaremongering headline of 'MORE FANS NEEDED TO PAY FOR SUCCESS' reintroduces the yarn, which stretches back to the club's earliest days, that more people from the town were needed to push fivers through the turnstile grilles whenever the Shakers were at home. 'Bury face two home games in the next five days and unless more people can be tempted through the turnstiles then two more wins would add to the financial headache' the article reads.

This is not a plea that without cold, hard cash the club would close, in the way that it was in 1990 before Andy Hill left for Manchester City or in 2002 when the 12,000 blue and white tip-up seats which made up Gigg Lane's capacity were sponsored by generous donors. The article even claims that the panic button is nowhere to be seen, because the story is actually a ploy to increase income that will help to pay the players' win bonuses. 'Like most other clubs in the country Bury operate a bonus scheme, their first team squad players receiving extra payments for wins and draws. The payments vary according to their position in the Fourth Division: the higher the placing, the better the bonus,' the piece continues on a day of publication when Bury were unbeaten and fourth in the table.

Chairman Terry Robinson is revealed to have boarded the supporters' coaches after the win at Chester to thank the fans for their backing. 'I just wanted them to know that their efforts to help the team had not gone unnoticed. The players and manager both commented on the noise they made,' he is quoted as saying.

'I would now like to see that happening at Gigg Lane and I'm sure it will if the team keeps playing as well as it has done. It would be terrific if we could generate the sort of vocal support which is worth a goal start to the lads every time they run out at home.

'I'm not saying that people SHOULD come to watch us. That would be wrong,' he continues. 'What I am saying is that fans who have been to our games have been giving glowing reports of our matches. To those who have listened but not yet come down, could I ask that they make an effort to see the next two matches and use them as a basis for determining whether the team is worth watching?' he asks.

The benchmark for attendances is given as 3,800 in the story's rousing last paragraph, written by John Dyson. 'The best way to win back the fans...is for the team to play entertaining football. They need to win more than they lose, be in with a shout of promotion from start to finish of the season and make the supporters feel a part of the club' goes its breast-beating close.

There's a line in the official film of the 1966 World Cup, *Goal*, when the narrator repeats the England supporters' chant in one of the group games that was spliced into New Order's official song for the 1990 tournament: "We want goals' – against Mexico they got one, a beauty scored by Bobby Charlton,' it says in plummy tones. In much the same way, Dyson was asking for entertaining games in that *Bury Times* article – and the very next day his wish was granted in the game against Colchester.

With the crowd creeping just over the 2,000 mark, Bury won a thrilling game by the odd goal in seven. While an undoubted spectacle, the local paper's report chooses to highlight the positive aspect of attacking football rather than defensive frailties that meant Bury had now conceded six goals in the first four league games: 'It matters not...provided the success rate continues at the other end. What they must guard against, though, is going to sleep when comfortably ahead, a fault which could have cost them dear on Saturday.

'As it happens, the six goals which were scored in the last twenty minutes gave Bury an "all's well that ends well" scoreline and gave everyone plenty to talk about as they made their way home,' it continues.

Andy Hill once again impressed, in this game coming up against future Arsenal star Perry Groves, but it was Wayne Entwistle who opened Bury's account – and his own for the season – following a flick-on from Craig Madden. Dyson's report then goes on to single out two David Brown saves from Tony Adcock, which had they been converted may have seen the match swing Colchester's way, as being the turning point of the game.

Instead, a Leighton James run and cross fell to Madden to head home. Three minutes later, the Bury striker was hauled over in the box and had his penalty kick parried by Alec Chamberlain, only for Winston White to smash the rebound home and make it 3–0 to the hosts. Roger Osborne, who scored the winner for Ipswich in the 1978 FA Cup final, pulled a goal back before Stewart Houston, who would later manage Arsenal, headed a second for the visitors as

Bury's defence stood 'transfixed'. Thankfully, a Trevor Ross palm-stinger fell to Craig Madden who restored Bury's two-goal cushion with two minutes left, only for the visitors to put another dent into Bury's *goals against* column with the last kick of the game.

The match report was printed on the same day that Bury faced former Manchester United star Lou Macari's Swindon Town side at Gigg Lane. With such a small squad at his disposal without any external forces getting in the way, it's not hard to imagine Martin Dobson's headache which led to the headline 'FLU SCARE MAY FORCE A CHANGE IN THE LINE-UP'. Wayne Entwistle, fresh from his goal and performance against Colchester, apparently called the club on the Monday to inform the boss that he was running a high temperature and shivering. He was told to stay away and decide for himself on the Tuesday if he was fit to play. In fact, it's something of a non-story following the hyperbolic headline, as he was apparently the sole player who was feeling a little peaky.

The story also credits Dobson with taking advantage of games on the Wirral taking place on Friday nights, describing how he went to see Swindon at Tranmere the day before he played himself versus Colchester. Another subliminal plea to get the number of bums on wooden seats up is made too as the seed is planted in the heads of 'neutral' United fans that they'd be able to see former hero Macari on the field of play once more.

As it was, Enty not only played that night, he also scored Bury's second goal of the evening as a 2–0 win saw them push through to the top of the table. In front of 2,769, the biggest crowd for almost two years and more than double the amount who saw that whimpering final game of the previous season against the same opponents, Bury's 'combination of effort, teamwork and skill was too much for Town' according to the local paper. It can't have taken Bury long to show the newcomers in the stand and on the terraces that this was a side worth watching as they reached the summit.

Craig Madden bagged yet again to give Bury the lead inside ten minutes before the free-flowing passing that the team would become known for took over. There was to be no respite for a Swindon team featuring former Bury favourite Andy Rowland. '[Bury's] intelligent and willing running off the ball maintained the momentum with goalkeeper David Brown a virtual spectator,' says the match report.

Having risen from his sick bed to play, Wayne Entwistle rose to meet a Trevor Ross cross halfway through the second half, scoring a goal which the report claims was fully merited thanks to his consistently strong work-rate. The new league leaders are described as leaving the field to a standing ovation, which may have been mostly brought about thanks to an astonishing eighty yard Leighton James run which began in his own penalty area, before Craig Madden headed straight at the 'keeper from the resulting cross.

Each issue of Bury's match day programme in the 1984/85 season carried an advert for Warburton's Travel, the coach company who were based in the town centre Bus and Rail Interchange that was then still only four years old. It says how they are 'proud to have been coach operators for [the] Bury FC team and supporters' club for over 23 seasons'. Whether this actually means anything from twenty-four seasons to fifty is unclear, but the advert also boasts that their fleet is made up of 'modern luxury coaches' and features a picture of the squad posed in front of one of the company's vehicles in the potholed car park behind the Main Stand.

The coach looks decidedly un-modern by today's standards of the land yachts that glide players to away games, seemingly having more in common with the kind of basic vessel that ferried children to Chester Zoo on school trips. En route to Bury's game at Exeter, which followed on the Saturday after the win over Swindon, the players were to get to know this particular bus very well indeed.

Despite leaving for Devon at 8.45am on the day of the game – overnight stays being a frippery that Bury could ill-afford – the planned pre-match meal in Bristol was abandoned after the coach got stuck in roadworks on the M5. The *Bury Times* of 25 September

notes how traffic was restricted to a single lane crawl that at one stage made Bury's arrival for kick-off look unlikely, while pre-match food was made up of sandwiches which had been prepared for the journey home. In the same article, Martin Dobson praises his players' attitude as he talks about their determination in the face of what he rightly calls 'hardly ideal' circumstances, as stiffness was setting in from five hours spent in the same place without a break.

"We were in the massive traffic jam on the M5," remembers Bury fan Paul Greenlees today. "The coach had only just passed an intersection when we got caught up in it and we asked the driver to reverse back to it. He refused, obviously, but told us that he didn't think we'd make the kick-off. As we inched around the bend, we saw the team coach in front of us so we knew we'd make it," he adds.

After a hurried warm-up, Bury took control of the game with ease at St James Park. With the added dimension of Dobson's predecessor Jim Iley being in charge of the hosts, it was Wayne Entwistle who handed Bury all three points as he took his tally to four goals in a week with a superb brace. Wayne's burgeoning relationship with strike partner Craig Madden showed more signs of the innate understanding between the two growing as he headed in a Madden flick-on for the first. His second came after the goalkeeper could only parry another Trevor Ross missile, with the Bury striker nipping in to wrap up the points with eight minutes of the game left.

Hoping for no repeat of the nightmare journey to the game, the Bury squad boarded the now-familiar coach as joint top of the league following a Hereford United win elsewhere which put them level with the Shakers. Celebrating his side's fifth successive win, winger Leighton James remembers getting on to the bus and making straight for Terry Robinson.

"I said to him, 'Mr Chairman, if you think we're going to play like that after every game that we're delayed getting to, you've got another bloody thing coming!'" laughs the Welshman today.

With both his confidence and position in the leading goalscorer table rising, Wayne Entwistle presumably enjoyed that game at one of the farthest outposts for Bury that season. Born in Bury and signing professional forms in 1976, Wayne had something of a nomadic career after he left his hometown club for Sunderland a year later, and it was Jim Iley who brought him back to Gigg Lane

from Grays Athletic six years after that. The old cliché about a player having more clubs than Jack Nicklaus could be applied to Wayne as he moved from team to team in the North West, but the town retained its magnetic pull to Wayne, which is how I came to know him when my age was still a single digit number.

Wayne Entwistle's 1984/85 season pen picture.
(Copyright: Bury Football Club)

In the late-eighties, Wayne's van carrying the cooked meats that he was selling following his retirement from the game was a familiar sight around Bury. I got to know him when the same van's doors would be opened following services at All Saints in Elton and he'd sell sliced ham, turkey and chicken to the congregation. Having considered each other as friends for more than twenty years, he agreed to be interviewed by me at the family farm which he grew up on, on Woodhill Road.

"The surrounding estates hadn't been built when I was a kid on Higher Woodhill Farm, as it's called," explains Wayne today. "It was all land belonging to Harry Fitton's farm that was owned by the Stanley family, which is why the cottage that was built in 1710 is called Stanley Cottage. The wall outside was my goalposts, and because there were no other kids around at the time I'd just kick a ball against it, hoping to be seen by Matt Busby if he ever drove down Woodhill Road," he laughs.

Wayne found himself back at Bury when Iley was looking for a striker with the local touch in the summer of 1983. "The promotion season came, for me, after Jim had brought me back to the club the season before Martin came in. Bury had no money to sign players from a distance because they couldn't afford the removal fees for players moving in to the area, so they were all fairly local," he reveals.

"I'd never criticise Jim because I thought he was a great bloke, but I don't think there's any doubt that when Martin came in he made us more professional. It was the Burnley connection: most of the lads had played under Jimmy Adamson and everything was much more structured. Training was pass and move, pass and move, which I really enjoyed.

"Martin retained about eight players at the end of the season after he'd been in charge for eight or nine games. I'm sure I'd have been given a free transfer if Jim Iley was still manager, but he'd gone, of course, and so Martin took me to one side to have a chat with me. I'd come close to quitting before, when I walked out of my contract at Wimbledon, and

Martin said it was my last chance to have a career in football. I have to admit that under him I felt I became a better player," he says.

It wasn't just his manager's self-belief that spurred Wayne on. The players that an ex-England player has the potential to lure to the club were just as important to him. "When I think about playing with the likes of not just Leighton and Trevor but Kevin Young too, when you go out on to the pitch with them, you know you're playing with good players. Leighton is an intelligent bloke as well as probably the best crosser of a ball I've ever seen, and Trevor is strong and comfortable on the ball as well as off it. Kevin was a typical product of Burnley because he was a very classy player. He was clearly coached the Burnley way and it helped develop our left side, which I thought was particularly strong when you factor in Andy Hill too. We were a strong side full stop, but our strength was definitely over on that side of the pitch.

"As a team I think we felt we were stronger than anyone else. The defence was strong with Pash and Bram too, but with Martin playing as a sweeper and reading the game so well, he made it look easy. It gave us the confidence that we showed with the pass and move and the width that we played with," he says.

News headlines may have made the mid-eighties seem retrospectively glum, and they weren't the best of times for Wayne on a personal level either. "I was going through a separation as the season progressed and football helped me get through it, I'm convinced of it. The ninety minutes when I went on the pitch was an escape for me as much as it's a release for supporters who've been at work all week. Training and away trips with the lads were a sanctuary. There was one game we played, I can't remember the opposition, but I really didn't want to play because my wife and I were splitting up. I played, though, and it got easier as the ninety minutes on the pitch tended to help me through," he reveals.

It's no surprise that Wayne has fond memories of going on the road, even if it was in one of those basic Warburton's coaches that didn't have a toilet, the preferred design option being a card table instead. "They were jollies, there's no doubt about that, but if you're doing well then you're more relaxed and you travel to games expecting to win. We only had a small squad so there was obviously the comradeship, but even when we suffered heavy defeats we didn't dwell on them. We just saw them as a blip and thought we'd win the next one," he says.

The training routine that Wayne utilised to forget about his troubles was equally as important. "I'd had a good pre-season before the promotion season began and scored five goals in the Lancashire Manx Cup and in games at Macclesfield and Penrith. I used to run and run and run on the track on Market Street and I owed a lot of my fitness that year to Bury Athletics Club, but I was substituted for Kevin Young about three-quarters of the way through the second half of the first game of the season up at Darlington because I was out of sorts," he remembers. But it was a revelation from the Dutch way of looking at football that really brought Wayne into his own as he settled into what would become his finest season.

Wiel Coerver was a coach from the Netherlands who managed, among others, Feyenoord, with whom he won the UEFA Cup in 1973. His Wikipedia page states that he was known as 'the Albert Einstein of football' because of his forensic studies of videos of the world's greatest players and the subsequent development of the technique which bore his name. His crucial theory was that skill was not inherent and something that a player was born with, with a sweep from the hand of God; it could be taught in an academic way as one might learn a foreign language.

"The coaching staff all went down to a seminar at the FA's school of excellence at Lilleshall that was hosted by Coerver. His way of playing was all about learning the basics before the rest followed. He taught the gaffer the drag backs and Cruyff turns which we then had incorporated into our training. It gave a lot of fluency to the Bury team's game, but it really had an effect on me too. The effect was such that Wilf McGuinness said that I was a different player after learning the techniques. I just felt that I became freer and that it gave me the confidence to try something different so I practised and practised the techniques," Wayne reveals.

When I was talking to his former teammates, the one factor of his personality that each and every one of them praised Wayne for was his bravery. The centre forward would put his head where angels fear to tread and this was best exemplified in the home game against Crewe in November 1984.

"I wasn't playing well and there was a clash of heads which meant I had to go off for nine minutes as I got stitches," he says. Presumably looking like Terry Butcher with a head swathed in bandages that were only ever going to take on a deep shade of crimson, Wayne rescued a point for Bury after re-entering the fray. "The ball came over, I can't remember who from, and I took it on my chest. I swivelled and smashed it into the roof of the net. I even had a chance later on with my head," he remembers.

Wayne wore the number nine shirt for every game of the promotion season except for one. The 3–0 defeat at Wrexham in the middle of December came the week after Bury had spent the previous weekend on the Isle of Man by virtue of the team not being involved in the second stage of the FA Cup.

"I injured my knee in the game we played over there against a team called Gymnasium. I'd done my ligaments and I couldn't walk or open my knee up at all. The following Wednesday we were at Peterborough who were up there at the top with us and I was fit again. The manager told me he wanted me to play because, with the exception of the Wrexham game, the team was on a good run and he wanted to maintain the continuity. I played, we won 4–1 in perhaps the best performance of the season, but I was very much a passenger in the team that night. We basically won with ten men and to this day my knee is still sore," he says.

Dobson's reasoning and eagerness in playing Enty on that chilly night at London Road were presumably just two of the causes for Wayne's good memories of working with the former Burnley pair who looked after team affairs. "I could sometimes be self-critical after a game, but Martin and Frank Casper took a different view. They'd pick out what they saw as the positives of your game and talk you through them, even if you felt you'd played poorly," he remembers.

Wayne's reputation among his teammates is unerringly similar to Paul Gascoigne's under Bobby Robson, as more than one described him in interviews for this publication as 'daft as a brush'. But listening to him talk with free-associating enthusiasm for his time spent as a footballer and the way he played the game, you realise that the former England Youth international is a very intelligent player. The twenty-one league goals which he weighed in with in the promotion season, just one behind top scorer Craig Madden, didn't happen by accident, and it's unsurprising that fans of one of his former clubs, Sunderland, still revere him as 'the punk footballer' based on his Paul Simonon haircut and a goal in a Tyne-Wear derby.

The journeyman who played for eight clubs who have won the FA Cup – Bury, Sunderland, Leeds, Blackpool, Wimbledon, Bolton, Burnley and Wigan – now works in the building trade. The legendary fitness that enabled him to chase everything with a relentless energy, like a dog chasing a tennis ball well into the twilight, can still be seen as he cycles to and from work each day as well as pushing his pedals over the weekend, for charity events just as much as his own wellbeing.

The following day from Wayne's heroics which earned Bury three points at Exeter, the horror of nuclear war, which had previously only been imagined, was brought to life on BBC2. The Americans had tried to tell the story of what would happen following a blast made up of dozens of megatons of warheads with *The Day After*, but as a film it was Hollywood-like and scarcely believable in its protagonist-led, almost saccharine ending. *Threads* told the visceral, disturbing story of what would happen to an ordinary place in this country – Sheffield – if The Bomb was dropped.

The film is undoubtedly a tough watch. Written by Barry Hines, who gave the world Billy Casper and the childlike PE teacher played by Brian Glover who worships Bobby Charlton in *Kes*, the build-up to war is depressingly mundane. The world still continues with news reports forming the background noise in factories and pubs, but all the while preparations are being made by the authorities. At Sheffield Town Hall an emergency committee, which includes Bury-born actor Steve Halliwell [*Emmerdale*'s Zak Dingle], is being formed as fears mount.

The world changes forever when the on-screen caption shows that the Soviet Union detonated a warhead over the North Sea at 8.35 on the morning of 26 May. Among the horrifying images that follow are burning bodies, dead babies, limbs being amputated in the dark without anaesthetic, a population succumbing to radiation sickness and a progressive First World country resorting to a Stone Age hunter-gatherer life. The captions are also brutal in their simplicity: a small knot of people wrapped in rags huddles around a fire as we're told that the date is 25 December, while later in the film, as the blast continues to take its toll, the population of the country is described as having fallen to medieval levels.

After watching the film, Albert Einstein's famous assertion that the fourth world war would be fought with sticks and stones seems grimly accurate. No data is available to back up the theory, but it can't be beyond the realms of possibility that CND received an awful lot of queries regarding membership the morning following the film's broadcast on this country's *Day After*.

The Shakers' last game of the month involved them hosting a team from close to the city that was obliterated in *Threads*. Bury wouldn't have been far enough from Chesterfield to escape any of the radiation that would have rained down after a nuclear holocaust, but it was with only football in mind and not self-preservation that fans of the

Spireites came to Gigg Lane on 29 September. The game was to be played the very next day after the High Court had ruled the strike which Chesterfield's miners were engaged in was unlawful.

"Some of our younger support saw the strike as an opportunity to wind up their opposite numbers. They'd chant about cockneys if we played a club from the London area, and if we played in Yorkshire, Nottinghamshire or Derbyshire, they'd sing about the miners' strike. They didn't know what they were singing about, they just wanted to cause bad feeling," remembers Malcolm Parr.

It wasn't just Bury fans who displayed gleeful ignorance at the political situation in vast swathes of the North, though. Tales of southern visitors waving ten pound notes towards their hosts at grounds beyond Birmingham are legion. Users on Bob's Board, an online community for Chesterfield fans, remember low crowds that should have been higher as the Spireites did well in the league for the duration of the strike, as well as turnstile operators turning a blind eye to the occasional fan hopping over the wrought iron, circular gate into the ground. Chesterfield's games against neighbouring Mansfield, a town located in the Nottinghamshire coalfield, were always tasty occasions before 1984 anyway, but the Orwellian year took the rivalry to unprecedented levels when the latter's miners defied the strike and kept on working. One can only imagine how little Christmas spirit was in evidence as the two met on Boxing Day that year.

Gary Buckley, replacing Terry Pashley, made his first start of the season in the 0–0 draw against the visitors from Derbyshire that ended a depleted Bury side's 100 per cent home league record. Referee Peter Willis, who just months later took charge of the 1985 FA Cup final, disallowed no fewer than four goals as the two sides played out what the *Bury Times* of 2 October called 'one of the most entertaining goalless draws imaginable.'

Stockport County fans keep the name of referee Willis in their bad books to this day because of two farcically contentious decisions against Manchester United in a League Cup game from the 1970s. A Bury player who found his way into Willis's book on this particular afternoon at Gigg Lane was Leighton James, who was booked as his passion spilled over into an argument as he left the field at the end of the first period.

Bury's second half performance saw them throw everything at Chesterfield's stand-in 'keeper Chris Marples who, the paper tells us, was also Derbyshire's second XI wicket-keeper. His most impressive save came from a Buckley volley struck from outside the area, but as Bury poured forward, a dive at the feet of Craig Madden was also singled out. David Brown was described as being equally as brave as his youthful counterpart as he saved from Bob Newton and Gary Bellamy.

Dobson waits until the final two lines of his understated notes in the game's programme to declare that his joint top side's confidence is 'sky-high' and that he was looking forward to a 'good confrontation'. It's a peculiar description that's shared by the *Bury Times*, whose banner headline for the match report reads 'RECORD GOES BUT ONLY AFTER FIGHT'.

Despite their cultured nature, Bury had faced a stern test in the top of the table clash and they came through it unscathed. The first of many hurdles that the season would put in front of the Forgotten Fifteen had been cleared.

October 1984

Before its occupiers went into freefall and wound up in the Conference North, Edgeley Park in Stockport was never a great ground to visit as an away fan in the Football League. The Railway End which housed those travelling to North Cheshire was without a cover, so if the weather tended to the typical there was an odds-on chance of a drenching. If by some quirk the weather stayed fine, the sun was then always pointing directly at the away supporters, which would lead to a terrace full of supporters using their hands as makeshift visors. Plane-spotters would enjoy the view from the terrace, though, as the drone of planes coming in to land at Manchester Airport every other minute livened up monotonous encounters or those which ended in a loss.

The latter was precisely what happened in Bury's visit on the evening of Monday 1 October as the Shakers tasted the sharp tang of league defeat for the first time in the season. Writing in the *Bury Times* match report, John Dyson makes an attempt at fairness and balance in the introduction, but it's eclipsed by a harsh truth: 'The law of averages dictated that Bury's unbeaten run had to come to an end sooner or later...and yet the manner of that first defeat of the campaign still came as a big disappointment.'

The report goes on to note that the free-flowing football which

Bury had played as their confidence had grown was not evident that night. The starting XI, with Kevin Young rather than Gary Buckley now slotting in to replace Terry Pashley, simply weren't at the races and were harried into trying to beat Stockport at their own long-ball game. A defensive mix-up between David Brown and John Bramhall allowed Oshor Williams – a future colleague of Bramhall's at the Professional Footballers' Association – to nip in for County's first. John Kerr, who would end the season wearing the white and royal blue of the visitors, scored the second from thirty yards out; it was presumably a goal that Martin Dobson kept in mind when he was looking for a striker with fresh legs for the end of the season.

The equilibrium that Dyson sought in the opening paragraph of the report is again scrabbled for in its close: 'One setback doesn't necessarily mean cause for concern but Martin Dobson will be keen to impress on his squad the need for a swift recovery after his side's most ineffective display since the opening day of the season.'

It's a recovery that would obviously be longed for in the next game, in which Bury were due to host Southend United. Highlighting how different the game was in only fairly recent history, the visitors were managed by Bobby Moore, the former England captain who lifted the Jules Rimet trophy after he'd wiped his muddy hands on the crushed velvet that lined the Royal Box at Wembley on 30 July 1966. Less than twenty years later, and less than ten years after Moore led out Fulham in the FA Cup final at the same venue, he would be bringing his Fourth Division charges to Bury.

After Martin Dobson's five appearances with the three lions on his chest in 1974, the *Bury Times* match report which was printed on 9 October was keen to play on the mind games between two former international players. After a 2–0 win for the Shakers, John Dyson claims that it's the Bury player-manager who's emerging from the precarious world of management with more credit 'than his non-playing counterpart'. Wayne Entwistle got the first goal after a goalmouth scramble inside a minute of kick-off, while Andy Hill grabbed his first for the club and Bury's second after Jim Stannard misjudged his cross.

The newspaper's main headline on the back page of the same issue is 'BETTER NEWS OF THE INJURED' after it is revealed that both John Bramhall and Craig Madden emerged from the game battle-scarred. Bramhall apparently lost a tooth somewhere on the Gigg Lane pitch after his first tussle of the game, while Madden strained his ankle ligaments. Chris Cutler is also mentioned as having had an Achilles tendon operation during the summer, recovery from which could soon lead to a reserve team berth. Terry Pashley is also referred to in terms of the second string as his ankle trouble looked to have cleared up following his appearance for the stiffs at Formby. The treatment room was looking like a busy place as the nights started to draw in.

While the local paper focused on the two managers and their England connections in the Southend report, it overlooked the fact that there was somebody else sitting in one of the Gigg Lane dugouts that afternoon who had a connection with the national side. Not just any side, either: like visiting Shrimpers manager Moore, Wilf McGuinness was involved on that balmy afternoon in North London when the people on the pitch thought it was all over.

In place as Bury's physiotherapist in 1984, Wilf was perhaps the most popular member of the backroom staff. Born in Collyhurst in 1937, he grew up loving Manchester United and signed for his idols straight from school in 1953, making his first team debut two years later. In 1958, a torn cartilage ruled him out of a trip to Belgrade in the European Cup. Frustration turned to relief and then bereavement as the injury meant he wasn't on the aeroplane which skidded and crashed on its third attempt at take-off from the appalling conditions at Munich airport, killing twenty-three passengers and crew, including three back room staff and eight of his teammates.

A further leg injury forced Wilf to retire from the game aged just twenty-three. He was subsequently taken on as a member of the coaching staff at his domestic club where he worked with a successful youth team before he performed a role with the similar-aged lads of the England team, including Bury's own George Jones. By 1966 he was managing Manchester United's reserve side which led to Alf Ramsey, predating the tournament which earned him his knighthood, inviting Wilf to train his squad at Lilleshall. A photograph printed in the testimonial brochure produced to mark his ten years at Bury in 1990 shows Wilf beaming on the far right of the middle row next to the manager, with his former United teammate Bobby Charlton taking a similar position on the row in front. Future Bury star John Connelly, the only man ever to play for the club who won a World Cup winner's medal, looks over Wilf from the back row. In the text accompanying the picture, Wilf talks through how he and his wife Beryl were invited to the final, how he lunched with the players on that famous afternoon and travelled with them on the coach to the stadium. As the celebratory booze flowed after the game, Wilf was at Ramsey's right hand once more at the post-match banquet.

Following the infamous spell in charge of United after his mentor Matt Busby left the post in the late-sixties, Wilf worked in Greece and Jordan before returning to the UK with York City. He joined Bury in 1980 and spent a happy decade at Gigg Lane which culminated in the granting of the testimonial in the days when a club's loyal servants were still awarded them. The testimonial brochure is a fascinating document to look back on as it tells the in-depth story of Wilf's career and features contributions from a veritable who's who of characters present at each stage of his footballing life. George Best, Alex Ferguson, Busby, Charlton, Denis Law, Nobby Stiles and Tommy Docherty all contribute tales of life at Old Trafford. From the Bury contingent, Martin Dobson, Andy Hill, chairman Terry Robinson, Craig Madden, Paul Hilton and Sam Ellis add their memories of the physiotherapist. The local press line up to pay tribute as well: David Meek from the *Manchester Evening News*, John Dyson, Andy

Buckley from BBC GMR [later Radio Manchester] and Gordon Sharrock of the *Bolton Evening News* all feature. Everyone, it seems, has a Wilf McGuinness story.

Here's mine. In the 1988 close season, Bury sold children's season tickets for the princely sum of £10. I'd only been to one game before then and I think that my dad took a punt on one for me with the probable mindset that if I didn't enjoy sharing his Saturday afternoon passion then it was simply an inexpensive experiment. We went down to Gigg Lane to collect them on a blazing summer's day after England had blown out of Euro 88 without even scoring a goal, and while we were there we bumped into Wilf. I can imagine that he saw a seven-year-old boy looking a bit nonplussed at the whole situation he'd found himself in, so he took me by the hand and gave me a guided tour of the ground, stopping players as they passed and making sure they had a quick chat with us. It was an act that only took fifteen minutes out of Wilf's day, but it made sure that there would never be any other club for me than Bury. I once heard it said that a lot of football fans don't choose their clubs and that instead their clubs choose them; Wilf McGuinness certainly made sure that Bury chose me.

I got Wilf's phone number through a former work contact and rang him to ask if it would be possible to talk about his time at Bury. He agreed, and after I relayed my story to him about how he was so influential in me becoming a Bury fan and that I wanted to buy him a drink to say thank you, we arranged to meet in a pub near his South Manchester home. After I had unpacked my research for him to look through as we chatted, I pushed a pint of lager his way in return for a lifetime of pain and suffering that was worth every second when, on those rare occasions when the planets were aligned, the tides were in synchronisation and everything slotted together perfectly, Bury would achieve something beautiful.

"Martin Dobson was the best thing about the squad. Me and him were suited to each other, and the club, down to the ground," he now remembers. "The Burnley connection of him, Frank Casper and Ray Pointer meant that for a few years we played some really good stuff. Training was very similar to when I was at United because it was just pure football. The belief we had really started to show itself in the pre-season where we played a good, attacking game. If an attack broke down we'd just start again.

"The players he brought in were brilliant. The confidence of Leighton James was outstanding when he'd nutmeg players on the left wing. There was one opposition lad who got wind of it and as they were lining up to start the game he said 'I know you, Leighton James. I'll have you.' Leighton just said to him 'You don't know me, I've never played this low before!'

"Up front you had Craig and Wayne, two brilliant goalscorers. I loved being around Wayne, he was always a lot of fun, and at the back you had lads like Terry Pashley. He had a hell of a left foot on him, and in the warm-up he'd hold my legs as I did my party trick of doing a handstand and knocking the ball with my heels, years before that Columbian goalkeeper [Rene Higuita] did the same thing with his scorpion kick," he laughs.

"There were just so many talented players in that Bury team," he continues. "John Bramhall was a strong defender, Joe Jakub and Trevor Ross would run their socks off, and then you had the skill of Kevin Young too. The manager had a good run in the team in the promotion season as well. I enjoyed being part of it so much. We didn't have the biggest crowds because of the proximity of Bury to other towns and teams, but I've got wonderful memories," he says.

It wasn't just the players from the 1985 promotion side that Wilf remembered as we spoke. Lee Dixon joined Bury from Chester in the 1985 close season immediately following promotion before making a name for himself at Stoke and then Arsenal. "I saw Lee on the night of that FA Cup semi-final in 1999 when Ryan Giggs scored that fantastic goal as United went on to win the treble," he reveals. "I put my arm around him to console him, and after the game he accidentally got on the United coach. He said to me that he was so used to being on the winners' coach," he laughs.

After joining Bury initially as a coach working with Jim Iley, Wilf was tending to injuries with the magic sponge by the time Martin Dobson arrived. "Jim was experienced in a lot of areas, but Martin was learning, which I think suited him," he says. "I remember thinking that if he managed as well as he played then we'd be OK – and we were, of course.

"I was perhaps something of an unorthodox physio in the ways that I'd treat the lads. I'd done my diploma in sports injuries after I broke my leg aged twenty-two playing for United, and I did my work with the England squad, which was great. I was fortunate that not a lot of serious injuries came along, but if they did then I could always consult a doctor or somebody more qualified, even though I had my badges. Most importantly, I think, I knew what not to do with injuries after what had happened to me," he says.

"I'd use an ultrasound machine on injuries that got nicknamed 'the biscuit barrel' – I used it on one lad and asked him how his injury was once we'd finished and he said it felt fine before I noticed I'd not switched it on! I thought I'd better not tell him because I think psychology plays a big part in things like that too," he adds.

After having his playing career cut short so devastatingly, Wilf quickly adopted humour as his defence mechanism. "I missed the spirit of the dressing room when I had to retire. It was a lot of fun. Obviously I'd lost my hair by then so I'd wear the wig and take the mickey out of myself for the adults, and for the kids I'd take a bag of lollies," he remembers. It's Wilf's fondness for candy on sticks that led to the subtitle of John Dyson's page in the testimonial brochure: in a story about how Wilf defused tension between sets of fans, we learn that the pitched battle was quelled by 'A HANDFUL OF LOLLIES AGAINST AN ARMY'. Lollipops also covertly appear in the sign-off of Craig Madden's piece in the brochure, which hints at the players' nickname for the much-loved physio being 'Kojak' as he ends his affectionate tribute with 'Who loves ya, baby?'

Wilf keeps warm in the game at Colchester United. (Copyright: Simon Egan)

It's anecdotes such as those involving lollies and ultrasound machines which gave Wilf a lucrative sideline to run alongside his coaching work, which he still utilises to this day. "I discovered that I could make money just telling my stories on the after-dinner circuit and so I tried it. At one point I was earning more doing that for one night than I earned in a fortnight at Bury, but I loved Bury and didn't want to give my job up there," he says. More than one ex-player has since recalled how Wilf used them, prone on the treatment table, as a captive audience for his routines that would be later recounted at venues across the North West. Occasionally, the locations spread even further; Bury supporters who chose to attend an executive dinner package ahead of the club's Third Division play-off final versus Chesterfield at Wembley in 1995 enjoyed between-course patter from Wilf, who looked as comfortable with a microphone in his hand as he did with his treatment bag.

As we got near to the bottom of that pint glass on a warm evening in Sale, Wilf summed his time at Bury up. "It was just good fun. It was the people who made it, the people who've given the best years of their life to the club who do it because they're big fans. Gigg Lane is a lovely ground and with Martin's team the fans got some of the best football they'll have seen. There always seemed to be a big roar there, which I suppose is what you get when you're winning, as Bury always seemed to be," he says.

"United were obviously a massive club in my life, but there was York and there was Hull too. But after United, it's always Bury. There were times I'd even sleep there if I'd had a drink after a game," he laughs.

Maybe that's why Wilf was so keen to take seven-year-old me on that wander around the ground in the summer of 1988. I wasn't just seeing his workplace. I was seeing a place that contained happy memories of good times too: his home. Not his spiritual home, granted, but a place worthy of the silver medal ranking in an extraordinary footballing life.

The world awoke on Friday 12 October to the news that Margaret Thatcher had miraculously cheated death when her Brighton hotel was bombed in the early hours of the morning in what the *Daily Telegraph* called 'the most audacious attack on a British government since the Gunpowder Plot'. The Prime Minister's habit of running the country on only four hours sleep a night enabled her to tell reporters gathered outside the Grand Hotel that she knew when the bomb had exploded, because she was still working until moments before the detonation at 2.54am.

Provisional IRA member Patrick Magee planted the bomb weeks before the Conservative party were due to hold their annual conference in the seaside resort. He was given eight life sentences for the murders of the five people who died in the blast, but was freed under the terms of the 1998 Good Friday Agreement. In an age when both the threat from across the Irish Sea and warnings containing recognised code words were frequent, the organisation's statement following the bombing was especially chilling, as they ran with 'Today we were unlucky. But remember, we only have to be lucky once.'

Remarkably, just hours after Norman Tebbit was the highest-ranking member of the government to be pulled from the mangled facade of the hotel, the Prime Minister took to the lectern in the conference room as scheduled. Behind the scenes, it's not hard to imagine that troops were being mobilised to plug the gaps in defences which had allowed such an act to take place. Garrison towns such as Catterick or Colchester must have buzzed with the nervous excitement of imminent mobilisation.

One other such town might have been Aldershot, where Bury played the day after the explosion. Wayne Entwistle got his name on the scoresheet once more with the only goal of the game as the hosts struggled to breach the Shakers' defence on what the *Bury Times* match report reliably informs the reader is one of the biggest pitches in the league. Praise is heaped on Winston White, John Bramhall and Joe Jakub in the report, while Craig Madden's set-up for Enty's winner makes the latter's sweeping home of the ball sound like meat and drink for a striker who was bursting with confidence. Dobson would go on to call the victory 'the best away performance of the season' in his programme notes for the next home game, while also thanking the fans who made the five-hour trip to Hampshire for their vocal support.

If a visit to a town full of squaddies while the country is in the grip of a national emergency is an away day to force the raising of an eyebrow, Bury's match the following week would force the other eyebrow to arch too. Blackpool away in the middle of autumn is not a trip to get the heart racing with anticipation. Spray from the sea crashing over the tidal defences and showering the tram tracks, the lingering flicker of the illuminations coming to the end of that year's tourist season and a swift pre-match drink in the grim Manchester pub on the prom would all be infinitely more bearable if your team is riding high in the division. It's a good job Bury were, but standing on the huge Kop at Bloomfield Road as the elements threw all they could at the travelling contingent must still have been a struggle.

The game must have had a further dimension of challenge as a spectacle for those making the short trip as Bury missed no fewer than five gilt-edged chances in front of goal in the 0–0 draw. The match report from the local paper printed on 23 October says that the Tangerines were 'there for the taking' owing to their injury-ravaged squad, but that Madden, Entwistle and White were all guilty of fluffing easy chances in what John Dyson dubbed 'squandermania'. Rightly so, the concluding paragraph states that Martin Dobson would have been happy with a point before 3pm, but that 'finishing must now be the number one priority at Gigg Lane.'

The chance to put that right came on the same day that the newspaper was published as Bury faced Hereford United at home in a Tuesday night game. While everyone who goes to watch Bury has their own pre-match routine, those who watch the BBC's *Six O' Clock News* before leaving for night-time fixtures would, that evening, have seen a report which changed the world.

'Dawn, and as the sun breaks through the piercing chill of night on the plain outside Korem, it lights up a biblical famine – now, in the twentieth century. This place, say workers here, is the closest thing to hell on earth' are the infamous first words of Michael Buerk's report which alerted the early evening audience to the Ethiopian famine. From this piece of television that's just shy of seven minutes long came a view of charity through a new and different lens, which subsequently led to the reboot of music being used to help those in need which had last been seen with George Harrison's Concert for Bangladesh in 1971. Arising directly from the report, Bob Geldof and Midge Ure mobilised the cream of British rock and pop, grouped them together at Sarm West Studios in Notting Hill, called themselves Band Aid and recorded 'Do They Know It's Christmas?' on 25 November.

This would then lead to Live Aid, which was held on 13 July 1985. Rock concerts held at football stadiums were not a new concept at this point in the decade – Bruce Springsteen had donated $20,000 to the Northumberland and Durham Miners' Support Group following his concert at St James's Park in Newcastle the month before – but clearing the schedules and broadcasting them live on TV for more than twelve hours was unprecedented, especially as the concert from JFK Stadium in Philadelphia meant that every byte of new satellite technology that the world had to offer had to be utilised.

All of these things happened as a result of a news report that was broadcast as the white *Spray Breaker* shirts were being laid out in the dressing room, turnstile operators were being handed their floats and the switches to Bury's old floodlights, sitting at the top of their traditional blue steel pylons, were being flicked from the small control box at the bottom of the lighting rig that was located in the Main Stand-Manchester Road End corner.

The back page of the *Bury Times* which includes the report from the Blackpool game also includes a preview of that night's game against the Bulls. Headlined 'CLASH OF THE TITANS' – perhaps the only time that description has ever been applied to Hereford United – it outlines how no one would be keener than Winston White to knock the visitors off their perch at the top of the league table. Described as 'arguably the No 1 crowd favourite at Gigg Lane since his transfer from Hereford nine months ago' the winger is implored to supply ammunition for shot-shy strikers Madden and Entwistle, both of whom failed to score at Blackpool.

"I think it [the Hereford match] was first against second in the league and it was a game where we really had to show our mettle to the rest of the division," remembers fan Paul Greenlees.

In a game that the match programme tells us was sponsored by an Accrington menswear shop called Nobbut Lads – presumably 'Nothing But Lads' in East Lancashire dialect – it was Madden who grabbed Bury's second and winning goal with just seven minutes remaining. The first came from Leighton James, his much-yearned for first in a Bury shirt, which John Dyson writes about poetically: 'No-one could have anticipated the spark of individual brilliance which tipped the scales in [Bury's] favour five minutes after the break. James picked up an inside pass from Jakub some thirty yards from goal, looked up and suddenly unleashed a ferocious shot which dipped viciously at the vital moment to leave Kevin Rose helplessly clutching the night sky,' he reports breathlessly.

As wonderful as Taffy's goal was, it was a similar strike from Hereford's Jimmy Harvey which drew the visitors level with twenty minutes of the game left. Cometh the hour, though, cometh the man. As he had done so many times in the past, Madden seized on a defensive mix-up this time with the clock showing eighty-three minutes. There was no need for any of Winnie White's precision crossing as the local paper had requested, but the bulk of the bumper crowd of 4,147 wouldn't have cared less. After the disappointment of a face full of drizzle and only a point to show for those five missed chances after the Blackpool game, Bury were back on the up.

Or maybe they weren't, as in the last game of the month Bury lost 1–0 at home to a Scunthorpe United team containing former Gigg Lane favourite Alan Whitehead. Staying pragmatic, John Dyson breaks the seal of impartiality in his report as he refers to himself in the first person in a rousing introductory salvo in which he claims that Bury need to score more goals, reflecting the headline 'SHAKERS FIND GAPS BUT CHANCES WASTED'. Winston White, Joe Jakub and Leighton James all had good chances, while Martin Dobson had a header ruled out for offside with just seconds remaining.

Dyson's enthusiasm leaps from the page as he writes that the football played so far this season has been the best on display for the last three years. 'Why the gloom from so many people?' he asks before looking into the future and seeing success. 'Without hitting the high spots, they [Bury] certainly made their presence felt with a battling brand of football which raises confidence in this writer that, given the run of the ball over forty-six matches, there should be scenes of celebration at Gigg Lane next May,' predicts Mystic John.

Martin Dobson had presumably sold his philosophy wholesale to the *Bury Times* hack who was now repeating it back to his readers. In an accompanying story about Bury being drawn away at Preston North End in the first round of the FA Cup, the boss claims that he 'won't go overboard about one bad result' and that he took a lot of heart from how the team reacted to the defeat against Stockport earlier in the month.

Out of those forty-six games that made up the 1984/85 season, Bury had now played thirteen. Unlucky for some, but more than a quarter of the way through the season, things were looking good for the Shakers.

November 1984

The smell of prematurely detonated fireworks drifting over a football pitch on the Saturday closest to Bonfire Night is intoxicating. On this weekend in 1984, the smell wouldn't have been coming from fireworks bought in the newsagent on Parkhills Road and let off in Bury Cemetery, behind Gigg Lane's East Stand to which it lent its name. Instead, Bury found themselves travelling to the East Midlands and the ramshackle three-sided ground that Northampton Town shared with their county cricket landlords.

Bury were on top all afternoon before Kevin Young's late, late winning strike at the County Ground, which one can imagine *Grandstand*'s Bob Wilson commenting on as it appeared on the vidiprinter while other results were starting to come through. 'It was a timely reminder that the midfield players, too, have a part to play in front of goal,' writes John Dyson in the *Bury Times* match report printed on 6 November, sounding like he's sugar-coating a telling off to those in the centre of the park. He also describes Bury as having 'an embarrassing amount of possession' as he concludes the report with Young flicking the ball past the terrifically-named Peter Gleasure for the only goal of the game. The headline of the report performs its job of summing up the story below it perfectly: 'LAST GASP WIN BUT IT WAS WELL-DESERVED'.

Kevin Young proved to be one of the more problematic of the Fifteen to find. Despite undoubted good memories of the Wearsider who moved from Burnley in the 1984 close season, neither anyone at Bury nor the Clarets knew of his whereabouts. I'd heard vague rumours of him working in the prison service and so asked a mate who also worked in the same harsh, unforgiving environment if there was any way this could be confirmed. There was, and Matthew was subsequently able to pass on contact details for the former midfielder.

My insistence on conducting every interview with each player face-to-face meant that I would be catching a hideously early train to the beautiful city of Durham to speak to Kevin. Arriving slightly bleary-eyed, I alighted. The man waiting for me on a bench at the opposite end of the platform was unmistakably Kevin Young, so we made our way down to the River Wear. From there, we found a cafe next to the brown water which cascaded over the rocky riverbed and sat down for a conversation about the mid-1980s over coffee and cake.

"John Bond released me at Burnley in the summer of 1984 after I'd already been on loan down at Torquay," he says over the clatter of mugs and the gush of tea urns. "Martin Dobson had been in pretty much the same position when he left Burnley over Easter in the same year and he contacted me and asked me to come to Bury. He told me he was going to sign some more ex-Burnley lads, and living in the North West I couldn't not know about Craig Madden, so I signed. Being new to the team, I never felt that we were 'little Bury' or anything like that. I knew that in Martin and Joe Jakub and Andy Hill we had some great players," he adds.

Coming from Sunderland, Kevin could have had the ideal start in Bury's colours on the opening day of the promotion season. "I was only substitute at Darlington which was a bit disappointing. I'd have liked to have started my Bury career in the same area that

I came from, although I did come on for Wayne Entwistle. In fact it was disappointing not to start either of the first two games, because I'd been on loan at Port Vale too, who we played in the first round of the League Cup, but I made up for it in the first home game against Halifax when I scored. I thought then that my time at Bury was going to be good, though I also missed another game up in the North East at Hartlepool when my daughter was born," he remembers.

"I never really felt like I was a regular, though. Looking at the stats for the season I can see that I played thirty-five games and scored five goals, so I suppose I'm being a bit hard on myself," he admits. "But I loved it at Bury. The chairman Terry Robinson was a great bloke. He was one of the lads really, as we found out when we went to Ibiza on the end of season trip. I came back home after the holiday and was Vince Overson's best man. My wife was driving me mad, asking me questions about it," he says tantalisingly without expanding further. "The club was a family club that looked after its people and was very similar to Burnley in that respect.

"A lot of people still ask me for advice these days about the clubs their kids should join. I was born in Sunderland and moved down to Burnley when I was eighteen. In those days you'd join a club and you'd stay there, but that ended up not happening to me. When John Bond came to Burnley he just destroyed the place," he says, cementing his place in the hearts of Turf Moor regulars who feel the same way about the former manager.

Having played in the Second and Third Divisions for the Clarets, Kevin adapted to the basement well in his loan spell at Torquay that came before the move to Gigg Lane. "I found it quite easy as I had time on the ball and I was fitter than all the other players down there. Bruce Rioch was the manager and he wanted me to stay, but I decided I wanted to try out at Port Vale with John Rudge, so I played a few games there. Then Martin came in for me so I moved to Bury," he remembers.

Despite his talent shining in the Fourth Division, winter would always be a tough test in any season spent in the bottom tier of professional football. "Some of the grounds we played at were just awful," he remembers. "The Shay at Halifax was terrible, and although we were lucky at Gigg because we had such a great playing surface, the balls would be like rock during winter when the pitches would either be muddy or frozen solid at other grounds that weren't as well looked after," he says.

Conditions like these can't have helped Kevin's long-term health, which suffers to this day. "I've got arthritis in my left knee now which all stems from the football days and I reckon I'll probably need a new one in about ten years," he reveals. Such a debilitating ailment was the reward from a career during which Kevin carved out a reputation as an elegant player, which was the word occasionally used by the *Bury Times* to describe him, even in a match report from a game when he was sent off for a somewhat inelegant head-butt away at Chester City. Having never seen Kevin play, I told him that my dad's memory of him was of a classy player who played the game in a way that was pleasing to watch.

"I'd agree with your dad that I was skilful and classy," he laughs. "I was never a great crosser of the ball though. I'd get my target maybe four times out of ten or so, but someone like Leighton was in a different league. He'd get the lot. Of my other teammates, we had Joe, who was like an engine because he didn't stop running, and Craig Madden who was simply a natural goalscorer.

"When I was at Burnley we'd see that he'd score so many goals and we thought there must be something wrong with him because no one was coming in trying to buy him. He was a great trainer and one of the best people to have in the dressing room. We'd give him stick about his sponsored Lada from Bolton Car Centre and he'd give just as much back," he laughs, harking back to an age when Bury's star striker drove around in a Russian car that had all the handling capability of a Cold War tank.

When talking about the way that Dobson's teams played football, Young's eyes light up in the same way as when he remembers the dressing room camaraderie from underneath Gigg Lane's creaking wooden Main Stand. "We had so many options. We'd knock the ball about and keep it as wide as we could until you had Craig Madden coming short or Wayne Entwistle at the far post. Trevor Ross would be on the edge of the box, Joe Jakub would drive it in and Taffy or Winston White would be out wide. Leighton might be stifled every now and again, but we'd all step up to help each other when we needed to. We were a complete team. Trevor could take a cracking penalty and Taffy would address the ball in a particular way so he could ping it with accuracy with both feet," he remembers.

As the promotion season wore on, it soon became clear that Bury needed some fresh legs to allow those that had run themselves into the ground some much-needed respite. "We possibly needed a couple of new players towards the end of the season if we'd wanted to push on to the championship, and that's possibly where we went wrong," he remembers of Bury's fourth-placed finish.

Like his former Turf Moor amigo Joe Jakub, Kevin crossed the North Sea to Holland when he left Bury after eighty-eight games and ten goals in 1987. Where Jakub joined AZ Alkmaar, Kevin signed for the FC Utrecht team managed by Han Berger who would later manage various teams, including the Netherlands Under-21 side. After three seasons in the low country, including the campaign immediately after Marco van Basten's wonder goal against the Soviet Union made the national side the champions of Europe in 1988, Kevin moved back to the North East and Murton Colliery Welfare, with whom he turned out in local non-league fixtures.

Despite that pressing need for a new knee, Kevin is today very similar to Wayne Entwistle in that his fitness is still very important to him. It has to be, as that's what keeps a wage coming into his home in his capacity as a physical education officer at one of the most high-profile jails in the country. Michael Stone and Ian Huntley are currently kept in HMP Frankland, the UK's largest Category A jail, while in the past it has also housed Charles Bronson, Dominic Noonan and, most notably of all, Harold Shipman.

Never regarded as a particularly hard player, for Kevin Young it was all about skill. But as he organises daily activities in the gymnasium or exercise yard of his workplace, one can only admire his mental strength in going about his work in a more punishing atmosphere than Saltergate, Field Mill or Edgar Street ever had.

Bury's tumble into the basement at the end of the 1979/80 season put two whole divisions' worth of space between them and traditional local rivals Bolton Wanderers. While they languished in the bottom tier, the Shakers would have to make do with games against Rochdale for matches of geographical significance. The first meeting between the two in the 1984/85 season was to come at Spotland on the Tuesday after the victory in Northamptonshire.

If there'd been a common, not-so-subtle thread in match reports of recent weeks leading up to the game, it was that the strike force of Madden and Entwistle had needed to sharpen up. The game against 'Dale finished 1–1, and in his report that was printed on Friday 9 November, John Dyson's understudy Neil Burton goes for the jugular to the point that the sub-editor felt compelled to give the piece the damning headline 'BETTER FINISHING WOULD MAKE IT SO MUCH EASIER'.

Reporting largely in the first person, Burton claims that the colossal number of Bury's travelling fans would have been disappointed 'like me' at having to share the points with their neighbours. As Bury's attempts at free-flowing passing were abandoned in the face of derby day blood and thunder, Wayne Entwistle is perhaps unfairly singled out in a bold standalone paragraph: 'It is a pity that Entwistle's unquestioned enthusiasm and ability to get in the right place at the right time should be let down by his lack of finishing power,' notes

Burton in a passage that follows on from a reeled-off list of missed Enty chances.

Bury's goal came from Craig Madden and is described as being on a par with the disputed third goal of England's 1966 World Cup final victory as it ricocheted down from the crossbar and behind the line. The hosts then equalised with a penalty awarded for a foul committed plainly outside of the box, as seen from Burton's vantage point, before Bury took control of the game in the second half but failed to capitalise. Kevin Young and Gary Buckley are mentioned honourably in dispatches, but it would be another frustrating point for Bury that should easily have been all three.

Wayne Entwistle took the first step on the road to redemption on the day after the paper was published as he grabbed one of Bury's goals in a 2–2 draw with Crewe Alexandra at Gigg Lane on 10 November. This was the afternoon when Wayne became the physical hero of the Bury promotion side who would let nothing get in his way in pursuit of the win. 'WOUNDED WAYNE SAVES THE DAY' is the headline of the match report printed the following Tuesday, while the main story on the same back page focuses on Wayne's never-say-die nature and is headlined 'PAT ON THE BACK FOR MR COURAGE'. The latter story was written in response to his bravery at having left the pitch for eight stitches to a head wound before returning and claiming an equaliser.

Neil Burton's match report obviously gives Entwistle an easier ride than the *Bury Times* had done in recent weeks because of what he calls 'the Roy of the Rovers script' of how the game panned out. The hack also criticised fans who left with ten minutes to go as Bury found themselves 2–1 down before Wayne's woozy turn-and-shot which constituted the second goal. It was a strike which followed Joe Jakub's that brought Bury back into the game after they were initially 2–0 down against perennial bogey side Alexandra.

Martin Dobson's caring attitude towards his small band of brothers is again highlighted in the 'Mr Courage' story which dominates the back page of 13 November. 'His determination to get back out there and battle on was an example to everyone. Wayne tends to get frustrated and he knows he isn't perfect, but he always gives absolutely everything whether things are going well or badly,' Dobson beams to the local newspaper after he had sat out the game with a broken nose sustained in training. Despite the arm around the shoulder for his striker, he also reveals that the rest of the side got a half-time tongue-lashing, as 'only the agility of David Brown saved us from further embarrassment' and Kevin Young made way for substitute Gary Buckley 'in a tactical switch.'

The boss's nose had failed to heal in time for the next game, away at Preston North End in the first round of the FA Cup. While it was mercifully not at the hands of a non-league side, Bury fell at the first hurdle of the oldest cup competition in the world in a 4–3 humdinger. Neil Burton was again in place in the press box to describe the Shakers as 'more than a match for their Third Division opponents in a sparkling cup tie which provided ample entertainment.'

Both defences were labelled 'vulnerable' in the report, which subsequently alerted the reader to the fact that Preston's was actually the most generous in the Football League at that point. Despite this, the hosts raced into a 2–0 lead inside the first five minutes after some suspect interpretation of the 'not interfering with play' rule meant an easy tap-in for North End's first. A David Brown rush of blood to the head gave ex-England striker David Johnson an irresistible opportunity to slot home from thirty yards to double the home side's lead.

Burton praises Bury for not letting their heads drop and claims that Wayne Entwistle was having his best game of the season by the time he made it 2–1. Enty then won a penalty for Bury only for Trevor Ross to blast the spot kick against the post, but Bury reportedly had cause to feel optimistic going in for the half-time break.

It was an optimism that would dissolve after just twenty-six seconds of the second half as Preston made it 3–1 immediately after the restart. Despite the hammer blow, Bury didn't resort to desperate tactics and got a foot in the door with a Craig Madden toe-poke with half an hour left, only for the home side to force the very same door shut with a quarter of an hour to go with a fourth goal that took a wicked deflection off the last man in the wall to leave Bury 'keeper Brown stranded. With eight minutes still to play, Trevor Ross made amends for his penalty miss with a thunderbolt free kick that made it 4–3, but for all of their indomitable battling spirit an equaliser was just beyond Bury's grasp. The match report headline 'ROUGH JUSTICE IN THIS EARLY EXIT' sums things up well, but the silver lining of this particular cloud would be that the Shakers' mini-squad would now be free to concentrate solely on the league.

"It was one of those rare occasions when being knocked out of the FA Cup didn't really bother me," remembers supporter Malcolm Parr. "We could see how things were developing, and even though we were losing a stream of revenue, we had other priorities," he says.

The mini-hiccup that the *Bury Times* claims had developed in the last four games, in which Bury only won once, away at Northampton, is blamed squarely on the absence of player-manager Martin Dobson. After presenting the reporter with the fact that the seven goals conceded in that period matched the same number that had gone past David Brown in the preceding ten games, Dobson claims to now be fully fit before he switches the reporter's focus and apportions blame to the momentary lapses in concentration that are costing his side dearly. He also praises the supporters who travelled to Deepdale for the cup tie and claims that Bury didn't let them down with their performance.

The manager also makes a bold statement about the stage of the season that had been reached as he is reported as saying 'Promotion hopes can either be strengthened or crushed.' While this was undoubtedly true on the playing side of things at Gigg Lane, there was obviously a financial bearing on the hopes for success too. A small side bar on the back page of the paper from Tuesday 20 November advertises a public meeting that was to be held at Bury Town Hall two days later: 'To all interested in Bury Football Club – THE FUTURE?' reads its tantalising and ungrammatical headline, before offering a glimpse of glamour in the body text with the claim that players and directors will be in attendance.

It wasn't just those immediately connected with the club who were there either. Ed Stourton, future presenter of the *PM* programme on BBC Radio 4, was reporting with a camera crew from his then-employers ITN on what emerged as the launch of the Bury Football Club Life Line. Nat Lofthouse, who had launched the same scheme at Bolton Wanderers, had also made the short trip along the A58 to act as a mentor to the Bury players who were tasked with getting fans to sign up and donate £2 a week to the plan.

The report has survived on the itnsource.com website and is one of the precious few video snapshots of the Forgotten Fifteen. The players are shown being given their pep talk by Lofthouse, listening to their instructions intently while wearing rosettes the size of beer mats. As they make their way through the crowds, we see Winston White in a natty lemon cardigan and hear Leighton James espousing the scheme's virtues to some star-struck fans. Then come interviews with the fans themselves, all of whom talk about their love for the club and how an extra £2 a week isn't a great deal if it means professional football is kept in Bury.

Two days after their good deed at the Elizabethan Suite, in the building opened by the Queen in 1954, Bury repaid the fans' faith in them with a 2–0 win at Mansfield Town on 24 November. They had to work hard for the victory against the division's meanest defence and also lowest scorers, but it was the 1984/85 season's classic strike pairing who did the damage, with Craig Madden and Wayne Entwistle both grabbing a goal each to take the Shakers to joint top of the table.

Champagne corks popped on the trip home, not in deference to this run-of-the-mill victory, or even because of David Brown's penalty save from future Bury stalwart Mark Kearney. The reason is made crystal clear in the *Bury Times* match report headline from 27 November: 'CRAIG'S CENTURY GETS A 'BUBBLY' RECEPTION' is the reaction to Craig Madden reaching a ton of goals for the club.

In what reads like a terrific game to have attended, goalkeeper Brown is described by John Dyson as an 'imposing barrier' behind returning player-manager Martin Dobson, while praise is also lavished on Kevin Young and Trevor Ross for their lung-bursting runs from deep positions. Despite such a heroic performance, Trevor is spoken of in more cautionary terms in the other story covered on the same page of the paper. 'ROSS UNDER A BAN CLOUD' highlights once more Dobson's stern stance with his side as Trevor's walk of the disciplinary tightrope was causing him concern.

'We could do without suspensions hanging over our heads but I won't be telling Trevor to change his style of play. We have got to remain competitive so the odd booking is inevitable, but I won't tolerate them for dissent or retaliation,' he is quoted as saying, before revealing that Andy Hill was fined for such a yellow card after the trip to Nottinghamshire and that John Bramhall also had to pay up for the same reason after the FA Cup defeat at Preston.

Trevor Ross was one of those names from Bury sides of the mid-eighties that I remembered my dad talking about before I was old enough to go to games. When, aged about fourteen, I stumbled over a player of the same name in Nick Hornby's love letter to all things Arsenal, *Fever Pitch*, I remember chuckling at the coincidence of there being two players of the same name playing at such polar opposites of the Football League. I had no idea that the two men were in fact just one.

Having interviewed Trevor for Bury's match day programme in the mid-part of the 2000s, I called him again and asked if he'd be interested in talking about just the promotion season. He said he would be, and so on another lovely early summer's evening I circumnavigated the M60 to his home in Oldham and sat in his

Trevor Ross in action in the 1984/85 season. (Copyright: Bury Football Club)

back garden with him as we talked about how he arrived at Bury and rejoined his former Everton teammate Martin Dobson via Greece.

"Dobbo and I were friends at Everton and got on well. We'd had good times there," he now remembers. "Then when I came to Bury and was introduced to Frank Casper I got on well with him too. He was my kind of coach because we had a laugh straightaway. I was told what they wanted from the club and I signed. It was a bonus that it was only twenty minutes down the road and I think my sponsored Fiat might have swung the deal too," he laughs.

Being immersed in his native North West must have been a colossal relief to Trevor as the move to Gigg Lane came after a spell at AEK Athens in the Greek capital. "I should have gone to Sheffield United after leaving Everton and everything was pretty much signed, sealed and delivered. But then AEK came in for me and offered me a deal I couldn't refuse. My heart ruled the move, not my head, but it was a bad place for me to go," he reveals.

A short spell at Bramhall Lane followed on his return from the Aegean coast, but it was his old pal Dobson who won the race for Trevor's signature just after Andy Hill had also committed to Bury. "There was a lot of positivity around the club when I signed and there was a good team spirit, not least because I suppose I'm a bit of

99

a character and there were one or two others like that in the squad too. The morale was great on the training pitch. Everybody had a laugh and a joke and we'd have a beer afterwards. We played for each other and that's what got us through the season. As well as not having any injuries too, of course.

"The game was more basic then than it is now. It was certainly a lot more physical. Maybe it's slightly faster these days, but you've still got to get through your ninety minutes. If I was still playing today I'd probably be suspended more than I'd play. I didn't take any prisoners and if there was a ball there to try and win then I'd try and win it. It's not about being dirty, or going in intentionally to hurt someone because I'd never do that. I think Martin wanted me to be the player to put it about and get a few good tackles in early doors to help one or two of the younger players.

"There were players like Gary Buckley in the squad who were good, physical and didn't shy away from a tackle. He was a nice footballer but he sometimes got himself into trouble, so we had the balance between the skilful and the physical. We didn't fear any one player, any team or any ground. Each match was just another game and we always expected a point at the very least from every one we played. We weren't fazed. I never heard anyone sounding worried about the next game. I'd have told them to get a grip if I had.

"David Brown had a great season in goal and big John Bramhall gave us confidence too. We had a fantastic goalscorer, Craig Madden, up front who put a lot of work in and covered a lot of ground. I played at right back a lot and I'd get allsorts thrown at me, so I'd just smile at people spitting at me, swearing at me and all that. If I was in a bad mood I might say something back.

"A lot of fans looked to me to protect other members of the team too. Say Craig Madden or Youngy or whoever had been badly tackled, they'd be singing to the lad who did it 'Rossy's gonna get yer!' if there was a bit of a to-do. That happened away at Blackpool. There was a big centre half giving Craig a hammering and chopping him down, banging him here, there and everywhere. I said to him, 'Calm yourself down or there'll be trouble.' He did it again to Craig so I went in hard on him to show that we were a team who'd do that kind of thing for each other.

"Winston White used to like playing behind me too because he knew he was safe as houses. He knew that I could see everything that was going on and then if there was something in front of him that he needed to sort out then I'd be right behind him," he says.

Like Kevin Young, Trevor also suffers to this day with injuries sustained in his career. He now remembers with affection how those injuries were treated at the time by Bury's physio. "Wilf kind of met his match a bit with me. I was a bit of a joker and I'd wind him up by hiding his clothes and stuff, but I loved him to bits. Before that cup game at Preston we were having the team talk on the Friday and Dobbo was telling me about their left winger who was apparently their danger man. He said 'I want you to take him out of the game' and I said 'What, for good or just for tomorrow?' It wasn't meant maliciously, only as a joke, but Wilf pinched it and put it in his after-dinner routine," he smiles.

"He was just a character, and I imagine he still is. He was always laughing, always joking, and he was Mr Bury. As much as he liked a laugh he wouldn't beat around the bush, though. If you were shite, he'd tell you, especially with me because we had a good relationship," he says, bringing to mind the possibility of McGuinness telling George Best or Denis Law the same thing during his spell in charge of Manchester United.

If any players had to go off because of a Trevor Ross challenge back in the day, there would only have been one substitute on the bench lined up to replace them. Today, a Football League team can name eighteen players in a match day squad, and the dip in quality is, according to Trevor, noticeable. "If you had two players injured you were buggered," he says. "These days you can put three on if you want to use them. They'll say that someone's running out of steam so they say 'We'll change him' – if someone ran out of steam when I was playing they had to carry on and dig deeper for that bit extra!" he says.

Trevor didn't earn anywhere near as much money when he called Highbury his home ground as today's players do at the Emirates Stadium, and he feels that this is another big difference between how the game was then and how it is now. "Players going down at the slightest touch are spoiling the game, but I also think that the mentality towards winning games has changed and that's due to money. When I lost a game I'd be angry. It'd hurt me because that's what had been bred into me from playing at school. But I go to games now and you sometimes see them coming off if they've lost and they can be smiling," he concludes.

I came away from Trevor Ross's house full of admiration for a man who still had a smile on his face despite the crippling injuries caused by the game he loved. It had only been a brief interview, but, as a key member of the promotion team who fans look back on so fondly, it was a privilege to spend time with him.

Back at the tail end of November 1984, the NUM's resolve in the face of the miners' strike was wavering. More than 3,000 had returned to work as the cold winter bit hard, taking the nationwide total now back underground to more than 62,000.

Bury may have ended the month on a high after that 2–0 victory at Mansfield in the Nottinghamshire coalfield where the miners had kept on working in opposition to their Derbyshire counterparts, and there was still going to be plenty of joy to come for the Shakers on the field in the month that followed, but it was to be a tragic Christmas in the town for reasons much closer to home than a strike in an industry which it had never relied on.

December 1984

As younger fans were opening the first windows on their advent calendars and getting excited by shop window displays and toy commercials on television, Bury were preparing to welcome Torquay United to Gigg Lane after a weary trip up from Devon. Despite it being 1 December, the Christmas spirit hadn't yet reached Martin Dobson, who doles out some tough love in his programme notes for the game: 'With three weeks having passed since our last home game…a lot has happened at the club. We made our FA Cup exit at Preston and I have kept harping on to the players just how important the first 10–15 minutes are in a game. It was disappointing therefore to concede early goals in each half, we just didn't defend professionally,' he blasts. On Andy Hill's retaliation at Mansfield, the gaffer leaves a figurative lump of coal in the nineteen-year-old's stocking, but the hope of an orange in those of others: 'With a small squad, injuries and suspensions could cause us problems but with the likes of Pashley, Buckley, Cutler, [Chris] Grimshaw and [Andy] Welsh itching for first team football, I would have every confidence in playing them,' he warns.

As it was, none of the fringe players started the game against the Gulls, though Gary Buckley made the subs' bench. John Dyson's introduction to the match report printed in the *Bury Times* of Tuesday 4 December declares that it's the sign of a good side when they win despite not being at their best. Reading the intro and knowing that Bury won the game 3–1 makes one wonder just how poor the visitors must have been to allow a result that looked like such a walkover.

Bury took only three minutes to draw first blood as Wayne Entwistle pounced on a cross spilled by the Torquay goalkeeper. Five minutes later, the visitors equalised in a move which Dyson claims was the only other activity in the first half apart from Craig Madden heading against a post. With ten minutes of the second half gone, the Shakers regained the lead as John Bramhall added the final touch to a set piece routine straight off the training ground before Leighton James rounded off the scoring after a one-two with his former Burnley teammate Kevin Young.

It's a tale about another former Burnley man that dominates the back page of the paper in a story underneath a photo and short write-up describing Ian Botham attending a sportsman's dinner at the social club. 'PASHLEY 'NO' TO AN ACHILLES OPERATION' is the banner headline of the story about the dependable ex-Claret Terry and his defiance of the scalpel for the good of his team. John Dyson reports that 'Pash' hobbled out of a 5–3 reserve team defeat to Manchester City in the Lancashire League and looked to be heading for the operating table and the same procedure that both John Bramhall and Chris Cutler underwent in the summer. 'But after a long chat with Martin Dobson, Pashley has decided to take a gamble by playing on match days and relying on rest and treatment for the remainder of the week in the hope that the injury settles down,' writes Dyson. Having started only seven of Bury's twenty-one league and cup games so far in the promotion season, his eventual tally of twenty-three appearances confirmed this bravery as the right course of action.

Still employed by Burnley, the club where he started his career in 1973 and whose backroom staff he joined after leaving Bury and retiring as a player in 1990, Terry was easy to find. A call to kindly Turf Moor

receptionist Veronica, outlining my reasons for wanting to speak to the former defender, resulted in his number appearing in my email inbox. I phoned Terry and asked if he'd be interested in talking about the promotion season and he agreed, so we arranged to meet in Blackpool on the Saturday of a bank holiday weekend.

"I had good times at Bury. I enjoyed my time there in good teams that played good football. In fact, I think I'd even go as far as to say that I played my best football there," he reveals in a busy cafe in the Lancashire market town of Poulton-le-Fylde, where we drove after negotiating the crowds at Blackpool North railway station.

"I joined from Blackpool in the 1983 close season after Jim Iley signed me, and it wasn't really the best time to sign for a new club after they'd come so close to being promoted the season before. After a pre-season game that summer at Wigan, Jim even said to me 'I'm not really sure why I signed you' before wandering off. It didn't leave the greatest impression on me and I never really connected with him, but when Martin came he brought good footballers with him. His philosophy clicked with me because I'd played with him before at Burnley, of course, and it was because of his connections that he attracted a good combination of youth and experience. Him and Frank were bubbly and you need that for success.

"I don't think Bury could have had a better person for the job than Martin, not least because he was still playing. It was his first job, and I knew when I played with him that he'd become a manager, just like I knew that Frank Casper had it in him too. The two of them made sure that as a team we went out every game thinking that we'd score goals and win games. They gave us freedom and that's to Martin's and Frank's credit. We were never the best supported side in terms of numbers on the terraces but it was a joy to be playing an attacking game, even from a full-back position," he remembers.

In fact, in the varied coaching positions that he has taken at Burnley since injury called time on his career in 1990, Terry still uses techniques learned from his former mentor who was the darling of the Bob Lord Stand at Turf Moor while he himself was playing for the youth team. "Martin embraced the Wiel Coerver methods that you can still teach youngsters today. He was truly innovative as far as I'm concerned," he says.

Like so many of Bury's promotion squad from British football's worst year, it was in East Lancashire that Terry received a dignified education in the game and its trappings. "We weren't taught to think differently about ourselves because we were footballers," he says. "We were living our particular dream and being paid well for it, but at Burnley we didn't play for money. We played for the love of the game and were grateful for a contract. We had families and bills to pay, and although we were paid more than I suppose what you'd call the man in the street, it wasn't to the extent of today," he claims.

When Dobson's managerial style found its feet after the learning curve that was the back end of the 83/84 season, Terry claims that it was easy for the magic to flow. "We worked hard with all of the running in pre-season and no one cut any corners. You've got to get amongst teams and try and upset those that play football, all the while trying to do the same yourself. We stuck to what we believed in, we were successful and we took our attitude from training into match days. If you're on a good winning roll then you're always looking to the next game," he claims, not unreasonably.

"Gigg Lane was always a great surface for playing football on, but our training pitch at Goshen wasn't the best. So many of the

106

grounds that we'd go to were more like that than what we were used to at Gigg. Hartlepool was awful, not just for the pitch but because of what the dressing room was like too. You could only get four people in the bath, and even if you did manage to get in it, there'd never be any hot water after the match. The wind would be whistling underneath the door so you'd just be desperate to get on the coach," he laughs, visibly shuddering at the memory.

Another ground of which the mere mention drags all sorts of repressed memories kicking and screaming to the fore is the Shay in Halifax. "I don't remember our game there in the promotion season, but on a wet and windy day there's nowhere else like it," Terry says. "It shows character if you can get something there, though. It's not going to be pretty, but you can grind out a result. If your attitude and mentality aren't right then you're going to struggle and get found out as a lot of teams did in the FA Cup third round there," he adds, side-stepping Bury's 4–1 defeat in January 1985.

The Achilles injury that Terry's stoicism prevented him from going under the knife to remedy developed as the promotion season progressed. "I initially did it in pre-season when we were running figures-of-eights on the hills at Pilsworth. They were steep, about twenty metres, and it happened and I couldn't shake it off. I found a physiotherapist in Cleveleys because I was still living in this neck of the woods and he diagnosed the problem and gave me exercises to do. I did them, avoided the operation, and the problem cleared up with plenty of rest," he explains.

The diagnosis of Pashley's problem from a different source than Bury's physio Wilf McGuinness wasn't a personal slight on the man with the magic sponge. "Wilf was a character and I loved being around him. He'd put the ultrasound machine over your injury and you'd sometimes have to treat yourself as he tested his gags on you and wrote down the ones he'd put in his after-dinner routine. If you dared titter at one of his stories, you were left to your own devices as he'd be writing down a tale involving George Best," he laughs.

As we looked through the old match reports that ran in the local press during the promotion season, it's clear that when Terry mentions his time at Bury as being a happy one, he wasn't messing around. "You wouldn't get much change out of playing against Andy Hill if he was at right back or centre back. Wayne Enty, who I used to room with on away trips, might not have been the most silky-skilled player, but he made up for that with his willingness and determination. His partnership with Craig Madden was phenomenal that season. Craig wasn't the biggest lad, but his instinct in and around the six-yard box was incredible. I coach kids now, but you can't coach an instinct. He'd get a touch from any part of his body – his left foot, his right, his head, his backside. He just knew what to do.

"Winston White could win games on his own, and I grew up in the same team as Joe Jakub so we were always good friends. He broke his leg twice when he was only young, but it never held him back. You'd see him flying into tackles leading with that very same leg! John Bramhall was another who wasn't particularly skilful, but you need players like that. You'd rather have the Bury lads in your team than against you," he claims.

The will to win among the Fifteen even spilled over in training when Pashley inflicted the injury on Martin Dobson which ruled the boss out of four games in November. "Taffy flicked another great cross in and we both went up to head it, him towards goal and me trying to get it away, and we collided. He wasn't going to play me the following Saturday, but he didn't have a choice now because he had plasters all over his nose and a black eye. I just had a small nick on my forehead," he claims, smiling.

Today, coaching the youngsters at Burnley, Pashley has a sensible philosophy to pass on to his young charges. "Burnley laid the foundations of my career and I moved on to Blackpool for the sake of that career. I struggled a bit when Sam Ellis brought his own players into the Bury team after Martin left, but that's football. I tell the kids that today as I coach them," he says plainly.

Keeping his interests in the game fresh enables Terry to stay up-to-date with some of his former colleagues. "I saw Wilf at the FA Youth Cup semi-final in 2012 when my Burnley team played Blackburn. He was there with his son Paul, who was manager of the Manchester United team that the winner of our game would play if his team got past Chelsea," he says.

Having already taken caretaker charge of the Clarets for a spell in 2007, Terry landed in the manager's seat at Turf Moor again for a temporary period in 2010, but this time in a joint venture with a man he knew well: Martin Dobson. "Owen Coyle had left the club to join Bolton and taken a lot of his backroom team with him. Martin and I stepped in, and though Brian Laws was in place for it, we pretty much oversaw the 3–0 defeat at Old Trafford in January that year," he says, all memories of training ground broken noses now presumably forgotten. In 2012, following Eddie Howe's departure from the Burnley job, Terry would go on to take the reins for a third spell as caretaker.

"Martin and Frank tested us," he concludes. "You need that if you want to be successful because otherwise it's a chore and you're not giving your best. They made us enjoy going to training each morning which, when you consider we'd be picking up dog muck before putting the cones down for our sessions, really is something!" he laughs.

Learning how to play the game 'the Burnley way' is a fine thread that connects the story of the Forgotten Fifteen, but in Terry Pashley there's a disciple who keeps the flame burning strongly. As we parted with a friendly handshake, I could picture a lot of eighteen-year-olds being on the end of a similar goodbye as they progressed up the footballing ladder following his coaching.

Bury's defeat at Preston North End in the first round of the FA Cup gave the players the dubious distinction of having the second weekend in December free. The last paragraph of the *Bury Times* story about Terry Pashley soldiering on in the face of his Achilles problem reveals that the players were to spend the weekend on 'an active break' in the Isle of Man. Fans, meanwhile, would be ruing the defeat at Deepdale as it almost certainly meant an afternoon of Christmas shopping on the windswept open concrete piazzas of Bury town centre.

Memories of the Manx trip are a little hazy for most members of the squad. After the voyage across the Irish Sea on the Heysham ferry, the chicken-in-a-basket entertainment at the hotel was provided by an iteration of soul stars The Drifters, and once they'd completed their set, the American superstars drank in the hotel bar with the Fourth Division footballers. As the majority of the players noted when thinking back to the trip: the team that drinks together, stays together.

On the same day that their victors in the first round of the cup were losing 4–1 at home to non-league Telford at the second stage, Bury were playing Manx side Gymnasium in front of a crowd recorded in Peter Cullen's 1999 history of the club as fifty. Craig Madden and Joe Jakub each grabbed hat-tricks and Gary Buckley weighed in with a strike. Leighton James spent part of the game in goal before Bury's final goal was scored by assistant manager Frank Casper, who was given a run-out as an early birthday present on the last day of his thirties.

Like his former player Terry Pashley, the assistant manager during the promotion season was also easy to find and request an interview with thanks to the kindness of Veronica on the Turf Moor reception desk. After agreeing to be interviewed, Frank arranged to meet me in a pub on a winding country road in the East Lancashire hills. In fact, it was an interview that had to be conducted twice as the voice recorder on my phone hadn't picked up the hour-long conversation from our first meeting. A week after we first met, we met again to talk about the same things, having made absolutely sure this time that the gauge on the recorder shows we are being listened to.

"It was a great season for us, obviously. We could have done better in that we could have won the championship, but for so few players to gel in the way they did was special," he says. "Martin and I looked at the players as a group and had to work out if that group was good enough to get us promotion. The nucleus down the middle of the team was David Brown in goal, Joe Jakub in midfield, Wayne Entwistle and Craig Madden up front with John Bramhall at the back, so we built the side around those five, with others like Andy Hill joining over time.

"We both knew Leighton, of course, because of the Burnley connection, and Martin had played with Trevor Ross at Everton. Both were approaching the end of their careers and nowadays it wouldn't happen. Back then, though, players needed to earn what they could in the last two or three years of their careers and Martin sold the club well to them. He didn't need to sell himself because of his experience. We held interviews with all kinds of players from the local area and we had a good choice.

"So we also signed Kevin Young, who I'd known since he was fourteen and up at Sunderland. I knew he could play higher [than the clubs he'd been on loan at]. The John Bond situation at Burnley and what he was doing with the youth team worked to our benefit. Burnley had always scouted a lot of players from the North East. There'd be coachloads of lads coming down from there because of the good training that they knew they'd get," he says.

Frank's new role on joining Bury at Easter 1984 was a distinct learning curve after Dobson persuaded him to join him at Gigg Lane. "We met in the pub where we're sitting now, The Ram, and he knew I was out of work even though I'd got my badges in 1978. He was looking at the Bury job so we came to a mutual agreement. He got the management job because he could still play so it gave Terry Robinson some relief on the budget. Despite that, Terry still couldn't pay me so I actually worked my first twelve months at Bury for nothing. Ray Pointer had joined the coaching staff just before me, and we'd played in the same game, me for Rotherham against him and Bury, when he scored five," he says of the game in 1965 when the record for the most goals scored by a single Bury player in one match was set.

"I had to be the go-between with the players and the management team. On the first day that Martin and I took a training session the dressing room was in a downbeat mood. The former groundsman, Rod Lester, threw the kit from two laundry baskets into the room and the players jumped on the pile as they tried to find kit to train in. You'd get players shouting 'I've found a sock!' and I felt that it was going against my principles – that you had to look smart if you wanted to play smart.

"I was at the PFA awards having a drink with a lad called Martin Protheroe who used to play for Burnley but was then working for Umbro after he'd not quite made it as a player. I thought I'd done a deal that he'd give us training kit for each of our lads. It arrived and they all loved it, except for the chairman who'd been landed with a £4,000 bill for it. He hit the roof," he laughs.

Despite such a setback, Frank's personality won him friends around the club. "At a small club you get to know everyone quickly. I got to know the girls in the laundry and the groundsman and struck up friendships with them. If they're not happy, the club's not happy. [Former secretary] John Heap would tell me stories that helped me settle and Reg [Smith, former director and former Rector of Bury, based at the town's Parish Church] would be down most days. It was a good club," he remembers.

Frank remembers the Lilleshall training session where he and Dobson learned the ways of Dutch maestro Wiel Coerver well. "Enty was a skilful lad but he wasn't consistent. Me and Martin went down to Lilleshall with the Dutch kids to see how we could work on this aspect of his game. We saw them doing their moves and it was almost as if they were wearing ballet shoes. Wiel said that every player should have a ball of their own and showed us films at night of dribbling, shooting, tackling and how to keep the ball. The next day we saw the kids doing what we'd seen on the screen. It was incredible," he reveals.

Also on the agenda was a meeting of other figures in the game at the bar in the sleepy Shropshire town. "We'd get in at three in the morning after having a few drinks and then be watching games six hours later with shades on," he laughs. "Me and Howard Kendall met Sam Ellis and Jim Smith in the bar and we eventually left Sam in a chair by the fire. That was around the time when Sam made Blackpool tough. That lad Greenall [Colin, who signed for Ellis and Bury in 1990 for £125,000] was a brute," he adds as an aside.

"Coerver taught us how to keep the ball and how to pass it, which I think players should still be taught today. We got back to Bury, and remembering what he said about everyone having a ball, I got in touch with a contact I had at Mitre who gave us twenty-four of the things. We conducted trials on new balls too, so we'd get new ones every two weeks," he says of the Mitre Deltas that would have been dribbled around the detritus on Lower Gigg or Goshen. "Eventually, Wayne Enty practised and practised on his own with his ball and got the knack of a lot of the commands," he adds.

It was also a system that enabled Frank to work with another lad who'd found his way down the football food chain after being released by John Bond's brutal regime at Burnley and who found himself at Gigg Lane in the 1985 close season. "We signed Lee Dixon from Chester and worked on him and David Lee [then in Bury's reserves] together. We taught Dixon the fundamentals of defending in a back four and helped him learn how to support wingers. He's an intelligent lad, Lee, and he picked it up quickly to the point that we lost him to a bigger club too quickly. We tried to keep him with a big signing-on fee, but it wasn't to be. When we signed Liam Robinson and Peter Butler they went to tribunals and we were told to pay low fees but with sell-on clauses. Stoke signed Lee from us for a small fee without a sell-on, which was extremely disappointing," he notes.

The assistant's nose for a good player came into its own in his and the boss's first close season. "We looked at the players we already had and who we wanted. We knew their backgrounds, their temperaments, when they signed. Look at someone like Andy Hill. If he's good enough to be at Manchester United at eighteen or nineteen then there's no question that he's going to be good enough for Bury.

"You're going to have to accept that your squad is going to get injuries, but you just hope that they're not long-term and that they're not going to be too niggly and disrupt your training routines," he says of the paper-thin squad. "We tried to keep training hard with different methods because we knew as players how we'd want to be treated. We didn't run the lads until they dropped, we ran them by yardage. When their yardage was done, they'd finished. That's not to say that Craig Madden, Joe Jakub and Wayne Entwistle couldn't run all day. They had good engines and could run for a whole game. You'd ask them before training, though, 'Do you want to run or play a game?' and they'd always choose a seven-a-side game at Goshen. A lot of the time they only thought they were tired, it was all about mental toughness," he laughs.

While Frank knew what to expect from one of Bury's big-star close season signings, he had to trust his gaffer's judgement on the other. "Martin had played with Trevor Ross at Everton, of course, and knew that he had a good two or three years left in him. He was ideal because he brought strength to the team. He was physical, he had a terrific shot on him and he could pass the ball well. We were lucky to get him because Sheffield United and Burnley were both after him at the time too. He could have easily gone higher up the league," he says.

With such a man as Ross in the team, and following his revelations about the blunt and direct team talks outlined in the interview conducted with him for this publication, one might imagine that if things got tense in the Bury dressing room then matters might have come to blows. Frank refutes this.

"Martin and I wouldn't shout. Some managers shout, some throw things or wave their arms around and some put their arms around players. We'd use some, perhaps, industrial language, but we'd never rant and rave because everyone is different and it's not for the benefit of the team to be like that," he explains sensibly.

Scouts were something of a luxury for Bury in the mid-eighties. "We'd look at games and do our homework on set pieces. We'd speak to managers of clubs who'd played against the teams we were due to be playing soon and write down positions, looking at how they got the ball from the back to the front, how they used the wings. We'd find out where their players stood for set pieces, how the midfield dealt with them, if they stood at the front post or the near post. If we got things wrong and it meant we conceded parts of the game, Martin wouldn't shirk his responsibility. He'd stand up in front of the players and admit that he'd done something wrong. I gave him a roasting after the game against Exeter when Wayne Entwistle scored twice and he took it, but at the same time it didn't mean that the rest of them had played like world beaters," Frank notes.

When looking through the match reports of the 84/85 season contained in a large lever arch file, further memories of the squad he oversaw came flooding back to the former assistant manager. "Craig Madden just had the knack of scoring goals. There's an art to it. We knew that a lot of his goals were tap-ins, but there's the anticipation that you need to be in the right place at the right time and he had it. We knew Taff from the Turf. He was the best crosser in the division by a mile, just like he had been at Burnley when we had Dave Thomas on the other wing. With Terry Pashley, I'd say to him 'I know you can do it out there, you know you can do it out there, so go and show them that you can.' If you tell a player he's crap he's going to believe that he's crap so you need to give them a boost. Pash would get his head down and he had a great first touch.

"You'd have Enty, who'd captained England Schoolboys, running sideways, waiting for the ball to drop with his arm up, putting into practice what he went over time and again in training. We instilled it into Craig and Wayne that it was a crime to lose the ball, which stemmed from when Martin and I played in a game for Burnley up at Middlesbrough which we drew 3–3. I told Jimmy

Adamson that I'd been crap after I gave two goals away and Martin had rescued us with two, but Jimmy said that although my first touch wasn't great, I'd never stopped running for the ball in comparison to some others who hadn't pulled their weight," he continues.

"Wilf was a great presence too. I knew how important physiotherapy was from my time at Rotherham when one of my teammates broke his leg. He had a hairline fracture in it and I stayed at his house on the Friday night before a game. I had to help him dress on the Saturday morning and get his boots on in the changing room. He went out, fell and it snapped. Players put themselves through horrific situations like that because of their mortgages," he remembers, before revealing that he himself was waiting for a knee replacement as we spoke.

It's nothing out of the ordinary to imagine Frank taking his two sons, Lee and Chris, to Gigg Lane while he was employed by the club. What makes this particular work experience placement more remarkable is that just over twenty years after Dad joined Bury, Chris would be stepping on to the next rung up and managing the Shakers after his own playing career came to a distressingly premature end while playing for Reading.

"He asked for my advice when he was youth team coach at Bury and the job came up. I told him not to take it and said that the job was too big and that management isn't a nice role because there's no money and you get all the rubbish thrown at you. He went against what I told him, though, and said that he was going to throw his hat in because he knew who the other applicants were and he felt he was better than them. He believed in himself as a person and as a coach, which is what you need when stepping up from coaching kids to the first team because it's the biggest step up. I wished him good luck on his first day and he let the players know that the preparation for Saturday began then. Those that were up for it would have shown him that they were," he says proudly.

As the conversation turned back to 1984/85, Frank wrapped up his memories with a remarkable comparison. "It was a brilliant season for Bury, and with the players we had we should have won the league. It was Dobbo's first job, it was my first job, and when you've got Fourth Division teams launching the ball at you it's an eye-opener, but we had players like Taff who'd let opposition players chase them. We were almost like Barcelona because we knew we could get it back within ten seconds and we could knacker the other team out," he laughs, yet also highlights just how technical his and Dobson's examination of opposition sides was.

After we said goodbye outside the pub, Frank would be heading back to his home in the town of Burnley that had embraced him following his move from Rotherham and his native South Yorkshire in 1967. His first stop after leaving Bury in 1989 was back at Turf Moor to take charge of the club where he was so revered, before he set up his own business, Super League, supplying football kits, including those which Bury wore in two seasons in the second tier in the late-1990s. It was a pleasure to talk to a man so inextricably linked with the two clubs.

Their drinking buddies may have had a top three hit in 1972 with 'Saturday Night At the Movies', but it seemed that Bury were still in the bar of the Palace Hotel in Douglas with the Drifters when they faced Wrexham at the Racecourse Ground on the afternoon of Saturday 15 December. A 3–0 defeat to the team that was propping up the rest of the Football League, in front of just 1,400 more people than saw the rout over Gymnasium a week earlier, can't have been the best way to prove that the mid-season jaunt across the Irish Sea had been worthwhile.

With the game taking place in a fog that wouldn't have been out of place rolling on to the Manx promenade in December, John Dyson in the *Bury Times* reports that many of those who'd travelled to North Wales from the blue skies of Lancashire would have been praying for abandonment. Despite a purple patch in which Bury hit the woodwork three times in ninety seconds, it was to be a fruitless afternoon, the worst of the season so far for the Shakers.

It's the kind of result that makes fans aged from eight to eighty grumble, "I'm not going again." The back page of the *Bury Times* from Tuesday 18 December which features the report also carries two other stories, one of which, if you were so inclined as not to want to go to the next game, offered an alternative with more than a hint of razzmatazz.

'GLITTERING PRIZE FOR TV WRESTLERS' is the headline of a story about *World of Sport*'s audience-pulling spectacle coming to the Castle Leisure Centre the following night. Johnny Wilson and Skull Murphy are named as being the men squaring up to each other in front of Granada TV's cameras for the Grand Prix belt sponsored by ITV's Saturday afternoon sports fest. Pat Roach, by now known in front rooms up and down the country as Bomber in *Auf Wiedersehen, Pet* is also reported to be taking to the canvas after travelling up from Birmingham, which strikes an odd chord given Bomber's West Country burr.

If you weren't prepared to give up on Bury just yet, the final of the three stories on the back page of the paper is a doom-laden preview of the Shakers' trip to Peterborough United on the same night that Kent Walton was to be commentating ringside at the sports hall on Bolton Street. 'Shell-shocked Bury must crack the best home record in Division Four if their badly-wounded pride is to be swiftly restored after Saturday's disappointing 3–0 defeat at bottom club Wrexham,' goes the intro.

The story goes on to note that Dobson wanted more mental and physical toughness from his men. 'Certain individuals didn't perform against Wrexham and they are as disappointed as I am. Looking right through the team, we didn't function in any department and we were waiting for things to happen instead of making them happen,' he is quoted as saying. John Dyson refers in the story to the way that the Bury team had picked themselves up and dusted themselves down after other bad performances earlier that season, with particular attention paid to the defeats at Stockport and Scunthorpe, but says that Dobson will be hoping for the side to bounce back at London Road. It would be tough, because as Bury took to the pitch in the freezing Cambridgeshire air on 19 December, the hosts had only conceded five goals on their own patch up to that point.

'THE WRECKERS!' is the simple headline that dominates the back page of the edition published three days later in commendation of Bury's tremendous 4–1 win. As the understanding between the two grew even stronger, Leighton James and Andy Hill served up some scintillating overlap play on the left that resulted in both getting on the scoresheet, Hill with a curling shot from the edge of the area and James with a stunning twenty-five-yarder. Craig Madden also got his name on the scoresheet twice.

"Peterborough had won something like eight of their home games up to that point and drawn one and we went there and hammered them," says supporter Paul Greenlees today. "It was a stunning performance that was probably Leighton James's best game in a Bury shirt. I'll still maintain that it's one of the best Bury performances I've ever seen," he adds.

"Peterborough away in December 1984 is one of the best performances I've ever seen by a Bury side in forty years of being a supporter," remembers Malcolm Parr in The Swan and Cemetery on Manchester Road. "We scored four but it could so easily have been seven. There was another exceptional Leighton James goal after he ran half the length of the pitch to score it. When that team clicked, like they did that night, nobody in that division could live with us. We ended up doing the conga on the away end singing 'Nellie the Elephant' by the Toy Dolls," he laughs, the euphoria of the victory meaning that the travelling army eschewed traditional Yuletide ditties.

It was a result that meant Bury went into Christmas on top of the tree as they looked down on the rest of the Fourth Division from its summit, but the festive season of 1984 in the town was a tragic one. At 4.50am on Christmas morning, emergency services were called to Massey Street, off Huntley Mount Road, after reports that a house was on fire. Despite the arrival of the fire brigade within minutes, six bodies were recovered from the house and three people were pronounced dead on arrival at hospital.

The first issue of the *Bury Times* published after the disaster reports that the fire 'wiped out' four generations of one family who were celebrating Christmas together. Four of the nine victims of the blaze, which Greater Manchester Fire and Rescue called 'the worst fire of its kind in recent years', were children.

"A former colleague's father-in-law was the commander at Bury fire station, and they told me all about it on the few days we had to work between Christmas and New Year," remembers Malcolm Parr. "It was an enormous tragedy and Frank always said that it was the worst incident he attended in his thirty years of service. Several of his men were traumatised by the incident," he continues.

An inquest into the fire was held in March 1985. 'Toxic gases from blazing foam-filled furniture gave victims of Bury's worst ever house fire less than three minutes to escape. A fire chief said the temperature in the house...could have reached 1,000 degrees centigrade,' reported the local paper on Tuesday 5 March. The inquest also heard how wrapping paper from opened presents was thrown into the fire grate and that blankets used by sleeping members of the extended family, as well as a settee, caught fire as they slept.

Today, little reference to the fire exists. It is not included in the *Chronicle of the 20th Century* and a Google search brings up only four directly applicable results, two of which are from regional newspaper websites. One is from the history section of the Greater Manchester Fire and Rescue website that mentions the fire in the same vein as the Woolworths fire in Manchester in 1979 which killed ten people. The last result is from Hansard, the record of parliament in the UK, and is a transcript of former Bury North MP, Alistair Burt, delivering a motion for the compulsory installation of smoke alarms in domestic properties. His plea goes into sobering detail of just how significant the presence of a detector in the house could have been.

With mass communication not being as it is today, it's hard to imagine how news of the fire spread. With the World Wide Web still seven years away, there were no news websites to look at or emails to be received. Facebook messages weren't sent, tweets weren't retweeted and texts weren't pinged off. Even picking up the landline phone and dialling a number, which now seems to be the method at the very bottom of the communication food chain, wasn't quite as easy because not everyone had telephones. Broadcast media covered the story, though obviously not to the saturation point of today's rolling networks.

"I remember national and local radio and TV news coverage of the fire on the basic bulletins that they have over the Christmas period," says Bury fan Mike Brooks today, "and I would have thought most people in the ground for the game against Port Vale on Boxing Day were aware of it."

Although it seems undoubtedly harsh to consider it today, many fans might have pushed the tragedy to the back of their minds that afternoon as Bury took their revenge on the Valiants for the defeat in the League Cup first round with a thumping 4–0 win.

The same issue of the paper that carries the tragic story on its front page runs with 'HEADING FOR PROMOTION!' as the headline for the match report. John Dyson gushes over 'the best finishing form of the season' as all four goals are praised to the hilt. Wayne Entwistle grabbed the first from a Leighton James cross which curled away from Barry Siddall in the visitors' goal, while John Bramhall found the net from a Winston White cross from the other flank for the second, just before half-time. Enty claimed a second from a Joe Jakub corner to take his season's tally to twelve, and Craig Madden wrapped up the scoring a minute later from a perfectly pitched Trevor Ross ball.

The back page of the paper from 28 December also pits Bury's strike force of Madden and Entwistle ('25 goals between them so far this season') against their counterparts up front for the following afternoon's visitors. Tranmere Rovers' twin forward threat of John Clayton and Colin Clarke is warned of in a story headlined 'MARKSMEN FACE-TO-FACE IN SHOOT-OUT'. Reporting the two strikers' haul of a remarkable thirty-five goals so far between them, John Dyson notes that 'playing on familiar territory will swing the odds in favour of the Bury duo'.

In the end, there was absolutely no contest as Bury cantered to a 3–0 win, taking their two-game tally over the festive period to seven goals scored and none conceded. In fact, in the report that was printed in the *Bury Times* on the first day of 1985, John Dyson describes Tranmere's attack as 'woefully lacking in ideas'. John Bramhall is singled out as having taken the game with his iron grip, while David Brown had 'an unexpectedly easy afternoon' between the sticks.

Not for the first time, a Tranmere Rovers side went to Gigg Lane and 'needled' the home side, but it was the Shakers' superior skill-set that won through. Craig Madden tried his luck with an audacious overhead kick that just cleared the goal, before the stalemate was broken as another delicious Leighton James cross was headed home by Entwistle. The striker got his second of the game with thirteen minutes left to play, with Dyson describing his volley from a Winston White cross as 'the killer blow'.

It's a bit of a flat description, particularly because a photograph of Entwistle that was taken just after the ball left his foot could justifiably be called one of the greatest pictures ever taken of a Bury player in action. The snap, which was printed in the next programme, shows Entwistle's face contorted into a 'Take that!' at the ball. Both feet are off the ground, his right leg as straight as a set square from his toes up to his huge calves. His left foot, revealing that his boots were made by Pony, gives perfect leverage to his stance. A Tranmere defender looks utterly dejected as he half-faces away from the ball while the visitors' goalkeeper, former Bury stopper John Platt, has both hands raised in surrender as though he's a bank teller caught in an armed raid. In the background, Craig Madden may have been expecting a cross as he's caught in mid-jump, looking as though he's levitating in the way many Bury fans actually thought he did. The picture gives the overall impression that the power of the shot would have removed the nets from the stanchion of the goal, until you look at the trajectory of the ball from its moment of impact. It's heading into the ground and so would have bounced past Platt before the 'keeper had the opportunity to react.

The afternoon's scoring was completed by Madden, who calmly slotted a Joe Jakub cross past Platt with six minutes left. It was the cherry on the cake for the Shakers' Christmas 1984 which they finished three points clear of the pack, as outlined in the story that the match report shares the back page with. 'NO XMAS LET-UP BY ELEVEN GOAL SHAKERS' is the headline of a report that fizzes with how Bury have proved the sceptics wrong in the three games since the 3–0 defeat at Wrexham. 'Ever since I came to the club, I've heard stories about how Bury start the season well and then fade,' says Martin Dobson, echoing every three pint know-it-all's claim from the bars of The George and Dragon to The Swan and Cemetery.

'It's the British way to be critical but I'm not interested in the past. I'm only interested in the present and the future of this club. We're trying to build something here and we've got ourselves into a nice position through hard work and application. The next game is always the most important,' he continues. With that next game being away at Terry Pashley's not-so-fondly-remembered ice box Hartlepool United on the second day of 1985, a touch more hard work and application than usual would be needed.

January 1985

Traditionally, it must be one of the most spirit-sapping days of the entire calendar. The Christmas tree is still up as you stumble downstairs in the morning darkness, but there are no presents underneath it. There's no expectation of the time to be spent eating, drinking and being merry that were in mind when it was put up. Instead, it's the second day of January and the world is getting back to normal after Christmas. What could possibly make today better?

Very few people would answer 'The opportunity to stand on a freezing cold terrace at Victoria Park in Hartlepool' to that question, but that was to be the next trip on Bury's agenda. Those who made the journey up to the North East for the Wednesday night match were housed in the ground's Rink End, which was certainly aptly-named as John Dyson in the *Bury Times* match report of 4 January refers to prevailing conditions of snow, rain and biting wind. Bury's 1–0 win against a team who had only lost once at home all season would have gone some way to warming the hardy souls who'd travelled. As for the players, and remembering Terry Pashley's tales of small baths, no heating and tiny changing rooms, it's not difficult to consider them wanting to be back on to the comparative fan-heated warmth of their Warburton's Travel charabanc as quickly as possible.

The match report reveals little in the way of chances for either side as the weather bogged them down. Bury's solitary goal, which gave them the maximum haul that saw them become the first team in the country to reach fifty points, came fifteen minutes from time as Winston White was first to react to the goalkeeper parrying a Leighton James special on to the crossbar. Caked in mud they may have been as they clambered back on to the coach after an inadequate post-match shower, but the trip back down the A1 (M) would have been a joyous one.

"There was always a bit of low-level racism in the game in general back when I started, about black players not wanting to get stuck in and that they didn't like cold weather," says Winston White in a Birmingham branch of Starbucks. When you think of the cold wind whistling off the North Sea on a winter's Wednesday night in Hartlepool, it's clear that this was utter nonsense in the case of this particular player – and during the process that I went through to enable us to be sitting at that coffee shop table, it emerged that this wasn't the only thing that made Winston a remarkable man.

Winston White's 1984/85 season pen picture. (Copyright: Bury Football Club)

Winston was, without question, the most difficult member of the squad to find. Pleas to his former clubs yielded nothing, as did enquiries to the company for which his Wikipedia page said he was working. National newspaper journalists retweeted 140-character messages asking after the right winger's whereabouts, but still there was nothing forthcoming. I asked friends with access to Directory Enquiries online to search for him under his full name of Eric Winston White and received two phone numbers as the fruits of their labours. Neither person at the other end of the line was the person I wanted, but there was no need for one of them to be so rude before I even had a chance to explain why I was calling.

Eventually, I called on the PFA to help me find the elusive Mr White. Somewhat irritatingly, they did so almost immediately and an email with the subject line 'Winston White here' soon arrived in my inbox. The reason my previous searches drew a blank was because Winston no longer lived in this country. His email had arrived instead from Antigua, which rather subdued my joy because I was hoping to interview each player face-to-face.

We kept the email conversation going for a short while before Winston helpfully revealed that he was due back in the UK soon. Having taken my phone number, he promised to get in touch when he next came back. It was a promise he kept, which is why I dashed from the bar in the Help Me Thro', one of Bury's most charming pubs, after I received a text as I waited to be served on a busy bank holiday. I went outside and was standing in the smoking area at the back of the pub having straightaway called the number from which the message arrived. Quickly we arranged to meet. The city? Birmingham. The place? New Street Station, which was considerably less glamorous than the right winger's current home.

I don't think I've ever been so relieved to see a person waiting in a train station as I was to see Winston White in one of the most charmless buildings in the Midlands. I shook his hand as though he was a soldier returning from war and we walked to the coffee shop. I didn't realise that this would be the start of our spending the next six hours talking about all things Bury in the mid-1980s.

"I signed for Bury when Jim Iley was manager. I'd been playing in Hong Kong, and Chesterfield wanted me when I came back. I stayed there for two weeks and made one appearance before I went to Port Vale, where I also only played once because my fitness levels weren't really up to scratch," he begins.

"I moved on to Stockport where my mate Oshor Williams helped me to get fit after I'd not really had a pre-season, but without wanting to show disrespect to them I felt I could play at a higher level and I felt I'd get that with Bury. I think Jim had seen me have a couple of good games against his team when I'd been at Hereford so he signed me," he laughs.

With such a journeyman's start to the 1983/84 season, few Bury fans could have expected Iley's signing to have such an impact. "I loved it as soon as I came to Bury," Winston now reveals. "I had the fans singing 'Sign him up!' at me and I just felt really comfortable. The other players, like Joe Jakub and Wayne Entwistle, were really welcoming so I decided that if I was offered terms I'd stay. I was offered a contract, and it wasn't the greatest, but I needed to get back into the game," he says of the beginning of his 125-match stay.

"I'd been there for about two months before Jim Iley was sacked and Wilf took over as caretaker before Martin was appointed manager. When he [Martin] came in, it moved everything to a totally different level. He was a name in football so he was able to attract names like Kevin Young, Trevor Ross and Leighton, of course. Leighton would challenge me because I was fast and black and he was slow and white.

"We'd see how many crosses we could get in and how many assists we'd get. He [Leighton] was quite languid in his approach, but he'd really make me think about my game because he was so intelligent. Early in the season, he was setting up goals and putting crosses in, whereas I was working twice as hard but not getting the same results. He made me think about my game and it was off the back of matching him in training and his economy of movement that I felt I became a better and more rounded player. I'd never tell him that though because he was a big-headed so-and-so," he smiles.

Like the rest of his peers, Winston got on well with the man who treated him after Fourth Division defenders got frustrated with his dazzling performances on the right wing and clattered him. "Wilf used psychology on us and I used to enjoy going into the treatment room. His stories are legendary and there were times when I'd not want to go home because I was having such a laugh. I can't help but smile when I think of him. He realised early on that I responded to an arm around the shoulder and he called me a ball player, which made me feel good when I thought of the players that he'd played with, managed and coached. He made you feel like part of the fixtures and fittings at what was already an extremely friendly family club. I remember the Rector too, along with directors like Ian Pickup and John Heap, the secretary. I can look at the programmes [which I had taken for Winston to leaf through] and I can recognise every name, which is how it should be.

"But we were fit too," he continues. "And we didn't have many injuries because of that. I didn't like being injured because I knew that my teammates were good enough to take my place because they could cover every position and I knew it would be difficult to get that place back.

"Our team had natural leaders like Joe Jakub, who's one of the funniest people I've ever met, and John Bramhall, plus the younger lads like Chris Cutler and Andy Hill who would have competitions related to their fitness. Trevor Ross played almost all of his football in the promotion season on the right side of the pitch in midfield, but Martin played him at right back which was another example of the manager getting people to play in other positions.

"We had so few subs that we obviously had a tight nucleus, but Martin was also very sophisticated with the way he dealt with our time off because it maximised our fitness," he claims. "He was a great presence on the pitch too because he was such an intelligent player. He wasn't a bawler or a shouter, he had a great level of fitness and he played as sweeper with a real ease. I'd have a knockabout with Frank Casper on the training pitch too because I was his favourite player," he laughs. The affection clearly remained some four years after Bury's promotion when, in 1989, Winston signed for Burnley after Frank took over the reins at Turf Moor.

Born in Leicester, Winston's hometown club was his first and he made history for them by being the first black player to turn out for the Foxes, despite Showaddywaddy drummer Romeo Challenger

Wayne Entwistle and Kenny Clements in Bury's centenary
celebration game versus Manchester City.
(Copyright: *Bury Messenger*)

John Bramhall heads clear in the home game versus Blackpool.
(Copyright: Ian Lunn)

David Brown dives at the feet of Blackpool forward Kevin Stonehouse.
(Copyright: Ian Lunn)

Winston White shoots in the game against Crewe Alexandra at Bury.
(Copyright: Chris Tofalos)

Winston White goes for goal in the pre-season friendly versus West Ham at Gigg Lane.
(Copyright: Simon Egan)

Craig Madden has an effort at goal against Chester in the Freight Rover Trophy
as Lee Dixon looks on.
(Copyright: Ian Lunn)

Gary Buckley's shot is saved by the Northampton 'keeper but the striker buries the rebound.
(Copyright: Ian Lunn)

Leighton James terrorising
a Hartlepool United defender.
(Copyright: Ian Lunn)

Shakers Review, the matchday programme
of the 1984/85 season.
(Copyright: Bury Football Club)

Andy Hill tussles with Halifax Town's Ces Podd on his Gigg Lane debut.
(Copyright: *Bolton Evening News*)

The look on his face suggests he can't believe it, but Enty's shot versus Mansfield
will hit the back of the net.
(Copyright: Ian Lunn)

Gary Buckley shoots at Layer Road in the away game against Colchester United.
(Copyright: Simon Egan)

How Gigg Lane looked after the 1984/85 season. The Boy's Stand, previously bottom right in the picture, had been demolished and the cage was erected around the 'B' Stand in the Main Stand.
(Copyright: *Bolton Evening News*)

Kevin Young surges forward n the home fixture versus Southend United.
(Copyright: *Bolton Evening News*)

Take that! The iconic picture of Wayne Entwistle scoring Bury's second goal
versus Tranmere on 29 December 1984.
(Copyright: *Bolton Evening News*)

Andy Hill is presented with the Player of the Season award by Terry Robinson.
(Copyright: *Bury Messenger*)

Pomagne for all as Bury's players and fans celebrate promotion despite the defeat
to Wrexham on 4 May 1985.
(Copyright: Pete Cullen)

being on their books as a youngster before White signed. "I never took it for granted, being a professional footballer. It's a great feeling when the crowd are singing your name, but I was the one who took the rough with the smooth because I was the only black player in the Bury promotion team, in an era when monkey chants were aimed at players who weren't white," he remembers.

The mid-1980s was a particularly upsetting time for the British game in this context. Paul Canoville was racially abused by his own fans in the Shed End at Chelsea, and although West Brom's 'Three Degrees' of Laurie Cunningham, Cyrille Regis and Brendon Batson had made great strides in shoving racist abuse right back at its perpetrators, attitudes were still far from being overcome.

A game which tried to remedy this was the testimonial of former West Brom – and future Bury – midfielder Len Cantello. The match, which was played at the Baggies' home ground the Hawthorns, featured white players versus black players – one of whom was Winston, then playing for Hereford United – drawn from across the Football League.

"I looked to Cunningham, Regis and Batson when I was at Hereford. Players like them and Remi Moses gave me something to aspire to, to achieve, and that was to play in the First Division. I'd had limited opportunities after making my debut for Leicester the year before because I had to try and dislodge Keith Weller from the side, which is why I moved to Hereford," he remembers.

"I'd get stick when I was warming up, oddly mostly in the North. You can either live with it or shrink into your shell, and as one of four boys growing up I had the character and mentality after always standing my ground in our household, so I could meet the situation head-on," he adds.

One occasion that Winston remembers in particular didn't happen in the North. It happened at what was then one of the most notorious grounds in the country, a name that is still synonymous with football violence. "My biggest inspiration was always the manager at

Leicester who gave me an apprenticeship, Jimmy Bloomfield. We'd played at Millwall, the old Den, in a pre-season game and he'd named me as a sub. I came on at half-time and there was a crescendo of boos because I was the only black player on the pitch," he reveals.

"I played well, and when we got back on the coach after the game, we got stuck in a queue on Cold Blow Lane. Some of their fans started throwing bricks at it and then came right up to the windows and started trying to topple the thing over, venting all of their aggression at me. I could see the hatred in their eyes and it sent a chill through my body.

"Jimmy called me into his office on Monday and said to me 'As long as you're playing, racism will exist because it's the sick society we live in. If you're being noticed to that extent, it means that you're having a good game.' So with that in mind, whenever it happened I tried to turn the negative into a positive. It wasn't always so easy, though, because when my dad and brothers would go and watch me they'd sometimes be in the thick of it and I'd sometimes fear for their safety," he continues.

"I have never been racially abused in a dressing room, because in there you're judged by your ability, and I've never used it as an excuse either. If you're looking for racism I think you'll find it, and I think some players might have done that and shrunk and left the game because they couldn't deal with it. A famous chairman made the comments about black players only playing in good weather and I laughed at him when I heard it, especially when I thought of some of the games I've played in, and played well, when it's been freezing. You just have to be as good as the other players you're fighting for a position and I think it was my family who gave me that strength," he concludes.

In total, I spent six hours with Winston before his work commitments, as founder of a personal training academy in the Caribbean, brought an end to our interview. "My team and I deliver internationally approved health and fitness courses to students and exercise professionals across the Caribbean," he explains.

"My goal is to leave a positive legacy across the Caribbean where highly qualified fitness professionals can go into their own communities and work with those who suffer from non-communicable diseases like hypertension, type II diabetes, obesity, particularly in children, stress-related illness, asthma and chronic obstructive pulmonary diseases.

"I designed a business model that suits government and associated bodies in the Caribbean. This has certainly created challenges, but I am receiving excellent feedback on the project and I'm still optimistic about the academy's growth as a key educator in health and fitness in the Caribbean," he says.

Antigua wasn't Winston's first port of call after hanging up his boots. "After retiring from football I qualified as a sports therapist and personal trainer. I gained a degree in business and leisure management and then went on to studying for an MBA specialising in leadership. I continued to work in various roles in football and the health and fitness industry, but I always had a desire to return to my Caribbean roots. I have always been passionate about helping to improve the health of the Caribbean region through physical activity and education, and after over thirty-five years in the sports, health and fitness industry I decided the time was right," he finishes.

It had been a brilliant way to spend a day's holiday from work, especially given that I'd gone through something of a quest to find Winston in the first place. We said goodbye in a pub around the corner from the station – no pint for Winston, of course – and I felt I'd made a new friend: one of the most fondly remembered players from a squad I wish I'd been able to see.

The *Bury Times* of Friday 4 January – which contained the report of Winston's match-winner versus Hartlepool – didn't have a match to preview for the following afternoon. As it was the halfway point of the season, the fixtures had come full circle and Bury were due to host the team to whom they travelled on that balmy August first day of the season, Darlington. But the visitors were still in the FA Cup and were facing a tough tie against fellow North Easterners, Middlesbrough, which meant that the Shakers would be left twiddling their thumbs on one of the best days of the football season.

Hooliganism was undoubtedly the spectre which contributed greatly to 1985 being the worst year in the British game, and it staked this particular reputational claim early, on the first calendar weekend of the year. Future Bury manager Neil Warnock was still a chiropodist in Sheffield at the time, juggling the curing of bunions with managing Burton Albion in the Northern Premier League. In that most romantic of competitions, his side had made it through to the third round and the company of teams from the First and Second Divisions. Warnock's men had been given a dream draw, at home to a Leicester City side from the top flight which contained, among others, Gary Lineker and future Bury midfielder Andy Feeley.

The Brewers moved the game to Derby County's Baseball Ground for safety reasons, which turned out to be the height of irony given what was to occur. With the score at 1–1, Burton goalkeeper Paul Evans was hit by a piece of wood thrown from the stand behind his goal and knocked unconscious. As he staggered around his area, periodically vomiting, the goalie conceded five more, including a hat-trick from Leicester's future crisp vendor and two from Alan Smith. The media took up Burton's case for a replay, and Warnock was summoned to the FA to be told that the game would be replayed behind closed doors at Coventry City's old Highfield Road stadium. In the replay, Evans was beaten only once – and his teammates were a whisker away from claiming a draw as they shaved the post in the final minutes.

'It really was a crazy few days,' Warnock told the *Independent* newspaper in 2013 when the two were again drawn against each other in the cup.

*

With the free weekend, it wasn't until the edition of the *Bury Times* dated Friday 11 January that John Dyson could get back to writing about the Shakers. It was their current league status as the most successful team in the land that prompted the back page story 'BURY'S HALF-TERM REPORT IS PACKED WITH PROMISE' in which Martin Dobson notes how proud he is of his players, as they were, in his words, 'Showing talent, working hard, [have] a good attitude and could go all the way' after the transformation that had followed the Jim Iley era.

Dobson continues: 'I'm delighted with the way things have gone so far. I believe in certain principles and the way the game should be played...Our success so far stems from the day the players reported back for pre-season training. We worked them very hard and it is standing them in good stead in the latter part of games when we wear teams down.

'We've played every team in the division and I'd like to think we've earned their respect. If we continue with the same approach we have nothing to fear,' he told John Dyson before going on to thank the fans for their support in home crowds which were up 1,133 on the previous season's average.

Kevin Young missed Bury's game at Hartlepool on the second day of the year, and in the same edition of the paper which contained the halfway point assessment of the season so far is a short story explaining why. His wife, Karen, had given birth to daughter Joanne earlier that day, and Kevin is pictured receiving a bouquet of flowers in congratulations from the rest of the squad. It's a tremendous vision of togetherness from such a tight-knit squad, and contains one duty-bound player making a bunny ears gesture above the head of another. Step forward Craig Madden, making Winston White look like the unsuspecting rabbit.

The third and final story relating to the Shakers on the back page of the paper has the headline 'THUMBS DOWN FOR £250,000 AID SCHEME'. John Dyson reports how the club had approached

Greater Manchester Council for a package worth a quarter-of-a-million pounds, which would have enabled them to wipe out their overdraft debt to Lloyds Bank and pay off a loan given by Bury Metropolitan Borough Council in 1984, in return for opening up Gigg Lane for the wider use of the community in a bid to bring in extra cash. The package also subsequently included £50,000 which the club hoped to spend on all-weather pitches in the car park and better floodlighting. The latter improvement, if that's the correct term to use about the elongated lamp-posts which eventually replaced the elegant blue floodlight pylons standing proudly in each corner of the ground in 1985, would eventually come to pass ten years later. So did football pitches in the car park, but to describe the walled-in rectangles of concrete painted green as all-weather pitches would be something of an overstatement.

Chairman Terry Robinson told Dyson of his disappointment at how the club was turned down for the money on the inside back page of the 11 January edition. 'The club is no worse off but it is another channel which is now closed as we seek to keep plugging away and doing our best for the town's football club,' he is quoted as saying, his furrowed brow instantly visible in the mind's eye as he wondered how he'd clear the £155,000 debt with Lloyds, the £70,000 his club owed Bury MBC and the £26,000 that unpaid creditors were owed.

The word 'avuncular' could have been conceived with Terry Robinson in mind. After he became chairman in 1983 following on from his reluctant predecessor Ron Clarke, a generation of Bury fans grew up seeing Terry in the social club after moments of rare success with a pint of stout and a cigar, or on TV as the club's figurehead. I was no different, but after I'd spent a portion of my teenage years watching games from Gigg Lane's Centre Stand I'd got to know Terry's daughter Katie, and in the age of social media was friends with her on Facebook. It was therefore easy to find him and request

Terry Robinson in 1984.
(Copyright: Bury Football Club)

an interview, despite his presence at some of the top tables in the British game. I imagine that most Bury fans watching the teams being presented to guest of honour Kofi Annan before the 2009 FA Cup final said the same as my dad and me as we half-watched in the pub: "Was that...Terry... walking behind him?"

As bluff and straight-talking as ever, Terry and I met in The Red Lion in Hawkshaw. "When I think back to the season my first memory is always of Leighton James because he brought something so different to us. We'd taken a bit of a risk bringing Wayne Entwistle back to the club when Jim Iley was still manager, but Martin was brilliant with him and I thought he was going to go on to be a great manager in the game. It was a season where you could live it without vividly remembering it because of the team spirit. It was first class," he says.

Compared to the heartbreak of his first close season in the chairman's office a year earlier, after Bury had missed out on promotion in the final game, the summer months of 1984 were an exciting time for a boyhood Bury fan to be in the corridor of power under the Main Stand.

"Martin brought in the kind of players we'd not seen for a long time. It was unbelievable getting Trevor Ross on a free transfer. Together with Leighton and Martin himself, they were named players.

135

With the local aspect of Wayne Entwistle in the team and Craig Madden continuing his form, we thought we were on to something.

"We weighed up at the start of the season how many Madden and Entwistle would each score and we came up with fifteen each. We signed John Kerr as another striker towards the end of the season and I got criticised for it, but we had so few players that we needed another option, and as soon as he was on the bench, the two other strikers burst into life," he says.

Despite Terry sitting down to work out with Martin Dobson how many his strike pairing would score, he would mostly take a back seat as far as team selection was concerned. "I left everything to the manager unless the transfer fee was very large because I knew that Martin could work within the remit I'd set him. Wayne had left Wimbledon and been working at Edward Andrews on Walshaw Road before Jim Iley signed him for his second spell with us.

"Wayne was a bit of a revelation with Martin managing him. My mother used to have a pie shop in Elton and she said that if Wayne went in she'd give him a pie because he needed building up," he laughs.

"Of the other players, Craig was signed by Dave Connor and was still scoring, so Martin could bring some youngsters through. He brought Kevin Young in who was a very skilful player, but if you ask me of my memories of the season they're always of Leighton James," he remembers.

Having watched Bury from the Boys' Stand in between the Cemetery End and the South Stand himself, Terry remembers the disappointment of goal-scoring sensation Ray Pointer being sold over Christmas 1965. "It was before my involvement with the club, obviously, but I always thought that if I did move into a position where I could influence it, that I wanted to get Ray back at the club in some capacity," he says.

"We got him into the commercial department first before he became a coach, and then Martin got Frank Casper on board. Jim Iley, from whom Martin took over, was a thoroughly decent chap, but he was a bit old-fashioned. His reputation was cemented by the Wimbledon game in 1983, but I remember when he came back to Bury with Exeter in the promotion season, something happened which showed me the mark of the man.

"It had finished as a 2–2 draw on an awful pitch, and despite the two clubs' relative positions in the league he didn't gloat. I saw him after the game and said 'It's like a home match, at least it's a short trip home for you' because he was still living in Bolton. He said, 'No, I'm going to go back to Exeter with my lads and then I'm going to drive back.' He wanted to show his team that they were all the same and I respected him for that," he reveals.

"The team was a tight and compact unit. Thankfully there were so few injuries, the pitches were in a decent condition and the team wanted to win, so the seeds were out there on the pitch. Martin ran everything like an army general which made my job in the boardroom much easier. He'd arrived during the previous season and knew the areas he wanted to strengthen and I trusted him and Frank," he continues.

Terry's connections meant that it wasn't just on the pitch where new personnel were arriving. "Ray Jacks was a Burnley fan who was a bit disillusioned with what was happening at Turf Moor. I knew him through business and asked if he wanted to join our board. He gave us £5,000 which he didn't want back so we put his product's name, *Spray Breaker*, on the front of our shirts as our first shirt sponsor. We had to print the explanation of what it was in every copy of the programme because no one knew," he laughs.

It was also the time in the club's history when Bury got their chartered accountant backer, the man who made the news in 1999 when it emerged that the money with which he'd bankrolled the club's success in the 1990s wasn't actually his to spend. "The share issue in August 1984 was when Hugh Eaves got involved in the club. There was an issue of between £30,000 and £40,000 and the board of directors had bought about £20,000 worth. Hugh Eaves rang me from London and asked me if the scheme was still available and I told him it was, to the tune of another £20,000," Terry says.

"So he asked me if he could buy them. He explained that he was born in Tottington and he worked in London. He asked if he bought the shares whether he could join the board. I said that of course he could, but why he was asking. He told me that he didn't know if there was any room, to which I replied that we wanted as many people as possible," he continues.

"Hugh said that he wanted to buy all 200,000 of the shares as an open offer to the town. At that point, Ian Pickup and I had been starting to buy up the shares which were previously owned by former chairman Billy Allen from his wife Milly, so Hugh bought all of these which enabled Milly to live the rest of her life comfortably. The rest of the Hugh Eaves story is for another time," he concludes with a laugh.

Terry left Bury in 2002 and moved on to many different areas of the English game, including representing the Football League on the FA Council, which culminated in his most recent position as director of football at Leicester City. It was an enjoyable conversation over a pint, and perhaps there's a degree of the rose-tinted to it, but I felt that he looked back on his first position in football at the club he supported as a boy with a terrific fondness. I felt that the interview brought back a lot of good memories for him, both of his position in the board room and, perhaps more importantly, as a fan.

If the prospect of Hartlepool on the second day of the New Year wasn't a game to look forward to, the thought of Bury's second match of 1985 was enough to fill the most positive of fans and teams with dread. The Shakers were due to visit what was comfortably one of the worst grounds of the ninety-two as they made the short trip over the Pennines to Halifax and the Shay – less the name of a stadium and more a name which immediately resonates with the thought of crunching tackles, driving rain and mud. It's a venue that separates the men from the boys and brings to mind another West Yorkshire sports arena, Belle Vue in Wakefield, where Richard Harris starred in the film *This Sporting Life*.

The hosts hadn't won in the six games leading up to Bury's visit. The script was already written and Bury played along with it word-perfectly as they crashed 4–1 in front of a crowd that John Dyson notes was Halifax's biggest of the season. The 2,854 crowd comprised possibly more away fans than home and far outstripped Town's previous best that season, the 1,870 who had seen the match against Blackpool on the opening day.

The week after that opening day of the season, Bury had comprehensively dismantled the Shaymen 3–0 at Gigg Lane, but this game was to be an entirely different story. In a report alliteratively-headlined 'SHAY SHOCKER FOR SORRY SHAKERS', Dyson writes of treacherous conditions underfoot as the rain that features in the mind's eye when thinking of the ground name was replaced by snow and the temperature dipped below zero, which would have had those away followers bouncing up and down for warmth on the terracing in front of the ground's speedway track.

Bury took the lead halfway through the first half, after a Winston White cross-shot that looked destined for the goal was latched on to by Craig Madden who made absolutely sure that the ball would end up in the back of the net. The Shakers then remained largely in control until a Town equaliser which caused Bury's game

Bury concede one of four goals away at Halifax Town on an awful afternoon in January 1985. (Copyright: Johnny Meynell)

139

to disintegrate. Poor covering from Leighton James allowed a Halifax player to get a cross past him which was met successfully by a Town striker, then David Brown allowed a Trevor Ross back pass to bobble out of his safe grasp, leading to the cross from which Halifax grabbed their second.

'Suddenly too many of the Bury players were filled with self-doubt and disappeared from proceedings for long stretches. Halifax repeatedly got to the ball first, were more prepared to take risks and seemed better equipped in the footwear department,' wrote Dyson, the last point referencing a 7–0 defeat for Bury at Chesterfield in 1976 when Bury wore hopelessly ineffective boots on a similar ice-rink of a surface.

Halifax were reportedly lucky still to be in front as their goalkeeper Paddy Roche made some excellent saves from Joe Jakub and Wayne Entwistle, but they sealed Bury's heaviest defeat of the season with two goals in the last five minutes of the game.

On the same page of the *Bury Times* of Friday 18 January that the dissection of the Halifax game appears is a short piece that's slightly at odds with such a catastrophic defeat. Without a game the following day, fans are instead offered the opportunity to book on to the supporters' coach for the long, long trip to Colchester on Saturday 26 January. Few can have read the report and thought that what they really, really wanted to do after consuming the detail of Bury's hopelessness in West Yorkshire was to commit to a coach fare of £8.50 for a journey which would begin at 8am.

Coaches had been in the news just over a month before the match after pop group Bucks Fizz had been involved in an accident on board their tour bus as they left a show in Newcastle. Singer Mike Nolan was the most seriously injured when their coach crashed into some roadworks on 11 December, and after he had 'died' on the operating table and was given the Last Rites twice, he was beginning to recover as Bury travelled to Essex.

Frozen pitches like Halifax's were still very much an issue on the day of the game, the same day that Third Division York City and Keith

140

Houchen's last-minute spot kick saw off Arsenal on a frosty, rutted surface at Bootham Crescent in the FA Cup fourth round. In Essex, it was to be a fruitless trip and what must have felt like an even longer journey home as Bury's winless record at Layer Road, which stretched back to 1960/61, had another season added to it. Goalkeeper Alec Chamberlain, who played for the hosts when Bury were promoted to the second tier at Watford's Vicarage Road stadium in 1997, was the main reason for this as he pulled off a series of fine saves before a controversial winner from Roger Osborne. Gary Buckley is described as being 'outstanding' in the match report printed in the *Bury Times* on 29 January headlined 'KEEPER HERO AS SHAKERS FAIL TO LAY THAT JINX'.

Elsewhere in the paper, Martin Dobson tells John Dyson that he is refusing to panic following Bury tasting defeat in two successive games for the first time that season. Injuries to Wayne Entwistle and Craig Madden and suspension for Trevor Ross might have reduced a lesser man to tears, but Dobson remained stoical. 'I said after the Colchester game that it was our best performance of the season and I see no reason to retract that statement. It sounds silly when you've been beaten but their goalkeeper gave an inspired performance and stopped everything. We couldn't have done more,' he is quoted as saying.

'There's no cause to panic. The players came off at the end of the game with their heads down but we've told them if they keep performing like that they won't have any problems,' he concludes about his team who were still at the summit of the division as the season moved into February.

The next game would potentially be difficult even without factoring in a squad not containing Madden, Entwistle and Ross. It was a top of the table clash in Derbyshire as Bury faced the only side who were their equals in the division: joint leaders Chesterfield.

February 1985

The winter of 1984 going into 1985 would have been a cold one in Chesterfield. The town's miners were still on strike and their resolve, together with that of the others who had stopped working back in the spring nearly a year ago, was slowly being broken. One of the few tiniest crumbs of comfort which the Derbyshire town could take was that they had an excellent football team to watch. In fact, they were unbeaten at home since before the strike began.

'SKIPPER JAKUB INSPIRES AS SUPER SHAKERS WRECK A 13-MONTH HOME RUN' goes the banner headline of the *Bury Times* from 5 February for the report of a game in which Bury were simply awesome. 'Although there was never a question of the Shakers repeating the 5–1 scoreline from the previous Christmas, this result [1–0 to Bury] was clearly far more significant in terms of the right of Martin Dobson's charges to be classed as promotion and title favourites in the latter half of the season,' writes John Dyson in a breathless opening salvo.

Wayne Entwistle and Craig Madden played, and together with Leighton James brought the best out of Chesterfield goalkeeper Chris Marples whose counterpart in the Bury goal, David Brown, had only one save of note to make across the whole game. But it was Bury's captain who ran the show, as the headline suggests, together with a man who wasn't ever-present across the season, but who was in the middle of his longest run in the side. 'Marathon man Joe Jakub ran miles in his enthusiasm to close down, block passes and make tackles and he was ably backed up by the sniping Gary Buckley, the net result being that Chesterfield were rarely allowed to make good use of their possession,' writes Dyson.

The only goal of the game came from Wayne Entwistle, who headed home a cross from his skipper. After dealing with the home threat competently for the remainder of the game, Bury's only anxious moment came when the wonderfully-named Brian Scrimgeour collided with Andy Hill and the defender had to be stretchered off. Terry Pashley replaced Hill for the last half hour and according to Dyson performed admirably as he didn't put a foot wrong. X-rays at the local hospital showed that Hill's ankle was unbroken, meaning he'd follow his teammates back across the Peak District in a much more relieved frame of mind than he might otherwise have done, to go with the joy at the Shakers opening up a three-point lead over their opponents at the top of the table.

The younger element of Bury support that had ignorantly taunted Chesterfield fans at Gigg Lane in September also made the trip. "There was some singing which upset the home fans," remembers supporter Malcolm Parr. "The game was already heavily policed and it felt like we were on a picket line before the locals took exception to the few who were singing. Our coaches were parked in this sterile area behind the away end and from there we had an escort back to the motorway. The strike was an issue when Chesterfield were at home and the way the game was policed reflected this. It was a shame really, as it was a good game and a great win where we had to dig in for the result, like all good teams have to sometimes," he adds.

On the same night that the day's paper reported the victory at Saltergate, Bury began their Freight Rover Trophy campaign with a game at Gigg Lane versus Chester. If early exits in both the FA Cup and the League Cup had drawn secret exhalations of relief that Bury could concentrate on the league, the prospect of a further three games in the group stages of the competition in front of small crowds must have been frustrating in the extreme. A thoroughly underwhelming 1–1 draw, against a Chester side containing future Bury defender Lee Dixon, featured a Bury side made up largely of first team regulars, though Chris Cutler started up front in only his second start of the season. The apprentice accompanied the sorcerer Craig Madden, who grabbed Bury's goal in front of an impressive crowd for the competition of 1,814.

A 2–1 win at Sealand Road in the reverse fixture a fortnight later was followed by a 1–0 defeat at eventual competition winners Wigan in April, which ended Bury's involvement in the competition. The winning goal at Chester was scored by youth team star Heath Reynolds, whose day-to-day coach was former Burnley striker Ray Pointer who won the First Division title with the Clarets in 1960.

Five years later in the summer of 1965, Ray joined Bury and scored a phenomenal seventeen goals in nineteen games. These included five goals versus Rotherham which remains to this day the highest number of goals scored by a Bury player in one match. Astonishingly, Ray was sold to Coventry City over the Christmas period of the same year. It was a time of year which ensured the news would not be made public in the media and a generation of fans claimed they would never support the club and its underhand tactics again as Pointer's name became synonymous with stay-away supporters. He even added a further eleven strikes to his tally in that same season with the Sky Blues, before many years later he returned to Gigg Lane to work with Dobson and Casper and, among others, future first team star David Lee. Unfortunately, Ray was unavailable for interview for the Forgotten Fifteen project.

Following the home game against Chester in the Freight Rover Trophy, Cutler took his place on the bench for the game the following Saturday as Bury hosted Martin Dobson's predecessor Jim Iley's Exeter City side at Gigg Lane. Less than a thousand more fans than those who were at the preceding midweek game braved a biting wind and saw a nondescript first half that was saved by a Leighton James free kick which squirmed through the City keeper's fingers to give Bury a 1–0 lead. Joe Jakub only lasted three minutes of the second period before a knee strain forced him off to be replaced by Cutler, who lashed home his only goal of the season on the gluepot of a pitch shortly after entering the fray. That really ought to have been that, but an uncharacteristic clanger by the boss, who would later apologise to his squad for the effect his flu-addled brain had on his indecision, allowed Exeter a route back into the game. The Grecians capitalised further and drew level with ten minutes to go, but Bury held on to the point to remain four points clear of Chesterfield at the top of the table.

'I'm responsible for the mistake which let Exeter back into the game and I'll hold my hand up,' said Dobson after the game. 'It was the turning point in the game and it gave them a lift. Now I have to be big enough to get over it,' he said. The other manager from the day spoke to the assembled hacks underneath the Main Stand after the game with a refreshing pragmatism about his former employer. 'Bury will be Fourth Division champions and I want them to go up as champions because they are the best team in this division,' said Jim Iley before embarking on his long journey of solidarity back to Exeter and then the trip back to his home in Bolton which Terry Robinson remembered so clearly.

Chris Cutler was just twenty years old when he hit that delicious volley against Exeter which gave Bury a two-goal cushion. A photograph of Cutler scoring this, his third goal for Bury, which appeared in the match day programme for the next home game highlights just what a baby-faced assassin the striker was. But it was under Jim Iley that he made his first inroads to the first team as an even younger eighteen-year-old, making his first appearances on the bench at the back end of the 1981/82 season. Sporadic appearances on the bench continued until Iley was dismissed in 1984, whereupon caretaker manager Wilf McGuinness gave youth more of a chance and played Cutler in the games leading up to Dobson's appointment. The new manager then followed suit and frequently used Cutler as an effective super-sub.

Now working as a teacher in Cheshire, Chris was easy to find by virtue of him taking charge of his school's team with a lot of success. "I joined Bury when I was seventeen and played a lot of Central League football in the reserves. I made my debut against Wolves who had Emlyn Hughes playing for them and I went on to play against some really good players at really good grounds like Maine Road and Old Trafford. To be playing the likes of Norman Whiteside, Paul McGrath and Mark Hughes in front of 10,000 at Old Trafford was as good as playing in the first team," he now remembers in the restaurant of the Manchester Airport Marriott hotel, as the plates of a hearty breakfast enjoyed by the crew of an Emirates jumbo were being cleared up around us.

"Chances for me were limited," he continues. "Craig Madden was one of the best finishers I'd ever seen so it was difficult to get into the team. But it was different when Martin came in because he had a well-deserved reputation and he also employed coaching methods which were extremely different from Jim Iley's. He brought into the mix younger players like Andy Hill, which Jim hadn't done. There'd been a lot of older players before," he says.

Having been at the club for the final day capitulation versus Wimbledon in 1983 ("I went on to play with Paul Fishenden from that Wimbledon team at Crewe, and he remembers the game vividly"), Chris recalls there being a good feeling around the club in the 1984 close season as Dobson set about constructing a promotion-winning squad. "Craig Madden was always going to score goals as was Enty, and there were expectations after we'd signed Trevor and Leighton. We didn't think we were going to finish in the middle of the table like we'd done in the previous season. It was clear that we needed a bit of tweaking which is what Martin had done. When you look at some of the crowds that Bury were getting towards the end of the promotion season, there was a certain atmosphere where I think there was more pressure on the side to do well.

"Bury's was always one of the best pitches around and it undeniably helped our home form, but the pitches as a whole weren't as bad as you might think. When we faced other teams there weren't really any who wanted to boot Bury's more cultured side off the pitch either. Enty took some stick simply because of the way he played, but Charlie [Craig Madden] didn't. He was ever-present in the season we got promoted, and we had the enforcers like Roscoe [Trevor Ross] who didn't take any prisoners either, because the team had quite an old head, especially in comparison to the Crewe team that Dario Gradi put together which I'd go on to join. Within three years of joining I was the eldest there," he reveals.

Chris Cutler's 1984/85 season pen picture. (Copyright: Bury Football Club)

"Being a footballer was just very different back then from how it is now. I've got into various other things since I retired. I own a health club and I'm chairman of the Chester and district schools FA. In terms of preparation back then and basic things like diet, it was quite poor. There's more of an ethos these days about players being looked after. We trained in a small gym and there was no 3G or Astroturf when we'd trawl down to Goshen or Lower Gigg where Jim would boot a ball and we'd chase it," he continues.

The managerial change brought seismic differences in the way Bury did things, and Chris felt these as much as any of his counterparts who played in the largely settled first XI. "Frank Casper brought just

147

as many good ideas as Dobbo and he taught me things that have stuck with me. That's not to take anything away from Jim though, because he had some creative ideas too. For instance, having three or four big lads in the team meant that a lot of the time Charlie [Madden] could get ten goals a season just standing at the back post and having to move one step to nod it in. When I played in the Central League I scored a lot of goals like that. It was hard to defend against it and it's something I've taken into coaching at school level today, but I've never seen anyone do it as effectively as Craig Madden.

"Then, when we signed Taffy [Leighton James], having someone with such a phenomenal crossing ability in the team made such a difference. There weren't many teams in the Fourth Division who could say they had a player of that quality, were there?" he asks rhetorically.

"You had the kind of playmaker player like Youngy [Kevin Young] who made a difference and Joe, who was a fantastic captain. When he'd drop into the Central League for a couple of games if he was coming back from injury or something, players from the opposition would be saying 'He's a hell of a player, what's he doing at this level?' We were a classy team and a very good side to watch," he remembers.

It was through a combination of luck with injuries and sheer form that Dobson was able to name such a settled XI across the course of this season which is, of course, the principal reason why this book is being written. But for all of the joy at the string of games in which Madden or Entwistle or both got on the scoresheet, it was sometimes tough for the young Cutler to be watching from the sidelines, itching for a run out despite Dobson saying more than once in the press that he'd be considered for a place in the starting lineup.

"I still felt part of what was happening as the season progressed, but Enty and Charlie were two centre forwards who were scoring and that was the way it was going to be. I was twenty at the time and was something of the travelling thirteenth man, and other than Andy

Chris Cutler lashes home his only goal of the 1984/85 season in the draw with Exeter. (Copyright: *Bolton Evening News*)

Hill there was no one really within three or four years of me. It was totally the opposite of when I joined Crewe," he says.

"I'd started in the defeat at Wrexham the weekend after we'd been to the Isle of Man in December – not a weekend I remember much about given how much we drank with the Drifters in the hotel bar – and it wasn't until the Exeter game in February that I got another chance in the league when I was on the bench. I replaced Joe and had what was probably my best ever game for Bury. I played in all of the Freight Rover Trophy games too and I must have been watched because I joined Pallo-Iirot in Finland on loan shortly afterwards. I knew that Dario [Gradi, Crewe Alexandra manager] was at the Exeter game too and it was on the strength of it that he signed me. I knew that Bury were going to release me, and although going to Finland would certainly be an experience, I had something more settled lined up for when I came back," he explains of his move to the Railwaymen.

So that's how Chris Cutler was absent from the picture of the squad celebrating promotion in the dressing room in May 1985. As the Pomagne corks popped, Chris congratulated his colleagues from afar and was getting used to the idea of his new teammates, one of whom was to have a very bright future in the game. "I was at Gresty Road with David Platt and we became really good friends. We got promoted in the 1988/89 season by when he'd gone to Aston Villa, and I did my anterior cruciate ligament (ACL) in my left knee at the start of the next season which finished me off after I was tackled badly from behind. After the World Cup when David really made a name for himself, he came to see me, which I really appreciated," he reveals.

"I was still wobbling because I never really recovered from the operation so I retired at twenty-seven. I bought the health club and had another operation to straighten my knee up, but from the time I decided to finish it was another seven years before I kicked a ball again. I played a bit in the Chester leagues and managed the Chester Nomads to a decent standard. I played for them too and scored twenty-five in twenty games in my last season," he laughs.

"We played at a reasonable standard, which I could say because I loved football so much, but I didn't play for so long," he says. "I'm active. I run the school's Duke of Edinburgh award scheme and I enjoy researching sports psychology. Life's fulfilling. About the whole teaching thing, I've actually got a cutting from the *Bury Times* that my parents gave to me from the season before Bury were promoted [1983/84]. While I was at the club I went to Bury Tech and finished my A-Levels before I signed professionally. I told the club that if I was good enough then they'd wait for me, but they wanted me to sign straightaway which was reflected when Wilf put me straight in when he was caretaker manager. I was doing well up until Dobbo was appointed when I got a freak injury in training. I fell down a rabbit hole on the training pitch," he says, smiling at the memory.

"I'd waited eighteen months under Jim Iley to get close to the first team and Wilf put me in straightaway. Jim actually turned down £50,000 from Barnsley for me too after they'd followed me around the Central League. I had words with Jim about how he wouldn't play me but he wouldn't let me move to a club which might. It was Pat Howard who'd recommended me to them, because he was retiring as I was coming through at Bury," he reveals.

"It's probably why one of my favourite moments was going back to Gigg Lane with Crewe and scoring twice," he says, smiling again. "What goes around comes around!"

Postponements were taking their toll in the ravaging winter of 1985, but they occasionally brought some good. Bury were due to host Stockport County on the same night that the report on the Exeter game was published in the local paper, but referee Neil Midgeley called the game off the day before because of the heavy frost that carpeted the Gigg Lane surface. John Dyson reported that this was good news for captain Joe Jakub because it meant that his 135-consecutive-game stretch in the team wouldn't be disrupted by the knee ligament trouble that forced him to hobble out of the Exeter game. With Trevor Ross still having one game of a two match ban to serve and Andy Hill's ankle still not fully mended, the postponement of the visit of the Hatters, and also Bury's trip to deepest Wiltshire and Swindon Town the following Saturday, meant that the absence of three key players could be reduced to just one as March brought warmer weather.

As it was, Jakub's injury meant that he still missed Bury's next game, the third and final match of February, when a Northampton Town side, not yet managed by comedian Alan Carr's father Graham, came to Bury. Sitting as they were in ninety-first out of ninety-two places in the Football League, the visitors were totally overwhelmed by the fortnightly novelty of playing in front of four stands rather than their County Ground's three, and it was one man who displayed the difference between the two teams.

'INSPIRATIONAL BUCKLEY AS BURY NAIL DOWN COBBLERS' is the headline which makes no bones about nominating Gary as the man of the match in one of his fourteen starts across the promotion campaign. John Dyson's report highlights how it was the midfield dynamo's 'marvellous contribution [which] initially triggered the alarm clock which awakened Bury from their early slumbers'. This culminated in Winston White grabbing Bury's first, then Craig Madden and the man of the moment adding further strikes – the latter his only goal for Bury – before the visitors scored to give the scoreline the thinnest veneer of respectability.

Gary Buckley was something of an enigma to track down, and was eventually rendered contactable by a freelance journalist who had done a short 'Where are they now?' feature on the 1985 squad some years previously. As it turned out, if I'd widened my request for Buckley's whereabouts to other Bury fans, I could have found out from much-loved – and now, sadly, much-missed – pub landlord Keith Freeman.

When I rang the number given to me for Gary and explained my reasons for calling, the conversation turned very quickly to reveal that he and Keith were still very much in touch. If I'd looked at the programmes for the season more closely after my friend Craig Clarkson lent them to me, I'd have seen in black and white that Keith was one of four people who sponsored Gary's blue and white kit. As it was, Gary and I arranged to meet in The Ostrich pub opposite Heaton Park for the interview, where we talked beneath the hubbub of post-work drinkers and the whoop-whoop of a fruit machine.

"I've got good memories of the season because of the promotion but bad memories because I ruptured my cruciate in the away game at Swindon and I never really played again," he reveals, allowing an understanding of why he was in a smart shirt and tie in the promotion celebration photograph taken in the dressing room rather than his kit. "But the memories of the promotion and the team spirit that we had are just great," he continues.

Buckley began his career with Manchester City, with whom he made six appearances, before a move to Preston where thirty-four appearances were forthcoming for the Lilywhites. It was following a spell at Chorley that Gary arrived at Gigg Lane in 1984 after a call from the caretaker manager Wilf McGuinness who'd taken over the reins on a temporary basis after Jim Iley's sacking. "Wilf remembered me from Preston. He asked me to go down to Bury and speak to him. I got on well with him and signed on non-contract terms, then when Frank Casper and Dobbo came to the club I signed full time," he says.

Having been a fresh-faced nineteen-year-old when he made his debut for City in the 1980/81 season in which his side reached the FA Cup final, Gary took the new arrivals at Bury in his stride. "When the experienced players arrived, I wasn't in awe of them," he says now. "I'd played with big names when I was younger at both City and Preston, but I must admit to thinking that when they signed it made you feel as though the club was going places," he says.

Big name teammates weren't the only similarity to the time Gary spent training at Platt Lane and playing at Maine Road. "The training that Frank and Martin introduced was very similar to what I'd done at City. Frank took a lot of the sessions and he was a great coach. The two of them had up-to-date ideas where maybe things had been a bit old-school under the previous regime and we were able to get the ball down well.

"There were so few of us that there was probably a bit of a siege mentality," he says of Bury's paper-thin squad. "There's no doubting that we were one of the better footballing squads in the division, but we also had the players who could get in the mix if we needed them to as well. They're the kind of players that you needed on pitches like Wrexham, Halifax and Rochdale.

"We all got on really well. We'd have a kick at each other in training, but that's only normal whichever club you go to. There'd be five or six of us after training who'd go for a drink and the management weren't totally strict about it.

"We played at Torquay towards the end of the promotion season after I'd got injured, so I wasn't playing. I travelled with the team regardless on the day before the game and on Friday teatime I went for a drink with two or three others. I had a couple of pints, someone else was on shandy and someone was on orange juice. Martin and Frank walked into the bar and every drink on the table got pushed in front of me," he laughs. "Martin didn't say anything. He just looked at us. The following morning he said at breakfast 'I'm not going to say anything about last night, we'll just have to see how we go on today.' The lads put that bit of extra effort in and we won 2–0. We worked for each other," he says.

After such a sustained spell in the starting XI came to a juddering halt away at Swindon, Gary faced lengthy sessions on the treatment table. "I loved Wilf to bits, but I'm not sure he should have been treating my injury as it was so specialised. The aftercare was missing after my operation and I wasn't insured by the club. My rehabilitation just never came about," he says, before embarking on a full-on medical explanation of what happened to his ligament and how it wasn't fixed correctly.

Despite having to retire from the game in 1986 after it became evident that the cruciate damage wasn't going to get any better, Gary has remained philosophical about the differences between today's game and how it was when he played. "I don't look at players today and the money they get with envy. There are a lot of sports which pay better, and if you get even £5,000 a week and you look after it, it'll set you up for life when you retire. Some of the foreign players piss me off because I think they can be mercenaries, but if you look at a lot of the English players, they just love playing the game and are being paid the going rate for doing it. If people will pay to watch them, the club will pay the salaries," he explains.

We rounded off our conversation in The Ostrich and headed to The Waterloo on Manchester Road, just up from Gigg Lane, which Keith Freeman was running at the time. We were hoping to see the landlord, but he wasn't in that evening, so we left a message with his wife to say we'd called in. When I next saw him at a game, Keith made a beeline for me and told me tale after tale about Gary and it was clear there was a lot of mutual respect between the two. The kind of respect that Keith had for Gary was the kind of respect that Bury fans had for Keith when they saw him in an unfamiliar pub in one of the four corners of the country before an away game. He's missed by us all, not just the players whom he served post-training pints to as the most genial of hosts when landlord at The Horse and Jockey, The Golden Fleece and The Waterloo, a traditional Bury 'home' pub which closed in 2012.

With just three games played in each of the first two months of the year, Bury went into the month that comes in like a lion and leaves like a lamb still on top of the Fourth Division table. Two points clear of second-placed Blackpool, the Shakers faced a tough spring that would be dominated by squeezing as many fixtures as possible into an extremely short space of time as the race to the finishing line got more and more desperate.

It was to be the month when the popularity of the national scourge went through the roof. Kenilworth Road and Stamford Bridge both saw the worst trouble they'd seen for years. So did Gigg Lane, together with its accompanying warren of terraced houses and cobbled back streets, as hooliganism came to town on the Football Special from the Fylde Coast.

March 1985

Bury's weary March, in which they would play eight games, began with a visit to the club who pipped them to automatic promotion on the last day of the 1982/83 season. As the Shakers were capitulating in the drizzle in their game against Wimbledon, Scunthorpe were overpowering Chester City in their match and, having played second fiddle to Bury all season, surging into the promotion places past Jim Iley's luckless side. It was the day on which the story of the Forgotten Fifteen began and a moment when the time-traveller who crushes a butterfly changes the course of the world. If Bury had gone up, Jim Iley would have remained manager, Martin Dobson would not have joined and one of the most attractive footballing sides in the club's history would not have been assembled.

Having been relegated from the third tier back into the basement after just one solitary season, Scunthorpe's challenge for an instant return from whence they came was faltering. The Shakers went to the Old Showground as the division's top dogs and remained so after a tough 2–2 draw in which their classic pairing of Craig Madden and Wayne Entwistle – a partnership begun by Iley – grabbed a goal each. Bury fell behind in the first half and subsequently developed a nerviness that saw the ball being likened to 'a hot, over-buttered, roast potato' in the *Bury Times* report printed on Tuesday 5 March.

Madden scored a pearl of an equaliser from thirty yards, which was dubbed 'MADDEN'S MAGICAL MOMENT' in the report's headline, just after half-time. The Iron retook the lead as their main threat came from the right side of the pitch, while Bury's chances were coming from sterling Leighton James work on the same flank, culminating in Enty salvaging a point with twenty minutes still to play.

"I remember the game at Scunthorpe mainly because of something that happened after it," begins supporter Malcolm Parr with a laugh in his voice. "The police were leading us back to our coach and there was a common, or a patch of grass or something, on the way. This young lad was standing on it giving us the V-sign, but he didn't know that a police car had pulled up behind him. He kept doing it and we were gesturing 'Behind you! Behind you!' at him, but he hadn't picked up on it. The police came from behind him, grabbed him and threw him in the back of the car," he smiles.

The status afforded to Madden's opening goal that afternoon in the match report meant that an aspect of the story next to the report on the back page of the paper had more than a degree of appropriateness. Like the Fiat garage at Blackford Bridge had done for Leighton James and Trevor Ross back in that balmy August, Bolton Car Centre had stepped in to offer Craig a new car. The striker's car wasn't the International Car of the Year that Dobbo's former teammates were given, though. It was a Lada Riva 1300, the same model which the same garage gave to Bolton snooker player Tony Knowles. The registration of the vehicle, the paper gleefully informs us, is A436 GEM for 'a gem of a player'.

That status had been bestowed on Craig a long time before the promotion season began, as he'd been consistently finding the back of the net since joining the club in 1977. I'd interviewed Craig on a couple of occasions in the past and kept hold of his number, so I simply needed to call him to ask if he'd be interested in talking for a third time about the promotion season. He agreed, and so with my friend Craig Clarkson, who'd asked if he could come along to the interview with his childhood hero, I met him in a pub in Chorley near to where Bury's record goalscorer of all time – a feat which looks unlikely ever to be surpassed – lived.

Craig Madden's 1984/85 season pen picture. (Copyright: Bury Football Club)

I began every interview with each player by asking what they remembered about the season without looking at any programmes, cuttings or photographs as a way of relaxing them and easing them into the light grilling they were to undergo. I received varied answers about what it was like to play under Martin Dobson, but Craig Madden gave me the most personal, and most bizarre, answer of the lot.

"I remember I scored against Hereford and I fell over. It's the only thing I can remember about the season," he says in his rich, treacly Mancunian accent, before adding, "Did I score many?"

He most certainly did. Craig's name appeared on the scoresheet twenty-two times across the nine months of the season, from the sunny afternoon up at Darlington in the first game of the season via a cold night in Peterborough and a spring evening against Stockport to his last goal of the season in a home defeat to Wrexham after promotion had been sealed.

On being reminded of his ferocious partnership with Wayne Entwistle during the season, Craig remembered his 'telepathy' with his Bury-born amigo. "Wayne was into his reactions and stuff that he'd learned with Lenny Heppel's 'rhythm and balance' technique up at Sunderland. I've never seen someone get so pumped up before a game. You have people you like playing with as a forward and who you know where they'll be. That was how me and Wayne worked," he says.

"As a group of players, Martin inspired us. He sat me down when he arrived and told me to just keep doing what I was doing:

scoring goals. As a squad, we respected him because of his status in the game as a player and because he was able to bring people like Frank Casper with him. Frank was a dream for me and he helped me a lot as a forward, because that was the position he played too, and I learned some great techniques from him in terms of positioning and what to do with the ball when I got it," he remembers.

"Joey Jakub was a good player who never really got the credit he deserved, but he played some tremendous football. Trevor played football well because he'd been brought up to do that, and combined with the wide players we were a real force. We had Terry Pashley who was up and down all game, and Hillsy [Andy Hill] was just brilliant in his first season.

"When we signed Leighton James it felt like we were going places because he was respected throughout the game with his caps for Wales and his crossing ability. I admit that I had a few doubts with some of Martin's decisions, though. I thought Trevor Ross might not have had the ability that we needed. I thought he was there just to be our hard man, but he ended up being a great friend of mine who I'd socialise with," he says.

"Like Martin, we also had Wilf who was well-respected because of his past with United and England, but also for his knowledge and passion that he had about the game. That's not even mentioning his personality," he laughs. "I think we closed ranks a bit as a squad because we felt like we were better than people gave us credit for and we were being hard done by. It was that flair we had and the swagger which Martin gave us.

"Martin had a calming influence that brought a harmony to the dressing room, but he also brought a kind of intensity to training because everyone got on with the new methods he introduced with such little fuss. There were a lot of players with different personalities, but we all got on so well. It was reflected in the players he brought in too. I remember Leighton James saying 'Just give the ball to me' because he knew what he could do with it, and we worked with him on the basis that we knew where he wanted us to be when he played the ball to us," he explains.

Craig signed for Bury in 1977 from local non-league side Northern Nomads who, as their name suggests, didn't have a ground to call their own. He combined playing for them with working as a painter at the same company as his mother before his manager Fred Eyre recommended the slight striker to Bury manager Bobby Smith, in front of whom he scored a hat-trick for Nomads against Stalybridge. A reserve team bow followed, in which he scored at Coventry City's old Highfield Road stadium in a Central League fixture, before what was to be a record-breaking run in the first team began. He'd been scoring consistently in the seasons which led to the promotion from Division Four.

"I was living the dream, being a pro, because I'd never really enjoyed school and barely went during my last year. Some of the places we went to in the league weren't much different from the non-league grounds I'd been at with Nomads," he now explains. In the same way that Terry Pashley did, Craig notes Hartlepool as the worst-ranking ground of the ninety-two in the Football League ("A tiny gas fire and a square bath that was only big enough for two people").

"I started a plastering course and that was going to be my trade. Bury came in for me and offered me less money than I would have got for keeping up with that, but I thought if I was good enough then things would come," he explains. Things did indeed come as Craig's career progressed, including the receipt of what he called 'the laughable Lada' in which he would give future England defender Lee Dixon a lift to training when Dixon signed for Bury in the summer of 1985.

"I used to keep it in a garage at the back of the house because it got vandalised, what with it having my name down the side of it," he says with a smile. "I went to the garage one morning and saw that the door was open. I panicked, but the car was still there. It was only when I tried to start it that I realised someone had nicked the battery. The day I picked it up from Bolton it broke down on the M61. It just

Craig Madden is his sponsored Lada from BCC.
(Copyright: Bury Football Club)

stopped on the outside lane, so I had to just slump down in the front seat of this car with my name all over it," he laughs.

"Nobody had a bad word to say about Martin. He was an enforcer on the pitch who had to lead by example and when he spoke people listened," he continues, switching the conversation to happier times on the field under Dobson. "He was a class player who had a reputation for playing the Burnley way which we just took and went with. He gave you the time of day and as a manager was always very approachable, which I found extremely encouraging because there's always a good cop-bad cop thing going on with managers, which means that sometimes if you have a problem it's better to go to the assistant or another member of the coaching staff, but that was never an issue with Dobbo," he says.

"He got me my move [to West Bromwich Albion, then in the First Division, in 1986] and he even drove me down there himself on the day I signed. He actually told me that I didn't have to go, but the minute I walked in it was a different world. It broke my missus's heart because she was so settled in the North West," he reveals.

Craig's wife wasn't the only one to feel so upset by the move. After nine years at Gigg Lane, he had become the club's all-time leading goalscorer with 149 goals in all competitions, 128 of which came in the league. If players had worn their names on the back of their shirts in his time, and replica shirts together with printing facilities had been as widely available as they are today, there's no doubting that Madden's name would have been the number one request at the club shop for the backs of the Spall Sports baseball-influenced white-with-blue-pinstripe number.

It was a spell which had done damage to the striker's body, though. Like his friend Trevor Ross, Craig has also had to deal with football being unkind to his wellbeing in later life. "I've had trouble with both of my ankles since I stopped playing, including a full reconstruction of my right ankle, and both knees aren't great. My back gets sore now and again too. When I was at West Brom they'd give me jabs in my knee and my calf before games. I had them before playing Liverpool and I even scored, but I couldn't walk for two days after the game. It's only when you're older and maybe wiser you think 'What am I doing, having a jab behind my kneecap to help me play football?'" he says, seemingly staggered at his own relaxed attitude from the past.

"Wilf would put the ultrasound machine about three inches over your injury and then just disappear," Craig laughs. "He'd come back and ask you how it felt and you'd just say 'Er, yeah, it feels great' even if it didn't feel any different at all and he'd go and tell you to get in the gym and look busy. We used to say about Wilf that he always looked like he had one foot in the road and one on the pavement because of his limp. He did his after-dinner act for a reduced rate for a mate of mine and I know his son [Paul] really well because we work in youth football. He's different class, Wilf," he beams.

Gigg Lane's luscious surface undoubtedly helped Craig rack up those goals. "We'd hammer the groundsman in a nice way, saying 'Your pitch is rubbish!' at him, but it was the best in the country and people wanted to come and play on it. We made it our fortress and I think people didn't want to come to Bury because they were intimidated by the surface and how we'd play," he says.

"When we signed another striker, both towards the end of this season [John Kerr] but also at any time when I was at Bury, I never felt like it was to put pressure on me. I just thought that they were signed to play with me and help me become a better player," he reflects. It was a desire from his teammates to get Craig's name on the scoresheet which brought him national acclaim. "In the 1981/82 season, Pepsi ran their 'Golden Goal' competition when they'd give £5,000 to a player who scored thirty-five league goals that season, and I'd told the lads from Christmas that if I won the cash I'd share it with them. Well, after that they just left everything for me: free-kicks, penalties, the ball was forever coming to me," he laughs.

"I reached the target but missed out on being the top scorer in the entire Football League to Keith Edwards from Sheffield United. I withdrew £2,500 from the bank after cashing the cheque and gave it to Keith Kennedy, who was club captain. He dished it out pro rata amongst the lads, but it was funny he seemed to get the most," he laughs. "At the time, I was getting married that year so the money would have come in handy, but it just seemed the right thing to do," he shrugs.

Following spells with Blackpool and York which followed his time in the top flight with West Brom, Craig was mulling over a move to Hong Kong Rangers while training with Fleetwood Town, then deep in the bowels of the non-league pyramid. At thirty-one, with football having been almost all he'd known, he took the option of a job with the PFA while turning out for the Cod Army ("They paid brilliantly even back then, twenty years ago. I got a car and everything!"). Via coaching spells at Stockport County, including a period as caretaker manager, he's recently left the Lancashire version of Highbury where he had been assistant manager and latterly youth team coach.

"Bury was the best time of my career, without a doubt," Craig concludes. "I was happy in the environment I was in – the club, the fans – I was even happy with training at Lower Gigg and Goshen. I'd had a lot of knockbacks in the game, like when I had a trial at Stockport and I didn't even get on to the pitch, I just sat there in the stand at Edgeley Park with my dad. I eventually got into the Manchester Boys team ahead of Andy Ritchie and he got into the England Boys squad ahead of me. We were jockeying," he laughs.

"I was being paid £35 a week when I signed which was much less than I'd have got plastering, but I got to play at places like Newcastle, Anfield and Old Trafford in the Central League. I signed league forms after Eddie Quigley, who was on Bury's backroom staff, chased me to Whitefield train station one afternoon after training to let me know the manager was offering them to me. I got £250 in fivers there and then, which terrified me on the walk from Victoria Station to Piccadilly, where I got the bus home to Stockport from," he says.

It could, however, have been so much different for Craig following an argument with Jim Iley that kept him out of the team for a time. After learning of Howard Kendall's interest in him down the road at Blackburn, Craig demanded to be allowed to speak to him, only for Iley to decline permission. "So that was that," he says, "but I found out much later that Manchester City wanted me too. Billy McNeil was the manager at the time, in 1981, and years later their former chairman Peter Swales cornered me at a do. He said, 'Your lot, I offered them £250,000 for you but they wanted £300,000!' It was the first I'd heard of it. I asked him if he was for real and he realised that I didn't know anything about it," he says, and I don't think I imagined a note of regret in his voice.

And the nickname, 'Charlie' Madden? "We were playing

Plymouth away and their bloke reading the teams out on the speaker system only had me down as 'C. Madden'. He asked Alan Whitehead what the C stood for and he said 'Charlie' and it just stuck," he laughs. And if there was a word which exemplified my and Craig Clarkson's time with Madden, then 'laughs' is surely it as we were treated to a conversation which wouldn't have been out of place as an after-dinner routine. It was a heroic evening with a heroic player.

The very next day after that 2–2 draw at Scunthorpe in which Madden and Enty had got their names on the scoresheet, the National Union of Miners called off their nationwide strike. Ninety-eight delegates voted to go back to work compared to the ninety-one who wanted tools to remain resolutely down.

If there was any latent anger knocking around the country following the vote, it manifested itself on the day after the ballot. Sunderland travelled to Chelsea in the second leg of the League Cup semi-final defending a 2–0 lead from the first leg, played at Roker Park the previous month. It was to be the first game of the month at which events on the crumbling terraces of a football stadium made more headlines than the action on the pitch, as the full force of hooliganism in the mid-1980s took hold. In his book *A Serious Case of the Blues: Chelsea in the '80s*, author Clive Batty describes a hysterical crowd whipping up a starting Blues XI, on £3,000 a man to overturn the deficit and progress to the final, into an equal frenzy. Sunderland powered into a 2–1 lead and the Shed End was soon alive with the smash of glass and the rumble of boots.

Batty notes that one fan in particular headed straight for the villain of the piece, Clive Walker. The Chelsea old boy had scored both his side's goals, and it was only a timely intervention from his former teammate Joey Jones that stopped the attacker's fist connecting. Walker would go on to set up a third for Sunderland; as he crossed for Colin West to head home, a police officer was actually chasing a would-be attacker across the penalty area. Bizarrely, Walker was also almost attacked by one of his former teammates. David Speedie was sent off for Chelsea and Walker taunted him, asking if he wanted any tickets for the final as the Scot trudged the long walk back to the tunnel. Speedie saw red for the second time in as many minutes and had to be restrained from lamping his former brother in blue. As it was, he eventually landed the blow in the relative privacy of the players' lounge after the game, according to Sunderland goalkeeper Chris Turner who told newspaper reporters what had happened.

Chelsea chairman Ken Bates would go on to say that he 'wanted to put [his] head in a gas oven' after the crowd trouble – that the *Daily Mirror* referred to in no uncertain terms with their 'SAVAGES' headline on the back page the following day – forced a Far Eastern electronics company to pull out of a sponsorship deal. He soon perked up when he announced the installation of an electric fence at Stamford Bridge which would give any potential pitch invader a twelve-volt non-lethal shock, but although it was put in place, the current was never switched on. Its use was deemed unsafe by the Greater London Council and the Conservative Minister for Sport, Neil Macfarlane.

Two days after the riot, Bury faced a trip to the relative calm of Edgar Street, home of Hereford United. The Bulls were in sixth place, six points behind a Bury side which was now leading the division by goal difference only after Blackpool had clawed their way on to the same number of points as them. The *Bury Times* printed on Tuesday 5 March previews the game the following evening as a 'battle' which is a word that wasn't being used out of turn, as John Dyson explained. 'United have turned their compact home into a zealously guarded fortress…Their impressive record of having conceded a mere five goals in 13 home games is the best in all four divisions,' he writes.

The scene was set for a similar showdown to Bury's clash with Peterborough in December, and Martin Dobson was unwavering in his philosophy. 'We will not be sacrificing our style just because we're playing Hereford,' he is quoted as saying. 'We know how hard our task will be, but we will still travel full of confidence,' he added.

Bury blasted three against the Bulls which, given the stat which John Dyson uncovered, should have been cause for celebration. Unfortunately, it would have meant so much more if the hosts hadn't scored five in response. 'Missed chances cost Bury at least a point,' says the intro of the report, which brings to mind a brilliantly bonkers scoreline if the Shakers could have taken their chances, but it wasn't to be. After going one down, a Trevor Ross thunderbolt of a penalty brought Bury back into the game before Hereford stepped up a gear and pushed into a 3–1 lead in time for the half-time whistle. Ten minutes into the second period, Kevin Young pounced on a Craig Madden header which hit the bar to smash the ball home, before the hosts restored their two-goal cushion five minutes later. Winston White grabbed a goal against his former club with seven minutes left on the clock before Hereford put the game out of Bury's reach with two minutes left to play after misses from Ross and Craig Madden. It's no wonder that the breathless report of the action is headlined 'STANDING OVATION BUT NO POINTS FROM A THRILLER'.

"It was nip and tuck all the way, that game," remembers Bury fan Paul Greenlees today. "We got back to Bury and Ian Fitzsimmons kept the social club open for us to have a drink. Some of the players came in for one when their coach arrived back and Wilf came and sat with me and my friends. He asked what we'd thought of the game and I'd said it was great and entertaining. He laid into me, asking how we could have played well when we conceded five and that it was a shocking defensive performance. After he'd gone, my mates told me they agreed with me. I said 'Well why didn't you say that when he was sat here?'" he laughs.

The following Saturday, Bury welcomed Blackpool to Gigg

Lane. The Seasiders had also lost their midweek game, going down 2–1 at home to Tranmere the day before Bury's defeat at Hereford, so the two sides remained joint top of the division. It was, in every respect of the word, a grudge match at which the scourge of following football in the mid-1980s erupted even before a ball had been kicked in anger.

The game signalled the greatest outbreak of hooliganism that the town had ever seen and which saw the match make the front page of the *Bury Times* dated 12 March as well as the back. 'HOOLIGANS ON THE RAMPAGE' is the stark splash on the front page. Anybody shopping in Bury town centre before the game started – normally a fairly quiet, innocuous pastime – didn't need to be told this as visiting supporters took inspiration from the events at Stamford Bridge just days earlier. The report goes on to describe how a coachload of Tangerines fans were involved in ugly scenes at The Bull's Head in Breightmet before they'd even reached the town boundaries, resulting in the coach being intercepted and its occupants ordered to accompany officers to Bury police station.

"It was mayhem that day. I went with some Blackpool-supporting mates and by the time we arrived there it was clear that every barmy pub crew from the Fylde Coast had descended on North Manchester," remembers Blackburn Rovers fan Michael Taylor of those who weren't apprehended by the police en route. "There was no obvious trigger for the mayhem, other than a wanton need to smash somewhere up. Blackpool fans were just gripped by this collective madness driven by their own notoriety," he continues.

Meanwhile, Malcolm Parr believes that not all of the trouble-makers were from the Fylde Coast. "There were people from Merseyside, Cheshire and Staffordshire there as well as the Fylde, from what I heard. I wondered if it was a game that hooligans from all over the country had chosen to come to and cause trouble," he says.

Despite the trouble which had occurred before the game

Trevor Ross smashes home the winning goal against Blackpool as Gigg Lane's impromptu demolition is about to begin.
(Copyright: Chris Tofalos)

bubbling under the surface as the action took place on the pitch, the mid-game demolition attempt of the stands which housed them was begun by Blackpool fans only after Leighton James won a hotly-disputed penalty with twenty minutes left to play.

Trevor Ross stepped up and converted expertly. A photo of him scoring the spot kick appeared in the programme for the next home game, showing a look of single-minded gritty determination on Ross's face. His left foot is on its tip-toes, and his right leg is almost at a ninety-degree angle to the left as it's propelled upwards by his huge calf muscles. Behind him, Kevin Young is already starting the run to chase a rebound which won't come and a Blackpool defender remains static with a strange smile on his face. It's almost a maniacal grin by a player who knows that expending the energy to go after

169

the ball would be a waste, because there's only one place where it is heading.

"Sam Ellis was Blackpool's manager that day," Ross remembers today. "He told me that he'd hoped any other Bury player would take the penalty rather than me, because he knew I'd score," he says.

'Rival fans, who have been condemned by Blackpool's manager, reacted furiously by ripping out bench seating, attacking opposition supporters outside the ground and embarking on a trail of vandalism,' reads the front-page article from 12 March. Michael Taylor remembers the violence well.

"I was in the Main Stand watching the back of the away end getting kicked in. Then the panels at the front of the Main Stand started getting smashed as well. The police were pretty brutal in trying to crack down and were arresting people left, right and centre. This inflamed the situation even more, but they were faced with mobs intent on destruction and they had little choice. After the game it must have been horrible for the home fans as these gangs were roaming around looking for people to bully, which is what so-called football hooliganism is all about," he concludes.

'The trouble spilled over to the outside of the ground at the end of the match. A section of concrete wall adjoining the ground was pushed over as the swell of the crowd surged forward,' continues the *Bury Times* news reporter on the front page, before going on to note how houses and cars in the back streets surrounding Gigg Lane were also attacked. In a near-echo of 'Rusholme Ruffians' by the Smiths – side one, track two off the album *Meat Is Murder* which was released in 1985 – trouble also flared at the travelling fairground on Angouleme Way after the game. The total cost of the clean-up and repair operation was given as £2,500.

With the current thirst for knowledge about 'running with the boys' in the darker days of British football, from those who either weren't there to see it or those who were and view it as a peculiar badge of honour, it comes as no surprise that Blackpool's hooligan

Ugly scenes at the Cemetery End gates as Blackpool fans riot. (Copyright: Michael Taylor)

element has its own Wikipedia page named after 'The Muckers'. Its writer remembers this day in a predictably blustering tone and also refers to the pubs in the resort where the fans would meet. What's odd about this is that in the programme for Bury's game at Blackpool in October 1984, the very same pubs are featured but in more sedate references to placings in domino and cribbage leagues.

Even today, former *Bury Times* sports editor John Dyson remembers the violence clearly. He and the rest of the members of the fourth estate were in place in the press box at the back of the Main Stand in the block next to that which housed away supporters. When the stand was redeveloped in 1992 following the Popplewell and Taylor reports, the press box's location remained the same.

"They were throwing pieces of timber over our heads towards the Bury fans to our right in the stand. They were like javelins being hurled into what was then called the B Stand. It was extremely frightening," he says.

Greater Manchester Police's reaction to the trouble was to order Bury chairman Terry Robinson to erect a metal cage around the area of the Main Stand at Gigg Lane which was used to house away fans. It utterly destroyed the charm of the sixty-year-old structure for what were to be the final seven years of its life. In the words of Prince Charles in his famous speech to the Royal Institute of British Architects in 1984, the cage was 'a monstrous carbuncle on the face of a much-loved and elegant friend'.

By 2010, Blackpool had remarkably risen to the heights of the Premier League having been in the basement just ten years previously. A season of struggle boiled down to a showdown against Manchester

United at Old Trafford which both sides needed desperately to win but for different reasons. A United win would clinch their nineteenth Premier League title while a victory for the visitors would boost their chances of securing a wholly improbable second season at the top table. Predictably, Sir Alex Ferguson's side won, and, as well as the red and white ticker tape reception for the champions, the *Match of the Day* montage showed lots of middle-aged skinheads with tattoos in tangerine shirts crying as they accepted Blackpool's relegation. In a moment of tremendous schadenfreude, I can't have been alone as a Bury fan in hoping that some of those pictured had taken their frustrations out on the Cemetery End or the panels at the front of the Main Stand on 9 March 1985.

The trouble overtook the game itself in the annals of the season, and indeed the club's past, described as it was in the local paper as 'the worst crowd scenes in the 100-year history of the club'. Despite John Dyson referring to 'the flotsam and jetsam that arrived in the town from the Fylde Coast...who should be behind bars' in the report printed on 12 March, it was a tense afternoon played out in front of 7,798, Bury's biggest crowd of the season. 'Hardly anyone had time to dwell on the ball and slow down the helter-skelter pace. The pitch was no place for the faint-hearted,' he continues.

Winston White had to be replaced by substitute Terry Pashley, and Gary Buckley is described as being 'shaken' by one crunching tackle from John Deary. David Brown was courageous in diving at livewire Deary's feet before Leighton James shoved the Blackpool fans' 'fat' taunts right back at them as he set off on a mazy sixty-yard run and shot at 'keeper Billy O'Rourke, before minutes later earning the winning penalty after a clumsy challenge by future Shakers defender Colin Greenall.

'Blackpool are a very physical side, although I stress not dirty,' Martin Dobson told John Dyson after the game. 'We had to match them from the word go. The players responded magnificently and although it might not have been pretty from a spectators' point of view, the result was very important to us. There was a lot of tension out there but I always felt we might get the one break you need to win a match like that,' he added.

Physio Wilf McGuinness would have been the busiest man in Gigg Lane the day after the blood and thunder Lancashire derby. On the same page as the report of the crucial victory over the Seasiders, 'QUEUE FORMS AT TREATMENT ROOM' is the headline for a story about how the minute squad was coping ahead of that night's game against Swindon Town at the County Ground in deepest Wiltshire. 'Bury tackle Jekyll and Hyde club Swindon...with a team which needed almost as much patching up as those parts of Gigg Lane which were savaged by Blackpool's thugs on Saturday,' reads the intro, before the body text refers to seven players who needed Wilf's occasionally-unorthodox treatment methods.

Joe Jakub is described as a definite non-starter because of his lingering knee problem, but of the other six, the player-manager rated his own chances of playing as very doubtful after he took a knock to the shin that was later swelling abnormally. The remaining five players referred to in the story – Leighton James, David Brown, Gary Buckley, Winston White and Andy Hill – were all named in the starting XI that evening.

'TALE OF TWO GOALKEEPERS IS SAD FOR BURY' is the headline on the back page of the *Bury Times* from 14 March which paperboys would have been pushing through letterboxes that Friday morning. Bury surrendered the top spot in the division to Darlington after this 1–0 defeat which, according to John Dyson, hinged on the two goalkeepers.

'Scott Endersby was unbeaten in the Swindon goal but while David Brown was far less occupied he made one tragic error which proved fatal. It came in the forty-eighth minute when he moved out of his goal to collect, on the bounce, a punt up field by David Cole. He would have taken it 99 times out of 100 but, on this occasion, and perhaps with half an eye on Peter Coyne, he missed it and as Coyne tried to get round him the Bury 'keeper panicked and hauled down the Swindon forward,' writes Dyson in reference to how Lou Macari's side took the lead.

Coyne converted the resulting spot kick which was a signal of how Bury's night was going. In the first half, Craig Madden was kept out by a terrific save from Endersby while Winston White rattled the crossbar and big John Bramhall brought the best from the home side's goalkeeper. The season was clearly taking its toll on Leighton James as Dyson describes the Welsh wing wizard limping throughout the second half, and former Bury hero Andy Rowland performed an about turn to become villain of the piece when he brought down Winston White in the area only for the referee to wave away the resulting penalty claims.

In order to interview David Brown face-to-face, as I had interviewed all of the other squad members, the project had to go continental. I'd heard vague murmurings that the former goalkeeper was now living in Italy, but it was John Bramhall who confirmed them by handing me his Blackberry with Brown's telephone number highlighted while he looked through my file of match reports during our interview. It was a huge number that began with 00 and I made sure I copied it correctly before I nervously called it later that evening. One wrong digit could have taken me to somewhere totally different in Italy rather than the home of a man who played for Horden Colliery Welfare – the team from which Bury signed Colin Bell – and Middlesbrough and Oxford before he joined Bury.

I dialled the long number and heard the long tone which meant I'd connected with mainland Europe. The phone was picked up and the person at the other end of the line said what I can only assume was 'Hello?' in Italian.

I suddenly reverted to the Englishman abroad who steadfastly refuses to learn the native tongue. "HELLO," I bellowed. "CAN...I... SPEAK...TO...DAVID...BROWN...PLEASE?" My new Italian friend put the phone on a hard surface rather than the receiver and went to fetch someone.

"Hello?" asked a voice with a trace of the North East in its accent.

David was the last of the players I made contact with as part of my research. After I'd outlined the premise of what I wanted to do, he gave me his email address so we could keep in touch. The plan of a break in Italy formed in my head and it wasn't long before I'd made arrangements for a flight from Stansted and a hotel room in a charming village called Verucchio, not far from Rimini.

I interviewed the final player of the odyssey, but not the last player to be interviewed in this book, in a pavement café in the blazing Italian sun. "Team spirit is a wonderful thing and we had it, not because there were so few of us but because we were winning games. I can look back at that team now and I'd have a pint with any of them," he remembers.

"There were different characters in the squad. We'd all take the mickey out of each other, like we did with Craig's car saying it should have had a gun turret on it, and get on the bus home feeling happy. We didn't lose many away, but if we did then we'd get on the coach thinking we had a good chance in the next game.

"The bonding trip to the Isle of Man was brilliant. We were these young lads drinking in the hotel bar with two original members of the Drifters, and although we wanted to hear all of their stories, they wanted to hear ours too," he remembers.

Brown was very much the unsung hero of the promotion squad after starring in every minute of all forty-six league games. "Andy Hill stole my Player of the Year award," he laughs now. "We were confident from the start though. We'd spent part of the previous season in the top four until the West Ham defeat [covered in the 1982–84 chapter] and we thought there was no reason we couldn't do it again. I could always get away to Italy to see Vanna [Brown's then-girlfriend and now wife] and I'd do a lot of running while I was

175

there to rest my mind. I always went back expecting a good season.

"I loved being a professional footballer for Bury. I'd had a nightmare at Oxford, the club I'd joined Bury from, because it was a terrible club for me to be at, but I was terrible for them too. I remember one New Year's Eve when I was on their books crying down the phone to my parents back in the North East because I was so unhappy," he reveals.

"Oxford wanted me to leave and I wanted to leave too. I joined Bury under Jim Iley and was confident that things would be different, but just days later he signed another goalkeeper, John Platt, too. I remember thinking, Oh my God, I'm not going to get a game, but fortunately for me I got into the team and kept my place. When I look at players now, the money is more, but I was paid a living wage to do something I loved. When Martin and Frank came into the club with names like Ray Pointer joining them, I felt that we were in the big time.

"We'd play on the Saturday and because Vanna was in Italy I'd have a couple of pints in the club with my mate Steve Johnson and then go home rather than hitting the town. I'd speak to a couple of fans in the club with an openness that I always felt I'd appreciate if I was a fan, then get home at about 9.30pm. I'd sleep in on the Sunday and be refreshed on the Monday morning for training. I lived in digs with a wonderful lady called Madge Fox for four years and after training she'd have the kettle on and the biscuit barrel ready for an afternoon on the sofa. It was the life of Riley!" he laughs.

David remembers with fondness his teammates who would put pressure on an opposing team despite Dobson's reputation for nurturing a more cultured side. "If an opposition side had a player who'd go in and kick Leighton James or Trevor Ross, they'd give just as much back. John Bramhall was no angel either, so we'd have players who could do both," he laughs about the friend who passed Brown's telephone number on to me. "Martin wanted to play. He wasn't a hard man, but he knew that in the Fourth Division at that point in time he needed players he could trust with different roles in the mix," he says.

One game which stands out from the promotion season is the fixture at Mansfield's vast, windswept Field Mill ground. "Ian Greaves was their manager and he had been my manager at Oxford when it had all gone wrong, so I felt as though I had to up the ante when we played them. Colin Calderwood had given me a kick when I'd gone down for the ball at his feet and it spurred me on. I saved a penalty from Mark Kearney in the game, we won and Ian approached me after the game and said he was wrong to let me leave Oxford so cheaply. It felt good to get one over him," he admits.

Penalties were actually something of a speciality of David's. Despite Bury's rather premature exit from the Lancashire Cup at the group stage in the summer of 1984, a year previously they had reached the final of the tournament where they faced a strong Blackburn Rovers side at Ewood Park.

"Simon Garner had a reputation of never missing a penalty. He took two against me in normal time and I saved both of them, one of them being a real blaster. It was just typical that we lost on penalties after extra time," he laughs.

Perhaps because it was the ground in his home town, an area he still regards with such a fondness that his accent clings to his Italian pronunciations, David enjoyed the trip to Hartlepool that all other players seemed to dread. "I played eleven games up there in total during my career and won seven and drew four, so I was more than happy when Winston got the winner for us that January. Halifax was a different story a few weeks later, though, when we lost 4–1. It was icy, the pitch was rock hard and we were totally unprepared. I was lucky enough to be given the opportunity to play at some wonderful grounds in my career. The Shay wasn't one of them, but the worst was Springfield Park. I played in one game there under Jim Iley that was so muddy that you couldn't make out the lines of the eighteen-yard box," he says.

The effects of being an ever-present, particularly on bone hard pitches that weren't maintained to the standards David had enjoyed when making ten appearances in the First Division for Middlesbrough at the start of his career, soon became apparent. "We lost 5–3 at Hereford in that real humdinger and I knew there was something wrong with my back. I talked to Wilf about it on the way back and the club knew I had a problem. I remember Martin Dobson came and sat down next to me on the coach and told me that in his opinion I could be a Division Two goalkeeper. He meant it as a compliment, of course, but the pessimist in me thought, 'Oh, so you don't think I can be a Division One 'keeper, do you?'

"He was trying to tell me not to worry too much about the injury, but at the end of the season my back froze and I had an operation which meant I missed the first season in the third tier after promotion. Martin signed Phil Hughes, and although I was fit for six months and played fifteen reserve games, he and Frank let me go. I can't blame them, I'd have done the same if I was in their position," he says.

"I think Wilf knew John McGrath, the Preston manager. I think he must have asked him to give me a call because John rang me and I ended up signing for them. Alan Kelly was my understudy and we all knew he was going to be great. But I joined, started playing in the first team and was doing well until I got injured again. Alan and I ended up sharing the first team duties for the next two years," he says.

In a repeat of the FA Cup first round of the 1984/85 season, Bury were drawn away at Preston in the competition's first stage two years later and Brown was to face his former teammates. "We, meaning Preston, were winning 2–0 at half-time so I was feeling pleased with my team's performance as we ran out for the second half. I was going to have the away fans behind me for the half and as I got to my goal line, one of them shouted 'Brown! You're an effing traitor!' But that's football and football fans. I have to admit, it felt good to win 5-1 that afternoon," he says with a smile. "I played what

I consider the best football of my career at Preston, even eclipsing the promotion season with Bury. I gave a lot to my career and got a lot back, but when I came back from my second injury the Astroturf at Deepdale didn't do me any good at all.

"I enjoyed my time at Bury very much though," he says without missing a beat. "The fans were great with me. When I was in hospital, Steve Johnson's landlord, a fella called Bill, would give Vanna a lift to the hospital to see me. They were a lovely bunch of people and when we spoke to them we'd pass on our appreciation that they'd get on a coach and go to a place like Torquay to go and watch us. As a squad we'd socialise together, with the other players' wives too. Vanna and I would hang out with Andy Hill and his wife Marion, Terry and Sylvia Pashley and John Bramhall and his wife Anne," he says.

"I thought that the Bury fans were brilliant and that Bury as a whole was a lovely town too," says Vanna. "There were some good shops there that I'd visit when I wasn't teaching at MANCAT and we'd go to the Italian restaurant, Est Est Est, on Manchester Road," she says.

It's now teaching that concerns the Browns in their everyday lives as they use their bilingual nature to teach English to any Italians who'd like to learn the language at the school which they own. "We're always working," concludes David. "Even the youngest schoolchild in Italy learns English so we're always kept busy," he finishes.

That night, after the Browns had travelled back to their school, I went to a wine festival in the centre of Verucchio. As the heavy bass of a swing band reverberated around the cobbled piazza, I sipped my sparkling rosé and felt pleased that travelling so far had been worth it to meet such a lovely, unassuming former Bury player.

The day after Bury's defeat at Swindon Town, hooliganism in the British game reached its peak in the most recognisable incident of the entire 1980s. Probably not at all influenced by Blackpool fans' actions at Gigg Lane the previous weekend, Third Division Millwall and their notorious 'Bushwhackers' went to First Division Luton Town in the FA Cup sixth round. The visitors were third in their division while the hosts were second from bottom in theirs. Tensions were high.

Trains ferrying supporters from across London, not just Bermondsey, pulled into Luton all afternoon, most of them with smashed light fittings and torn seats by the time they reached their destination. Having wrecked their transportation, the passengers then set about causing carnage in the Bedfordshire streets, and by 5pm, two-and-three-quarter hours before what was amazingly not an all-ticket game, Luton looked like a war zone.

Despite turnstiles being rushed and a demolition job being started on Kenilworth Road's Bobbers Stand, the game astonishingly began on time after Millwall manager George Graham appealed for calm from his team's supporters over the stadium's public address system. Isolated fighting pockmarked the game in its opening fourteen minutes before the referee David Hutchinson felt he had no option but to take the players off the field. They remained in the changing rooms for twenty-five minutes, after which the game was completed. Brian Stein scored the only goal of the game after half an hour, and as the final whistle loomed tantalisingly close, all twenty outfield players made sure they were positioned by the tunnel for the sprint up it to the relative sanctuary of the changing rooms once more.

It was after the game that the violence really took hold. The BBC's pictures of marauding supporters throwing shards of orange plastic which were once seats are now synonymous with football's public image in the decade. Wide shots show the glow of streetlights of a town shell-shocked by its metropolitan invaders who had caused the local shopping centre to be closed in the middle of the afternoon. Of the eighty-one people injured in the riot, thirty-one were police officers, including one who stopped breathing after being hit on the head by a lump of concrete. He was resuscitated by a colleague who was being attacked by people there in the name of supporting Millwall while he administered first aid.

In his book *Luton Town at Kenilworth Road*, Hatters fan Roger Wash writes that he does not believe those there were all dyed-in-the-wool Lions: 'When George Graham came over to appeal to them, they did not have a clue who he was. It was a night out for every yob in London!' Thirty-one arrests were made, with the majority of those who had their collar felt admitting in court that they didn't support Millwall. Up in the commentary gantry, John Motson famously said that 'this is what British football has to contend with now'.

In 2013, the two sides were drawn against each other once more in the same competition's fifth round. In a piece for *The Guardian* headlined 'THE NIGHT FOOTBALL DIED A SLOW DEATH AT KENILWORTH ROAD', reporter Sean Ingle uncovered some terrific tales from that night twenty-eight years previously, including the 'miscreant' teenage Chelsea fan who was seen by his parents on TV throwing a seat at a police officer. On returning to London in the early hours, he found his bedding outside his house and was told that if he wanted to behave like an animal then he may as well sleep like one too.

Over in *The Times* on the same weekend in 2013, Tony Cascarino remembered astonishingly travelling to the game with Millwall-supporting friends, despite already being a professional with Gillingham. He gives a terrifying account of his own foolishness that resulted in him finding himself in the middle of the melee which was given courage by sheer weight of numbers, but also the divides on the away terrace between those hell-bent on destruction and those who wanted to prevent further tarnishing of the Lions' reputation.

In the apartment at 10 Downing Street, Margaret Thatcher had seen each piece of orange plastic that littered the pitch on that night's edition of *Sportsnight*. One of her MPs, David Evans, was the chairman of the home side and was, according to Luton's manager David Pleat in the *Guardian* article, 'a naughty boy...Mrs Thatcher's plaything'. The Prime Minister knew that it was time to get tough on hooligans in the face of such public events, as did Evans who proposed that away fans be banned from Kenilworth Road from the beginning of the 1986/87 season onwards and that the much-maligned ID card system be introduced. Due to the away fan ban, Luton were not permitted to enter the League Cup in the first season during which it was enforced.

The day immediately after the riot, England lost out to West Germany in the bidding process for Euro 88. Marco van Basten's wonder goal against the USSR in the final could just have easily been scored at Wembley rather than the Olympic Stadium in Munich, but the vote swung the Teutonic way. 'The scenes at Luton were the most disgraceful I've ever seen – and I've seen a lot,' raged England's bid chief, FA chairman Bert Millichip.

Under the thirty-year rule, in which previously confidential government papers are made public by the National Archives Office once that duration has elapsed, a number of memos emerged in January 2015 on how it was felt hooliganism could be handled after the Luton riot. Unsurprisingly, the government showed just what little understanding it had of the sport and its supporters by attempting to quell marauding hordes of the terrifying and tooled-up with a scheme called 'Goalies Against Hoolies'.

Mrs Thatcher's press secretary, Bernard Ingham, imagined 'an eloquent goalkeeper' – Manchester United's Gary Bailey was mentioned on account of him being a university graduate – speaking out against violence at matches because they were often the first victims in a pitch invasion. The movement never went beyond the planning stage.

Meanwhile, the Bobbers Stand at Kenilworth Road was torn down and rebuilt in 1986 as an emblem which summed up just how much football was changing: it was, and remains, a stand devoted exclusively to executive boxes covering one whole side of the pitch.

David Pleat told the *Daily Telegraph* that a third of Luton supporters at Kenilworth Road on the night of the riot never went to another game, such was their fear of what football supporters could be capable of. The people of Bury had no such qualms about attending matches. Although it wasn't as large as the crowd for the Shakers' previous home game when Blackpool fans had provided their own smaller-scale version of the Kenilworth Road riot, a crowd nudging 5,000 assembled at Gigg Lane for the rearranged game between the Shakers and fellow promotion-chasers the Quakers on 19 March.

Darlington had taken over from Bury at the top of the table only a few weeks earlier and opened up a five-point lead over the hosts. With such a hectic March fixture list only 50 per cent completed, Bury's tired legs required the luck that comes when it's most needed, and it was duly delivered in this game. Each side was looking at securing a point from the game before a shot from Andy Hill – who very nearly opened his league account within five minutes of the start of the reverse fixture, his league debut, on the opening day of the season – found a way through a tangle of legs with twenty minutes left to play.

As they had done all season up to that point, Winston White and Leighton James terrorised the opposition side's full backs, but it was a flat Tuesday evening for Wayne Entwistle and Craig Madden, who struggled to make any meaningful contribution once they got on the end of balls from the wing. The defence too was always looking a touch suspect before Hill saved the day, as he would go on to do many times in his Bury career, either up front with a workmanlike goal or in his native defensive position. Darlington's lead at the top was subsequently cut to just two points as Bury's tired legs dragged up reserves of energy to keep the title challenge very much alive.

The game was Bury's first for seven days since the defeat at Swindon, a postponement of the home game versus Aldershot coming in between the two. The country was in the grip of a wet spring that continued into the long, long trip to Southend on Saturday 23 March for a game which supporter Malcolm Parr wrote about in a fanzine article over a decade later, under the pseudonym The Grim

Reaper. Titled 'TEN CANS OF BITTER AND A PACKET OF CRISPS, PLEASE', the article is as vivid a piece of writing about watching Bury on the road during this period as anything that was published in the *Bury Times*.

Now a very well-respected fan in the online world for his measured and considered opinions of all things Bury, Malcolm describes being tasked with buying as much beer as possible with the £35 that was gathered in a whip round. He fortuitously stumbled on a supermarket selling booze at vastly-reduced prices and bought seventy cans and seven bags of crisps, thankfully in a variety of flavours. It was only when the first can was cracked open at 8.15am – by which time the coach presumably hadn't yet made it to the Simister Island motorway junction – that it was discovered the alcohol was considerably past its sell-by date.

Paul Greenlees organised the coach which ran to Roots Hall. "The supporters' club had run a coach to every game up to that point and we decided for the long journey to Southend that we'd hire an executive coach for the fifty people who'd been to each game. We had the beer that Malcolm had bought and told the driver that we wanted to get to Southend for about 2pm, but he took no notice and by midday we were there. We had three hours to kill before the game so went to their social club and carried on drinking, having far too much," he remembers.

Malcolm Parr's written descriptions really come alive when describing the match action. While he and his fellow fans were getting soaked in the away end down in Essex, John Dyson was ensconced in a notepad-preserving press box which enabled him to write the report headlined 'YOUNG'S SUPER STRIKE PLUNDERS A POINT IN SIX-GOAL THRILLER' which appeared in the local paper dated 26 March. Despite the disappointment of slipping down to third in the league, Dyson keeps a brave face on things by referring to Bury's reputation as one of the best teams on their travels and quoting former England captain Bobby Moore who still had control of the opposition's reins. The former national team skipper told the post-match press pack that 'Bury played some quality stuff. I have not seen many better teams in this division and we did well to hold them.'

Nevertheless, Bury had to come from behind twice to earn their point. The Shakers took the lead through a Wayne Entwistle strike, but Malcolm Parr and his Burtonwood Beer brethren weren't in a position to see the goal. After asking stewards if they could be moved from an open terrace to the shelter of a side stand, their relocation was in progress as Bury took the lead while they climbed the wall between the two. The locals took umbrage at Enty's goal and forced the Bury fans back on to the soggy terrace that they'd just left.

"I'll never forget the sight of Pat Holt, a Bury fan who everyone knew, on her hands and knees looking for her glasses after the melee when fifty of their fans had charged at us," remembers supporter Peter Cullen. "Pat Mason was berating the Southend manager about the behaviour of their fans causing trouble, too. Pat Mason versus Bobby Moore!" he laughs.

Wet, miserable and not feeling any of alcohol's supposed warming qualities, Bury's support stayed murmuring in the rain as Southend went 2–1 up, only for Craig Madden to draw Bury level from a Terry Pashley cross. A Trevor Ross error allowed a United player to make it 3–2 before Kevin Young ensured his place in the banner headline with a terrific chip with twenty-five minutes of the game remaining. Leighton James poured forward as Bury's most immediate threat, but the visitors, and manager Moore, held on just enough. "We had a bit of a sing-song with the rest of the beer on the drive back to Bury," remembers Paul Greenlees, presumably thinking of soggy clothes settling into the coach seats too.

Even though both of Bury's dynamic strike duo found the net at Southend, Martin Dobson was starting to worry that Wayne Entwistle and Craig Madden were flagging at a point in the season when scoring goals to win games was even more critical than ever. On the same page of the Tuesday 26 March edition of the *Bury Times* as the dissection of the Southend game is the headline 'KERR TUG-O-WAR!' in reference to the Stockport County striker John who was being trailed by Dobson. The deal is described as a mystery by John Dyson, but is confirmed as being off ('...for the time being') ahead of that night's clash with Kerr's then-side at Gigg Lane. Chairman Terry Robinson claims in the article that his counterpart at Edgeley Park has not told him why the £15,000 deal for 'the right man for the job' is now off. The transfer deadline was just two days away, and Dyson warns that Bury may well turn their attentions elsewhere if the Kerr move was to fall through.

Bury were now into the long home straight of the season, and it was a 'home' straight more than anything else, as eight of their remaining fixtures were to take place at Gigg Lane. Match night for the game against County began with John Dyson presumably cursing how quickly football transfers can veer from one extreme to the other, as it was confirmed before the game that Kerr would indeed be signing for Bury for £17,000. He played no part in the 2–1 victory, though, with both of Bury's goals coming from Craig Madden to take him through the twenty barrier for the season. 'DOUBLE TOP FOR MADDEN' is the headline of the report in the edition of the *Bury Times* published on 29 March in relation to what should have been a perfunctory win against a team kicking around the lower reaches of the division.

This wasn't the case though. Terry Pashley is singled out for praise after taking command in a new, more attacking role following Stockport taking a surprise lead within ten minutes. It was his leadership which enabled Bury to develop a hold on the game that County could only hope to compete with by using strong arm tactics, particularly against the laughing cavalier attitude of Leighton James, who let his feet do the talking. 'Seven repeat home wins in the next six weeks would virtually guarantee a champagne celebration at Gigg Lane,' ends the report.

If there's one thing Bury fans through the ages have become

accustomed to, it's that just mentioning what needs to be done – even in your internal monologue, never mind saying it out loud – is enough for the smooth-running train to be derailed. Such a view as Dyson's in the Stockport report of the supposed ease ahead meant that the promotion charge wobbled on the very same evening that the report was published with a 2–2 draw at home to Rochdale. Enty and Charlie Madden both weighed in with a goal on the night that their new colleague John Kerr made his bow from the bench to replace the latter, but it wasn't enough as Bury were in fact lucky to come away with a point. The Shakers went behind on the stroke of half-time before Madden equalised, and a sustained spell of pressure saw the home side hit the bar twice in sixty seconds. 'Dale retook the lead with just twelve minutes to go before the hometown boy Entwistle grabbed an equaliser with six minutes still on the clock.

The point denied Bury the top spot in the division as Chesterfield held on to the summit. 'Is the relentless promotion pressure beginning to take its toll on fraying nerve-ends in the Bury camp? Did the presence of new signing John Kerr on the substitute's bench cause too many eyes to be directed warily at the dugout instead of concentrating on the job in hand? Or was Friday night's fiercely contested local derby clash…which ended with honours even, just a minor hiccup in the Shakers' final push for a top four place come the end of the season?' asks Dyson in a sledgehammer-subtle introduction. 'Yes, possibly, and my goodness, hopefully' would have been the response from every last voice in the Main Stand, the South Stand and the Manchester Road End as the finishing post got closer and closer.

April 1985

The madness and violence which had descended upon British football during March was to have one particular far-reaching ramification. On April Fools' Day, the government announced plans to restrict the consumption of alcohol at or around what they termed 'problem' football grounds. This was to become the Sporting Events (Control of Alcohol etc.) Act that was passed into law later in the year which banned the consumption of booze within sight of football pitches, but not those of rugby or cricket clubs.

The act has now become as much a part of the match day experience as the back pass or professional foul rule, other introductions which seemed unworkable when introduced but which have been accepted with gusto. Corporate hospitality areas of grounds up and down the country roll down blinds or shut curtains to adhere to the law. Concourses get uncomfortably crowded in the rush to down one last gassy can of lager served in a plastic container before kick-off (because obviously it was the sight of blades of grass that was a major cause of hooligans going on the rampage).

Thirty years after its passing, the act is still a topic which arouses much debate. The demographics of football fans have changed immeasurably since the large-scale crowd trouble of the mid-eighties and stadiums are now infinitely safer places than they were. Proposals have since been made to redress the balance regionally, which would allow local authorities to decide on a game-by-game basis if fans were allowed to sup in sight of the pitch, but the act remains in place.

If any squad deserved a pint after March 1985 it was Bury's. The eight games played were taking their toll and it's not hard to imagine a similar groan of acceptance from the squad, when looking at the calendar for April's seven games, to the one they'd have emitted when looking at the previous month's agenda. The finishing tape was very much in sight, but it was to be a long and hard final push, as draining mentally as physically.

Bury travelled to Burslem to play Port Vale on Easter Saturday, the first match of the month. A 0–0 draw was down more to the capabilities of Andy Hill, Terry Pashley and David Brown than the misfiring of Craig Madden and Wayne Entwistle. In fact, John Dyson writes in the *Bury Times* match report published on Tuesday 9 April that 'On his day, Brown must rank as one of the best keepers in the division and, when the Shakers were really up against it in the first half of this nerve-wracking encounter, he didn't let them down.'

This was very much Brown's day as he pulled off several fine, acrobatic saves from Robbie Earle and Wayne Ebanks. Deadline day signing John Kerr replaced Winston White with ten minutes to go in a move which saw Bury revert to all-out attack as opposed to trying to drill a hole down the centre of the pitch. The new man surged on a fifty-yard run and spread the ball to Trevor Ross to cross for Craig Madden who, in a position that you'd bet your mortgage on him at least finding the target, miskicked in such a way that it could have felt the season hinged on that one moment. All in all, it was not the best of days – especially for John Dyson.

"I was thrown out of the press box in the old Main Stand at Vale Park because I said it was like a pigeon loft. As far as I know, it's a ban that's never been lifted," he laughs today.

Due to the Easter printing deadlines, a small box placed in the

189

body text of the report informs the reader that Bury won 1–0 at home to Hartlepool in the Easter Monday fixture played the day before publication. The win came courtesy of a Wayne Entwistle goal and a fuller report appeared in the paper published on Friday 12 April. 'WAYNE HEADS OFF ATTACK OF NERVES' is its headline as it leads into Bury lurching tentatively towards promotion rather than marching confidently as the paper had predicted in the 1984 close season. The six-game unbeaten run that this game extended, that would surely be a cause for fulsome praise in any other season, is described as 'really hard work' given Bury's self-imposed standards from earlier in the season.

Wear and tear meant that the team were not firing on all cylinders, though there's a hint that there's more to the supposed dip in form than just tiredness. 'Disruption through suspensions and injuries as well as a greater determination by opposing teams to clamp down on Bury's strong points' are highlighted. Opposing goalkeepers choosing Gigg Lane as the stage for their own one-man show are also credited, and none basked in the Cemetery End's limelight more than 'Pool's Eddie Blackburn.

Photographs taken during the match show the custodian with a mass of unpredictable curly hair and an extremely impressive beard. It's almost as though David Bellamy is lining up between the sticks for the visitors. Madden and Leighton James both struggled to find a way past the goalkeeper, who was making only his third appearance of the season, after an Entwistle header found the net inside the first twenty minutes for the only goal of the game. It was a timely fillip for Enty, who stepped up to the plate knowing that new signing John Kerr was jogging up and down the Main Stand touchline in his role as substitute with an eye on one of the two forward berths. The win took Bury to seventy-three points and second place, a point behind Chesterfield.

Crewe, never the happiest of hunting grounds for Bury, was the next trip the day after the Hartlepool report was published. The Shakers hadn't won on the road since they dented Chesterfield's tremendous home record on 2 February and it was a record that would continue

190

after a 1–0 reverse in the railway town. 'BLOWN OFF COURSE ON A DAY OF DESPAIR' is the *Bury Times* match report headline printed on 16 April. Despite noting that Bury still had enough aces up their sleeves to be regarded as promotion favourites, John Dyson concedes that the team mustn't experience any more days like this in the run-in. As nerves continued to haunt the team, the match was settled by a David Brown own goal direct from a corner ball that had cruelly swerved and dipped in the bracing Gresty Road wind.

Despite not being as notorious as the Blackpool match at Gigg Lane in the previous month, trouble followed Bury to Gresty Road. "Because of the success of the team we'd started to attract a large away following, some of whom were the kind of people you wouldn't want supporting your team. I remember that several people were arrested that day in Nantwich after they smashed a pub up and that there was fighting in the ground. In those days at Crewe, away supporters stood behind the goal and the home supporters were to your left in a covered paddock. There was a lot of antagonism and a lot of stupidity between the two that day," remembers supporter Malcolm Parr.

John Kerr made his full debut in the game as he started the match partnering Wayne Entwistle up front. Dyson could hardly contain his disbelief in the report that Craig Madden, a man with more than 100 goals for Bury, was shunted into a midfield role to compensate for the injured Gary Buckley and the suspended Kevin Young. It was a reshuffle by Martin Dobson which didn't reap the expected dividends as Kerr struggled to form an immediate bond with Enty. 'Even assuming that Bury could theoretically afford to lose this game, it was the manner of the defeat which provokes concern as the season draws to a nerve-wracking climax,' the report ends.

At the time of writing, John Kerr is the only member of the 1984/85 promotion squad who is no longer with us after he died of a heart attack while on holiday in France in 2006. Craig Madden attended his funeral.

On signing for Bury, John told the local paper that he wasn't just aiming to get Bury into the Third Division, as was Martin Dobson's reason for signing him. He'd set his sights higher. 'I'd like both of us to be in the Second Division at the end of my two-year contract,' the twenty-five-year-old said. 'I'm ambitious and this move can be beneficial to my career. I hope the club gets promotion this year and I'd like to be part of it, but I can't expect to knock Wayne [Entwistle] and Craig [Madden] off their perch straight away because they've been playing so well,' he added.

John Kerr pictured on his arrival at Gigg Lane. (Copyright: Bury Football Club)

The short story about Kerr's transfer also quotes his new manager, discussions with whom about the boss's footballing philosophy influenced the move. 'We needed forward cover and his arrival increases our options. John already knows the standards he will have to attain to get into the side. This is a signing for the future as well as the present and I'm convinced John will be a useful asset to the club,' said Dobson.

Unfortunately, Kerr's Bury career didn't pan out like that. He didn't score in any of his eight appearances in the run-in of the promotion season, and in the third tier the following season he made thirty appearances in all competitions and found the net four times. Half of these goals came in a blistering burst from the blocks, the 4–3 defeat away at Chesterfield on the opening day of the season, while another was the 1985/86 goal of the season against Derby County when he controlled the ball with his knee before volleying it into the top corner of the Manchester Road End goal.

"He was very comfortable in his role as substitute towards the end of the promotion season. He chatted to fans during the game and asked fans what they'd made of the season," Bury fan Craig Clarkson now remembers.

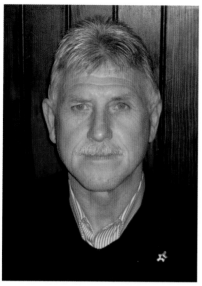

Joe Jakub in Chester.
(Copyright: author)

Wayne Entwistle in Bury.
(Copyright: author)

Chris Cutler at the
Manchester Airport Marriott.
(Copyright: author)

Terry Robinson in Hawkshaw.
(Copyright: author)

Trevor Ross in Oldham.
(Copyright: author)

Wilf McGuinness in Sale.
(Copyright: author)

Martin Dobson in Bolton.
(Copyright: author)

Craig Madden in Chorley.
(Copyright: author)

Terry Pashley in Poulton-le-Fylde.
(Copyright: author)

Kevin Young in Durham.
(Copyright: author)

John Bramhall in Manchester.
(Copyright: author)

Winston White in Birmingham.
(Copyright: author)

Gary Buckley in Prestwich.
(Copyright: author)

Andy Hill in Ramsbottom.
(Copyright: author)

Leighton James in Timperley.
(Copyright: author)

Frank Casper in Cliviger.
(Copyright: author)

David Brown in Verucchio, Italy.
(Copyright: author)

*Good Luck to "The Shakers"
from all at Cosgrove Hall*

Cosgrove Hall bring Danger Mouse to Gigg as they sponsor the game
with Wrexham in May 1985.
(Copyright: Bury Football Club)

The promotion train wobbles at Gresty Road in Crewe in April 1985.
(Copyright: Simon Egan)

The Manchester Road End in all its mid-80s glory. (Copyright: Bob Lilliman)

There's tension outside the Main Stand
before the game with Blackpool
in March 1985.
(Copyright: Michael Taylor)

An unexpected visitor on the away end
at the home game versus Blackpool.
Blackburn Rovers fan Michael Taylor was
not for turning.
(Copyright: Michael Taylor)

David Brown looks dejected as Halifax's Simon Lowe's header bobbles past him
in January 1985.
(Copyright: Johnny Meynell)

My dad's 'Ground Adult' season ticket for the campaign,
which allowed him into the South Stand or Manchester Road End.
(Copyright: author)

The no-frills advert from the programme for the no-frills
music shop in the town centre, which is now sadly no more.
(Copyright: Bury Football Club)

John moved to KV Ostend in Belgium from Gigg Lane, then to France, before he ended his career at Bangor City in the League of Wales. He then coached youngsters at a number of clubs and was employed as Cardiff City's director of youth when he died. As well as Madden, other mourners at the funeral included the Bluebirds' then-owner Sam Hammam and manager Dave Jones who went to pay their respects to the man credited as being instrumental in the setting up of Cardiff's youth academy.

The back page of the local paper containing the report of the defeat at Crewe also features a story focusing on how Martin Dobson was aiming to calm the jangled nerves of his squad in the last full month of the season. Fully aware that their tired legs were in danger of giving way beneath them and that all of his hard work in managing them up to this point might be undone, he claims that four more wins from the remaining seven games will be enough to get the Shakers promoted.

'We're still in a fantastic position and it's up to me and Frank Casper to take any pressure or doubts away from the players because we believe they have the ability to make it to the Third Division. I want eleven captains out there on the field, all accepting responsibility and showing that little bit extra belief in themselves,' he is quoted as saying.

The first of those seven matches was to come on the following Saturday afternoon when Mansfield Town were due to visit Gigg Lane. Bury's home form had, of course, played a massive part in their storm up the table. The Shakers had only tasted defeat once while holding this advantage and the record continued against the Stags, but, disappointingly, in the form of a 0–0 draw. The visitors restricted every conceivable threat from a Bury side desperate to find momentum which would carry them over the line, with Winston White, Leighton James, Craig Madden and Wayne Entwistle all having their game plans nullified. Results elsewhere meant that Bury had now slipped down to fourth in the table, but a 2–0 defeat for Hereford at fellow promotion-chasers Blackpool at least meant that the Shakers had a four-point cushion in the last promotion place.

The match report was printed three days after the game on the same night that Bury were set to welcome Chester City to Gigg Lane. Facing re-election, the visitors were in such poor form as to be likely easy pickings for the Shakers. Nevertheless, the *Bury Times* ran another rabble-rousing, breast-beating plea for support to the townsfolk at this late stage, which this time was delivered by assistant manager Frank Casper.

'CASPER APPEALS FOR A HOME HELP' has the former Burnley striker imploring: 'This is the time to dig in together. The players are uptight but take it from me they are doing their best and trying their hardest. After Saturday's match against Mansfield, they can't wait to get out against Chester because they badly want to bring success to the club. We understand the frustrations of the supporters but we're in a great position with only six games to go, so let's stick it out together.'

The assistant manager also claims that an early goal after the recent famine of one strike in four matches would lift the spirits of the home fans. 'It would certainly help to settle the players down and help them play more relaxed football, but games aren't won in the first twenty minutes and if we don't score early on we'll have to keep grinding on until we crack them,' he added cautiously.

The headline of the report for the Chester game shows that Casper was right to add a disclaimer on to the end of his quote. 'SECOND HALF GOAL SPREE EASES THE RUN-IN TENSION' describes the unbridled joy that a 4–1 win uncorks, with Winston White being John Dyson's main man following a mesmerising performance after some recently quiet, subdued games. Behind him in the pecking order, Terry Pashley was also praised to the hilt after not only a steely performance commanding the midfield, but also his first goal for Bury in fifty-eight appearances.

All of the goals came in the second period. The crowd was

almost 600 down on the number who'd attended the Mansfield game and those who stayed away must have felt their decision was justified if they'd heard a half-time update on the radio. However, after a burst of vocal encouragement from the Manchester Road End at the start of the second half, it wasn't long before a slaloming White run was brought to a premature end by the Chester goalkeeper. Trevor Ross smashed home the resulting penalty and the floodgates subsequently opened with a three-goal salvo in twelve minutes.

Winston grabbed the second goal before Leighton James added his name to the scoresheet with a drive into the corner of the net after collecting the ball on the halfway line, surging forward and selling a defender a dummy. Chester scored a consolation from the penalty spot, before Terry Pashley lifted the ball over the advancing 'keeper for his much-deserved goal and, after a worrying wobble, the promotion juggernaut was back on the road.

"Terry Pashley's goal was one of the most well-received of the season," remembers supporter Paul Greenlees. "We wanted every outfield player to score a goal and it was of course the only one he scored across the whole campaign. As it turned out, the manager didn't get one either," he continues.

Lee Dixon, who would sign for Bury just a few months later, was at the heart of the Chester defence and must have wondered where on earth his career was taking him. Having left Burnley on their relegation to Division Three in 1983, he was now staring the ignominy of re-election square in the face. Twenty-two England caps, Arsenal's title wins, FA Cup glory and European nights – or even a move to Stoke City, where he left Bury for after just one season – must have seemed an extremely long way away.

Football is now virtually unrecognisable from how it was in 1985. Space-age grounds are smarter and attract a wholly different kind of supporter, while club merchandise is in a totally different sphere to how it was when goods would be sold from a Portakabin in the car

195

park rather than dedicated superstores. Undoubtedly the biggest difference, though, is how much money players at the higher end of the league structure are paid. Even allowing for inflation, the amount that footballers were paid in 1985 pales when compared to their obscene salaries thirty years in the future. A player at a Premier League club, or even some Championship clubs, now only needs a couple of years at that level and some shrewd advice to be financially secure for life.

That's why you no longer get players seeing out their careers in the lower reaches of the Football League. They have no real reason to, beyond a love of the game. But it was that love which meant that Bury and, more specifically, his old Burnley teammate Martin Dobson were able to tempt Leighton James to Gigg Lane and the Fourth Division when he was ready to retire from playing after spending the previous season in the First Division with Sunderland. Gigg Lane was the next step on an illustrious career path that had taken in spells with Burnley, Swansea City, QPR and Derby County before he pitched up at Roker Park.

I'd interviewed Leighton before for the match day programme so already had his number, but it was through his daughter Jemma that I was able to speak to him and ask if he'd be willing to be interviewed. Still living in South Wales, the accent of which has never left his voice, Leighton agreed to speak to me but saved me an arse-numbing four-and-a-half-hour train journey to see him. Instead, he suggested we meet up in South Manchester, where he would be staying the night before flying out from Ringway on holiday.

Leighton James's 1984/85 season pen picture. (Copyright: Bury Football Club)

I arrived first at the designated meeting place, a Timperley Liberal Club, and took cover from the summer rain in the smoking shelter as I waited for the former Welsh international who is perhaps the most fondly recalled member of the promotion squad, owing to his exceptional skill.

"When Martin phoned me to enquire about my availability, I'd told him that I was planning to retire," he says in the games room of the club as the thud of darts landing in a board punctuates the audio recording of the interview. "He told me not to be silly and asked me to come over and have a look at the club and see what I thought of it. I enjoyed doing that because I'd become very disillusioned up at Sunderland. Alan Durban was manager with Pop Robson as his assistant. I was playing and looking after the youngsters and we were twelfth in the league with everything going fairly well. Then, for some inexplicable reason, Durban was sacked. Pop went too and I was sacked from my role with the kids, but I felt I'd had enough of the game so I was going to quit. Dobbo rang me and persuaded me to join Bury and I'm glad he did," he laughs.

"I only stayed for one season because I had the opportunity to become assistant manager at Newport County. I felt that Frank and Martin were fixtures at Bury and that I wouldn't be able to progress with my career in the way I wanted to.

"I knew Martin and Frank before I signed, of course, but I also knew Joe Jakub and Kevin Young from Burnley and Trevor Ross from playing against him when he was at Everton," he says. I'd mentioned in our preamble as we got a drink and settled down that Bury were renowned for playing 'the Burnley way' under Dobson, but Leighton refuted this.

"I wouldn't say we played the Burnley way, we just played good football. We played with the two wide men, me and Winston White, and two up front, Craig and Enty. We created plenty of chances, scored a lot of goals and we played in a very positive way which had been instilled into Martin and I at an early age when we were at Turf Moor. So I suppose it was influenced by Burnley, yes," he laughs.

"Basically, Winston and I were there to provide the crosses and create the chances. Looking at the stats for the season, we also scored five each, so it wasn't rocket science in terms of how you play the game, but I think we were very successful," he adds.

Leighton was very much the elder statesman of the team, joining the Shakers aged thirty-one. Years of running up and down the touchlines of some of the best grounds in the country had taken their toll, hence the consideration of retirement. But once Leighton got the bit between his teeth and regained his enthusiasm, as he absolutely did after he'd adapted to the Fourth Division and its less glamorous stadiums, there was no stopping him.

"Martin used to ask me if I'd like a couple of extra days off every now and again, but I'd always refuse because I was one of the team," he reveals. "I wanted to come in because training was good, I got on well with my teammates and it was a good time for the football club. I was still living in Burnley and those of us that lived over that way would sometimes travel in together and share the driving. Even if I did the journey alone, it was no real distance without any laughing and joking so I didn't mind however I got to training. I just always wanted to be there for it," he says.

Leighton is the first to admit that the division took some getting used to. "I took a bit of time to settle. Without wanting to be disrespectful to the other players in the squad, their speed of thought wasn't always quite as quick as mine. So you'd get the situation where sometimes I'd play a ball and it might have gone out of play because the person I was passing it to wasn't expecting it. If I was being marked tightly I'd flick the ball past the full-back for our centre forward to run on to and they'd get used to that after we worked on it in training. But let's face it, at my age I couldn't be running thirty or forty yards down the line, so with Andy Hill behind me, he'd do a lot of my running and I'd cover for him. I took Andy under my wing a bit and I'd like to think I had an influence on his career when he went into the First Division with Manchester City," he says.

Leighton turns a Swindon Town defender inside-out.
(Copyright: Chris Tofalos)

"The first game at Darlington was a bit of a culture shock, coming straight from my time at Sunderland," he laughs. "I'd played on lower division grounds in cup competitions, but it was a shock that places like Feethams were going to be my bread and butter. It was boiling up there, and despite what I said about wanting to be one of the team, I stayed at the house I'd bought when I was at Sunderland after the game because I was playing in a cricket final the next day, in the same team as people who would have been watching me during the football season. I drove straight back to Bury for training on Monday morning," he remembers.

While the Fourth Division of the mid-1980s might conjure up all kinds of images in the mind's eye, Leighton was happy to put right a few pieces of received wisdom. "People might say that you get kicked more in the bottom division, but I don't agree with that. I was able to keep hold of the ball and develop more time to move with it and we established that way of playing together as a team. That's what the team spirit was like. There was so few of us and we were getting tired by the end of the season, but nobody said anything because we were playing well and everybody wanted to be in the team.

"I always knew that Bury was a well-run club because I'd played on Gigg Lane in my youth days at Burnley. The credit for that had to go to the manager and the chairman, even though everybody made you feel welcome and you were never made to feel like an outsider. It was the little things that made it, like being encouraged to bring your family on match days. The pitch was brilliant too, of course, and even though the facilities at Lower Gigg were a bit rough around the edges, they were OK too," he says.

Affectionately known as 'Taffy', the nickname that was presumably bestowed on seventeen-year-old Leighton when he arrived at Burnley from deepest South Wales in 1970, the wing wizard doesn't remember any cliques in the team, just a solid unit who worked for each other. "Joey, Kev, Pash and me all knew each other from Burnley, Trevor knew Gary Buckley from Everton because Buck's brother [Mick, who died in 2013] had played in the same team as him and John Bramhall and David Brown were big mates. As a squad we'd probably have been better remembered if we'd won the championship like we should have done. As the oldest member of the squad barring the manager, I'd sit at the front of the coach with Wilf on the way back from away games and we'd drink wine from a bottle he'd keep cool with the ice he'd used to treat injuries that afternoon. He'd have a corkscrew in there and we'd get through a couple of bottles on the journey home. It was perfect," he smiles.

After we drained our drinks while going through the match reports and photographs, Leighton summed up, "I probably wouldn't have signed for anyone else other than Martin and an influential chairman like Terry Robinson and it was only the barrier to my coaching that stopped me staying."

As it was, he made twenty-eight appearances for Newport

in the dual role of player/assistant manager before the lure of the Longside was too strong to resist and he joined Burnley for a third spell in 1986. There's something in its own way sweet that as a player so fondly regarded by Clarets fans, he was in the starting XI on the day Burnley avoided relegation from the Football League a year later. It's almost as if the club's own personal Batman had seen the signal in the night sky and gone to help the club which was so close to his heart.

The 4–1 rout of Chester was the ideal birthday present to the club itself. The day after the game was the hundredth anniversary of Bury Football Club being formed in The White Horse pub on Fleet Street, where the NatWest bank now stands. Programme editor Peter Cullen produced a brochure to commemorate the occasion which included a potted history of the club as well as contributions from Graham Kelly in his position as secretary of the Football League and club president Major George Horridge.

However, it's the adverts from local companies congratulating the club on its first hundred years that draw attention today. When booking entertainment for a twenty-first birthday party in a local cricket club, who wouldn't be taken in by 'Greig Paul roadshows (formerly Kentucky Fried Disco)'? If you're on the lookout for some new attire for the office, Mike Summerbee has placed an advert for his made-to-measure shirt service. And because the former City winger would never leave you looking anything less than trendy, you'd be welcome in Reagan's Bar and Cellar on The Rock for happy hour. 'Free tasty dishes from our chef's appetizer menu' is the unique selling point of the bar's 5.30pm–7.30pm opening from Monday to Friday, as are the half-price double measures on offer during the same period each workday.

A number of different events were also planned by a Centenary Committee, chaired by Murray Birnie, to mark the milestone, which began in the September of 1985 so as to be as close to when the club

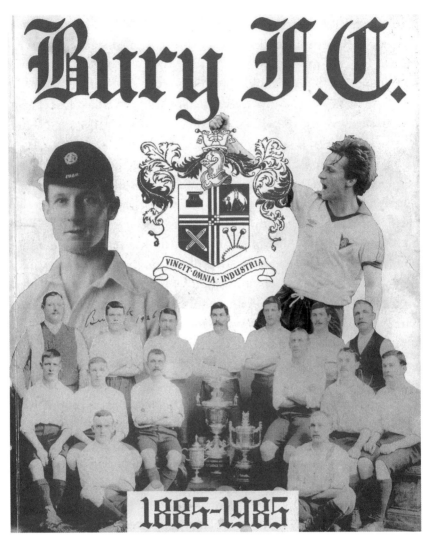

The brochure produced to mark the club's centenary.
(Copyright: Bury Football Club)

started playing matches as possible. A centenary dinner attended by
FA secretary Ted Croker was held at the Town Hall on 5 September,
ninety-nine years and 364 days to the day since the 0–0 draw with
Little Lever which was the club's first ever game. On various other

evenings throughout the autumn of 1985, cabaret nights, fashion shows and sportsman's dinners were held. The Houghton Weavers gave a concert at Radcliffe Civic Hall, an act called Champagne Charlie put on a music hall night in the social club and a gala night was held at the Piccadilly Hotel in Manchester as Terry Robinson's dinner jacket was given plenty of airings before the end of the year.

The last long trip of the season came on 27 April as Bury travelled to perennial strugglers Torquay United. The Gulls were in their somewhat customary place in the lower reaches of the table, two years before they were saved from relegation to the Conference in the final game of the 1986/87 season thanks to a goal scored in added time that was brought about by a police dog biting a player. Neil Burton was the *Bury Times* pressman who accompanied the players on the tiring journey after he was granted access to the team coach on what he called a 'spying mission' to the Devon coast. He writes of the superb team spirit nurtured by Dobson being as clear as the nose on your face and that he'd watched Bury have a morning limber-up in a field next to the motel in which they stayed on a rare overnight trip.

Just ninety seconds into the match, Bury's preparations were rewarded when John Bramhall's forehead connected with a Trevor Ross cross to give the visitors first blood. The second goal took its time, but came when some Winston White trickery, which evaded three lunging Torquay tackles, led to a cross from the right winger that was met by Craig Madden with six minutes left to go to seal the 2-0 victory. Bury's 300 travelling supporters would make the five-hour return journey home in a delirious mood after draws for Blackpool and Hereford meant that a first away win since 2 February had catapulted the Shakers into second place in the table behind Chesterfield.

"I went down to Torquay for the weekend," remembers Paul Greenlees. "I was amazed at just how many Bury fans had the same idea. We went out on the Friday night and I saw loads of people from

Bury. Not people I knew or that I could name, but people whose faces I recognised from Gigg. When I got to the ground for the game the following day, it felt like we had more supporters there than they did," he says.

Fellow fan Malcolm Parr also made a weekend of it in Devon. "One of my greatest memories of the weekend, away from pubs and singing, was walking along the cliff tops after the game. It was a really pleasant late-April evening and we all felt relaxed and happy. I knew we'd get promoted after a great weekend," he smiles.

John Bramhall's goal at Plainmoor might not have been decisive in the final analysis after Craig Madden had bagged the second goal of the game, his twenty-third of the season, late on. But the goal was a crucial nerve-settler for the away fans that day, which complemented Bramhall's solidity throughout the season when he wore the number five shirt in all but four league games.

I'd interviewed John before in his office at the PFA in Manchester, where he works as the deputy chief executive below another former Bury player, Gordon Taylor. After calling the players' union and asking if he'd be interested in talking in a bit more depth about the promotion season, I interviewed him in the afternoon following the morning I'd spent in Durham interviewing Kevin Young.

"Dobbo and Frank increased the professionalism of the club when they arrived. They brought a real calming influence with them, and when you look at the players they signed so quickly, we knew that we were going to be playing football," he now remembers.

"That's not to be critical of Jim Iley though," he continues. "We had a decent side in 1983 when we missed out on promotion. To be fair we should have really stormed the league that season, but it was an injury to Paul Hilton which did it for us. Paul was a class act, as you could see when he got his move to West Ham."

"Everything that Frank and Martin wanted to do was regarding possession, though. Training was bright and much clearer in its aims.

We had some really experienced heads like Leighton James, who was a massive influence on our season, and there was a good blend of the older pros and youth, like Andy Hill who was obviously a great prospect and who we knew would go on to bigger and better things. We were clear on what we wanted to do and how we were going to do it: playing football was going to be our main aim, and it's because of that that I'd say it was the best footballing side I ever played with.

"But with the older players who'd played at the highest level, like Trevor and Leighton but also Martin himself, the positive boost that they brought us was part and parcel of why we did well. The very fact that we were on the same pitch as them meant that their experience shone through," he says.

Those four games which John missed would have seen him being resident in the treatment room instead of the bench seats and clothes pegs of the changing room. The physiotherapist is another beacon that John remembers with the same fondness as the rest of his teammates. "Wilf was just Wilf. He had such a positive attitude that I suppose can only come when you've been to the big places that he'd been to with the game. He slotted into the jigsaw well because he had a good manner, so he had a massive tick against his name.

"We were responsible for his career on the after-dinner circuit, as he ran through his routines with us. But there was so much more to Wilf than his humour: he was a character, but he was so knowledgeable. You don't do what he's done in football without understanding it, do you?" he asks.

As well as the blend of youth and experience, Bramhall remembers the promotion squad as being a meld of footballing styles too. "In the Fourth Division, you'd have a strong side like Chesterfield who'd often be complacent in the way they played. We weren't. We played good football and stuck to it, though we knew that we could rely on Trevor to put a foot in, as could Gary Buckley. We could look after ourselves, but we could play too and that was a constant as the season went on. Massive squads just didn't exist back then, so in the first game of the season up at Darlington, I came back from an Achilles injury that I'd suffered in the previous season. I got blasted by Leighton James for something or other straightaway. Halifax was frozen solid too, like this desk," he says, rapping his knuckles on the hard wood. "I was desperate to get out there even though it shouldn't really have been played. It was nothing like the pitch at Gigg, which attracted good players to the club because they wanted to play on it," he claims.

As he's such a busy man with the interests of approximately 50,000 union members at heart, the interview with Bramhall had to be understandably swift. "We were paid to do something we loved, and after the Halifax game we went on to do well right up until we were promoted. Enty was unbelievable, the kind of lad you'd always want in your team, but we were all dedicated to what we did. The goals came from the service of Leighton and Winston, and although Leighton may have had his critics occasionally, he was a quality player. The same line-up was just really, really positive and when you get promoted you expect to remember it. It's just a shame that Bradford and Heysel came along to dominate how we look at the season," he concludes.

Bury faced yet another home game on the same Tuesday night that the report of the Torquay game was printed in the *Bury Times*. The win in Devon and how it propelled Bury into second place is the inspiration for a story printed in the same paper headlined 'BATTLE COULD BE WON BY END OF THE WEEK'. The report notes that should Bury beat Aldershot in that evening's game, it would put them nine points clear of Hereford with four matches to play 'and anything less than a three-point return in [Hereford's] next two games against Chester tomorrow [Wednesday] night and Halifax on Friday would guarantee Bury one of the four promotion places'.

Martin Dobson, heart presumably jumping like an excited child on Christmas Eve, kept a lid on his emotions with a plain quote to the reporter: 'We're in a great position now but nothing can be taken for granted in this game. It's up to us to get the points in the bag and not to worry about what the other teams are doing,' he stresses.

The giddiness would have continued on the three sides of Gigg Lane which housed home fans as a 2–1 win versus the Shots put Bury in command in the promotion race. It wasn't the prettiest performance ever dished up by a Martin Dobson team: 'The name of the game right now is winning and even a hollow victory is better than a nil return which would only serve to increase the end of season pressure on [the team],' writes John Dyson of the two first half goals from Craig Madden and Wayne Entwistle. Enty got the first, a terrific team goal that had Trevor Ross, Winston White and Joe Jakub all clearing a way to goal for him, while Charlie's goal was a throwback to a bygone age as he bundled the visiting 'keeper into the goal like Nat Lofthouse had done to Harry Gregg in the 1958 FA Cup final.

Aldershot attacked the game with a renewed vigour in the second half and pulled a goal back with twenty minutes of the game left. Despite some anxious moments, they didn't add to their tally. 'It was a leg-weary Bury side which headed for a welcome hot bath, perhaps not surprisingly after a run of four matches in ten days which has put the club a fingertip away from scaling the promotion ladder,' is the *Bury Times*'s closing line, while the *Bolton Evening News*'s report – written by future voice of Manchester City on BBC GMR, Andy Buckley – chooses to be more blustery in its opening. 'Bury are back in the Third Division after a five-year exile barring a miracle. Only a dramatic twist to the end of the season can prevent the Shakers from celebrating their centenary with promotion…And now they are ready to mount an all-out effort to snatch the championship from the grasp of Chesterfield.'

"The win against Aldershot was crucial not just for the points gained, but because the experience of the senior pros who knew how to win dirty in a game where the tension was almost unbearable," remembers Malcolm Parr. "We didn't play particularly well because the legs were going, but there was a pitch invasion at the final whistle through sheer relief more than anything else, even though the points difference meant that we weren't officially up," he continues.

Bury were sitting prettily on the cusp of promotion to the Third Division. The crowd for the Aldershot game was 3,252, considerably more than the 1,532 who'd seen the victory down in Torquay the previous Saturday. The Shakers' average crowd across the promotion season was 3,591, up massively on the 2,104 for the previous season and even more than the following season's 2,889 in the third tier. But nationwide, attendances were falling in line with David Pleat's assertion after the Luton-Millwall riot that people simply didn't want to attend games in the claustrophobic atmosphere that hooliganism was fostering. As such, fans were staying away in droves from the crumbling terraces that ringed professional football pitches.

However, sport was still the key to what would have been called water cooler moments back in 1985, had water coolers crossed the Atlantic to British workplaces by then. The day after Bury's win in Devon, Steve Davis continued to face Dennis Taylor in the World Snooker Championship final that they had begun while the Bury players and fans would have been travelling back north the previous day. Both players matched each other evenly before Taylor famously snatched victory with the final black ball of the final frame. There would have been bags under the eyes at water coolers up and down the country on the Monday morning as the game went on past midnight, but that didn't stop a staggering eighteen-and-a-half million people from watching the final.

If the result in the game between Halifax and Hereford went Bury's way on the Friday night, then the Shakers could look forward to at least one more bumper crowd before the season was out. But the events of May 1985 in the wider British game might just be an explanation of why Bury's average crowd was down for the following season. It was the best of times for the Shakers, it was the worst of times for the British game.

May 1985

'ON THE BRINK' is the headline which dominates the back page of the *Bury Times* published on 3 May. 'At approximately 9.10pm this evening Bury will know whether their promotion celebrations can begin or whether they still need to apply the finishing touch to their bid against Wrexham at Gigg Lane tomorrow. Anything less than victory for fast-fading Hereford at Halifax tonight will guarantee the Shakers a return to Third Division status in player-manager Martin Dobson's first full season at the helm,' reads John Dyson's introduction to the story.

Bury's victory over Aldershot on Tuesday 30 April had allowed them to open some space between themselves and Hereford. The Bulls' 2–1 defeat at Chester the following evening had widened the gap further to nine points with three games remaining. 'That was a great result for us and we're now in the nice position of knowing exactly what we have to do on Saturday. But I expect Hereford to win at Halifax and as far as I'm concerned our match against Wrexham is the most important of the season because we can clinch promotion irrespective of what anyone else does,' Martin Dobson told Dyson.

Dobbo may have expected Halifax's visitors to win the match played that night at the Shay, but a number of Bury fans travelled over the Pennines to lend their support to the Yorkshiremen. Paul Greenlees was one of them. "We were at the ground when Hereford arrived on their coach. I remember seeing them getting off it and thinking that they didn't look like a confident team at all. They just looked worried," he remembers today.

Halifax Town fan Martin Furness also remembers the game. "We'd won three on the trot and thought we'd done enough to stave off the annual fight with re-election, but I didn't think we were going to win that night because Hereford were so good," he says. "We'd played Stockport the week before and there was only about 1,200 on the Shay. For the Hereford game the crowd went up by about 400, so I don't think it's out of the ordinary to suggest that some Bury fans came over to watch us.

"We scored first through David McNiven before they equalised. We retook the lead through Simon Lowe, who'd scored a hat-trick against Bury in that 4–1 win in January, and that's how it stayed. It was a great win against a team so high up in the table, but obviously it meant so much more to Bury fans," he laughs.

Where Were You at the Shay?
The ground where Bury's promotion was sealed without the Shakers kicking a ball.
(Copyright: Bob Lilliman)

211

For the Bury fans who travelled east and were honorary Shaymen for the evening, it would be a celebratory trip home in cars that passed underneath Scammonden Bridge and past Stott Hall Farm in the middle of the M62 as Tommy Vance's *Friday Night Rock Show* on 1089 AM Radio One blared from the speakers. Baz Warburton still recalls the evening fondly.

"I was moaning that I was hungry when we arrived and went to their social club for a pint. A couple of old dears were eating some sandwiches and one of them gave me one. They were Hereford fans and their faces were a picture when I told them why I was there. I was proud that I was one of a small bunch of fans so loyal that they wanted to be there for the very moment that promotion was achieved, yet it's a bit sad that the players weren't there to join in with the celebrations too. It's great when fans and players can be in the moment together like after the promotions at Watford [in 1997], Chesterfield [in 2011] or Tranmere [in 2015]," he says.

In fact, the loyalty of those fans who went to Halifax went on to be recognised with the title of the club's first fanzine in the boom of fan culture that followed British football's worst year. As supporters across the country were putting together home-made publications that showed not all fans were intent on causing trouble, Bury's was launched with the name *Where Were You at the Shay?* as a test of the credentials for anyone claiming to be a true Shaker.

Bury had been promoted having used just fifteen players throughout the course of the season. Martin Dobson had done what he told the *Bury Times* he would do back in the summer of 1984, but the manager wasn't at the Shay to see the elevation confirmed without Bury having to kick a ball. He was listening to local radio for updates while other fans watched the local news bulletin which followed BBC1's *Nine O'Clock News* that Friday evening. Both confirmed the Hereford defeat which rubber-stamped Bury's status as a Third Division club for the 1985/86 season.

*

With promotion sealed, Dobson could look ahead to Bury's game that was due to be played the day after Hereford's defeat in West Yorkshire. In the same *Bury Times* story which outlines the boss's calmness ahead of the promotion-clinching result in Halifax, he also tells John Dyson about the Shakers' game versus Wrexham on Saturday 4 May. 'The championship has been our number one target from the opening day of the season and we're still on course to win it. We want to end the season on a high note. The shackles are off to a certain extent and I want to see the players perform to the best of their ability in the last three games and give our supporters a feast of entertaining, exciting and flowing football,' he tells the reporter.

Things didn't go to plan in the first of this trio of games. More than 4,000 home supporters spread themselves around Gigg Lane for the game against the visiting Welshmen only to witness the second home defeat of the season. The bogey side completed an unlikely double over Bury with a 3–2 win to complement their hammering dished out at the Racecourse Ground in December. 'Wrexham had no desire to be cast in the supporting role to Bury's celebration show,' writes John Dyson in the match report printed on 7 May as he describes the visitors taking the lead and Trevor Ross equalising from the penalty spot. Former Bury striker Dave Gregory made it 2–1 to the Dragons, before they racked up a third after Cunningham slipped the ball into an empty net. Craig Madden made it a personal quarter-of-a-century of goals for the season with eight minutes to go, but a point wasn't forthcoming.

But at the final whistle at Gigg Lane on 4 May, blown by referee Keith Hackett, none of this seemed to matter. Promotion had been confirmed and the crowd were there to celebrate. 'Whatever degree of disappointment had been felt by player and supporter at only the Shakers' second home defeat of the season was quickly swept away and replaced by those jubilant scenes – scenes which hadn't been witnessed at Gigg Lane in over a decade,' writes Dyson.

'The party spirit was transferred to the boardroom and finally to the social club where the promotion heroes ran a gauntlet of handshakes and back-slaps through to the players' lounge before being called back time and time again to the main lounge to take just one more deserved bow in front of their celebrating fans. Happily, the defeat didn't spoil the spontaneous scenes of gaiety that followed the final whistle,' the pressman concludes.

One of the main architects of those scenes was Bury fan Paul Greenlees, who made sure that the players had something to spray in celebration. "We snuck some Pomagne into the ground and left it on the pitch side of the perimeter wall," he says, smiling at the memory. "We got on to the pitch at the final whistle and handed it to the players so it's probably ours that they were pictured drinking in the changing room," he says.

"We stayed in the social club right up until closing time," remembers Bury fan Malcolm Parr with a smile. "The players came over after the game and made speeches and there was lots of singing and standing on chairs," he laughs about scenes predating promotions to come in 1996, 1997 and 2011.

The Sunday morning hangover from the party in the Tommy Marshall Lounge carried through into the following day, the May Day bank holiday, when Bury travelled to Tranmere Rovers. The edition of the *Bury Times* featuring the match report is missing from the local archive's reel of microfilm so it's Andy Buckley in the *Bolton Evening News* who provided the report used in the research for this publication. 'BURY TITLE HOPES ARE ENDED' tells its own story as a 3–2 defeat meant that silverware would elude Bury. Tranmere's formidable strike partnership of Colin Clarke and John Clayton, both of whom were so effectively snuffed out in the reverse fixture at Gigg Lane in December, took their joint tally to a whopping sixty-five goals for the season for the hosts, while Wayne Entwistle notched a brace to take his personal total for the campaign to twenty-two.

'The fans turned out in force at Prenton Park yesterday and it was a pity their excellent support was not better rewarded,' wrote Buckley, who also had to report on Andy Hill being stretchered off with an ankle injury that meant he would miss the last game of the season. Player-manager Dobson also missed the match as the thirty-seven-year-old playmaker began to contemplate semi-retirement.

The result on the Wirral meant that Chesterfield took the championship, while a 2–0 win for Blackpool at Hartlepool confirmed their promotion and shunted the Shakers down into third place. With the title now unreachable, Martin Dobson uses his extended programme notes for the game against Peterborough at Gigg Lane on 11 May to reflect on the season gone by like an Oscar winner giving an acceptance speech.

'I have been very fortunate in my first job in management to be able to rely totally on the people around me,' he writes. 'It is a very demanding job with many problems, but it would be a lot more difficult without the support of everyone at the club. Firstly, chairman Terry Robinson and the board. It is a new board containing several inexperienced members but everyone has worked tremendously hard throughout. In Terry Robinson, I couldn't have worked with a better chairman. A man who is a genuine number one Bury supporter, who puts the club first and foremost. Knowing the financial difficulties, he has slogged long and hard to raise money to keep Bury FC in existence and at the same time he has let me get on with the playing, coaching and training side of the job without the slightest interference,' he continues.

Loosening his figurative bow tie, Dobbo then moves on to thank his chosen few. 'Likewise, I have a very close working relationship with the coaching staff of Frank, Wilf and Ray. Every man knows his duties and responsibilities and has got on with the job without conflict. Football, though, is about players and it has been a pleasure to work with the playing staff here at Gigg Lane. We tried to instil a good team spirit at the club and I can honestly say that the spirit throughout has been one of the best I've ever witnessed in football. It can't be serious all the time, they have had a laugh and a joke along the line, but I would like to think that what we have said in training has made them into better players. They have listened and learned,' he writes.

'We ARE a club and everyone connected with Bury FC is important as I have frequently stated; the development staff, promotional side, the ground staff, office staff and Marion who turns us out immaculately week after week. Our supporters too have been super. It gladdened our hearts after losing against Wrexham and Tranmere over the bank holiday weekend, the way you shouted and cheered us even in defeat. We had all looked for good performances and your support was terrific,' he concludes.

Overleaf, Terry Robinson's comments echo Martin's but also feature the plea to sign up to the Lifeline, back the Town Tote and buy a season ticket – at prices cascading from £76 for a reserved chair to £48 for an adult on the ground to £28 for a senior citizen or junior – so that the club can keep money coming in during the summer months.

It's not hard to countenance Terry including this information in his piece in anticipation of a large crowd for the final home game of a promotion-winning season. Bafflingly, though, only 2,986 people turned up for the 1–1 draw with Peterborough. 'For those supporters with long enough memories to hope for a repeat of the 1974 promotion team's farewell party, it was all something of an anti-climax at Gigg Lane on Saturday,' writes John Dyson.

Bury's performance on the final day matched the air of indifference that had infiltrated the minds of the townsfolk. Winston White was the Shakers' star man as his trickery was the key to most of the hosts' creativity, but it was Trevor Ross who gave Bury the lead with a terrific strike from thirty yards, three minutes before half-time. The Posh were level within a minute before Ross received his marching orders for striking Errington Kelly eight minutes after the break ('It was a stupid thing to do and I regretted it straight away,' he told Dyson in a quote which was included in the newspaper report). The visitors' Trevor Slack was sent off five minutes later for laying out

216

Wayne Entwistle, after which Chris Grimshaw came off the bench to replace Leighton James for his only league appearance in the season.

Praise is reserved for John Kerr who 'hardly put a foot wrong and clearly revelled in his new role as an emergency central defender in place of injured player-manager Martin Dobson'. But like the other fixtures in the Football League on 11 May 1985, including Darlington's 3–1 win over Stockport which pushed the Shakers into a fourth-placed finish, the match between Bury and Peterborough at Gigg Lane paled into insignificance because of what was happening at two other grounds.

At St Andrews in Birmingham, Leeds United were the visitors on what should have been a celebratory afternoon. The Blues had won promotion to the First Division under Ron Saunders, but Leeds hooligans were intent on gatecrashing the party that Birmingham's own fans had planned. Avtar Gill was a twenty-year-old Sikh and Leeds fan who was at university in South Wales. He travelled to the Midlands with a friend.

"I'd been abused at or around Elland Road on match days because of the colour of my skin for some time," he remembers. "The game at St Andrews was just another end of season outing for us, but for Birmingham it was their promotion party. We arrived at the ground and had to walk across to the away end where we saw a group of around a hundred or so Leeds fans in the queue. It felt tense. The police had a couple of officers blocking the turnstiles and were only letting them through ten at a time because there were only two turnstiles open.

"It was starting to get out of hand when coach after coach turned up. There would have been a thousand fans trying to get past these officers, which was made even more difficult by the narrowness of the pathway that we were being herded down. There was a holding pen for away fans close to us too, which had a fence that was about fifteen foot high, where supporters were kept while the home fans dispersed after a game. Some of our fans started to climb the fence to avoid the queues, so the police sent in their 'cavalry' on horseback," he continues.

"Tensions were rising as dozens more Leeds fans tried to get into the holding pen to avoid paying at the turnstiles as kick-off was rapidly approaching. The police, in their infinite wisdom, decided to stick with their rigid policy of ten fans at a time, even though a number of well-intending Leeds fans suggested opening the other eight turnstiles which were closed. Birmingham officials eventually opened two more at 3.15pm," he says.

"A lot of people had got in through the holding pen without paying so you can imagine what it was like in the stand. It was clear that both the police and Birmingham had only expected one or two thousand away fans to travel, but I reckon there was more than double that," he says.

Birmingham won 1–0 that afternoon, but it's what happened after the game that has made the match infamous. "The rioting kicked off at the front of the stand during the second half when the police, who were standing in front of the Leeds fans, charged in to eject some of the unrulier supporters. They didn't get very far because the people they were after didn't want to leave, to put it mildly, so it was a game of cat and mouse that descended into a full-scale riot," Avtar remembers.

Images of the riot, recorded on primitive CCTV cameras, are available to watch on YouTube. Given a suitably apocalyptic feel by the blurriness of the pictures, what they show is truly astonishing. Wave upon wave of supporters pour from both home and away enclosures and cover the pitch just moments after the final whistle, only for them to be hastened back to the stands by officers on horseback. Police helmets and missiles – concrete from terracing, lumps of wood from advertising hoardings – litter the pitch as sporadic order breaks out from the violence.

"The defining and lowest moment of all, though, followed

numerous PA announcements trying to settle things down," remembers Dan Mackinder, another Leeds fan. "Our then-manager, Eddie Gray, was making his way towards the Leeds end in an attempt to plead for some sanity to be restored. As he reached the penalty area in front of the stand, a piece of asphalt that had been broken off the terracing was hurled towards him from our end and narrowly missed his head.

"I thought, 'Who are these idiots I'm surrounded by?' This is a man who just ten years earlier was part of one of the greatest teams I'd ever seen, and to this day scorer of one of the greatest goals in the club's history against Burnley in 1970. It was at that moment that I realised that perhaps I was one of only a few Leeds fans that genuinely wanted to be present. It seemed that everyone else was there for a riot," he says.

A crash can be heard on the audio which accompanies the CCTV film footage. It was the sound of a twelve foot wall collapsing under the weight of the crowds at the Birmingham End of the stadium. Standing beneath it was fifteen-year-old Ian Hambridge from Nottingham who was attending his first ever football match. He was hit on the head by falling masonry and died later in hospital.

"I wasn't involved in the trouble that afternoon, obviously," continues Avtar Gill. "Outside the ground, I was knocked a couple of feet in the air by a police horse and landed hard on a car bonnet. Another policeman tried to arrest me for it, and it wasn't until several Birmingham fans and a Birmingham steward intervened that they let me go on my way," he remembers, in an unusual act of the two sets of supporters that afternoon coming together.

In total, 125 people were arrested after the violence, ninety-six police officers needed medical attention and eighty spectators were injured. On any other day, these statistics and the images of the football-related violence at St Andrews would have dominated the news for days afterwards, just as the images of the Luton–Millwall riot had done only weeks before. But the riot and all that it encompassed has become largely a footnote in football history because of what had happened less than ninety minutes previously, 129 miles north of Birmingham.

It had been a great season for Bradford City. Manager Trevor Cherry had got his team playing attractive football, and after losing to Leyton Orient at the end of September, they went on a mazy thirteen-game unbeaten run as they surged to the top of Division Three. By February they were eleven points clear at the top of the division, and on the penultimate weekend of the season they wrapped up the championship with a 2–0 win over Bolton at Burnden Park. Cherry's Bradford-born skipper, Peter Jackson, was to be presented with the championship trophy before the home match versus Lincoln City on 11 May.

Simon Inglis, whose *Football Grounds of England and Wales* has become the go-to text for anyone interested in cantilever roofs, struts and Archibald Leitch signature styles, wrote in the first edition of his book that watching a game from Valley Parade's antiquated Main Stand was like doing so 'from the cockpit of a Sopwith Camel', such was the tangle of metalwork that formed its roof. In the summer of 1985, which Bradford would spend preparing for life in the second tier, this metalwork was due to be torn out and the stand's timbers replaced with concrete at a cost of £400,000. In the club car park, new steel had been delivered and was waiting to be erected on to the seventy-four-year-old structure. The local paper, the *Telegraph and Argus*, ran with the headline 'SPIT AND POLISH FOR THE PARADE GROUND' in their promotion special which was published on the morning of the Lincoln game in anticipation of the stand's redevelopment. It was to be a redevelopment which didn't happen.

More than 11,000 people had crammed into the compact stadium for the game, including representatives from Bradford's twin towns in Belgium and Germany. With the score at 0–0 with five minutes to go to half-time, the crowd was starting to think about how they'd spend the interval. Yorkshire TV's footage of the match, with commentary by John Helm, shows fans at the far right of the Main Stand as the camera looks at it streaming away from their seated area as the counter at the bottom of the screen records the time as 15:44:19. Nine seconds later, as a Bradford player plays the ball forward, Helm is saying 'We've actually got a fire in the stand on the far side of the ground.' By the time he's finished the sentence, the Lincoln goalkeeper, Dave Felgate, has intercepted the ball and booted it into Row Z.

What follows next in Yorkshire's raw unedited footage is horrifying. The glow of flame since Helm's initial observation has grown and fans are clambering over a high perimeter wall to the safety of the pitch. A close-up of a policeman waving people away from the fire shows a relatively sparsely populated area of the stand, which lends hope to the thought that it might not be too serious in terms of injuries sustained by fans. Helm even says, with a slight laugh in his voice, 'One hopes that the stand doesn't burn down.' It's as if he thinks the very notion of the entire stand succumbing to fire during a game and with so many people inside it is absurd.

More fans stream on to the pitch as Helm says that the fire 'is beginning to rage' during another close-up of the seat of the blaze. Thick, black, acrid smoke is starting to fill the air, but a lot of fans on the pitch don't seem to understand the gravity of the situation that's unfolding. Singing continues, as do people leaping in front of the ground-level cameras in 'Hello, Mum, I'm on telly!' poses. 'As that blaze grows, the stand has to be in jeopardy,' predicts the commentator, his tack noticeably changing.

With the on-screen timer counter showing 15:45:47, flames can be seen sneaking along the partition wall which divides the seating in the stand from the paddock terracing. It's a similar design to Bury's old Main Stand, which was built in 1924 from the same basic materials. The rest of the stand, away from the blaze's origin, is still full as the fire continues to spread. More fans tumble on to the pitch, by now in full-on panic mode.

The stand's roof had been lined and waterproofed using roofing felt and bitumen on tongue and groove boarding. This mixture was now catching fire too and dripping on to supporters below who found a passageway to what they hoped was an exit blocked. It would later emerge that those who thought the turnstiles through which they'd entered the ground would be a suitable escape route found them locked with no stewards available to open them.

As smoke peels off the stand roof, John Helm is by now in no doubt that the situation is grave. 'One can feel the heat…and that is a catastrophic sight for Bradford City Football Club,' he says as the camera catches the first sight of people climbing on to the pitch with burned clothes. A policeman is shown with his hair on fire that he quickly pats out as the majority of the stand is enveloped in flames. Two of his colleagues drag an elderly lady away from the stand to safety, while a group of others drag an unconscious man away from the smoke, his clothes hanging from him, shielding themselves from the heat as they do so.

The pall of thick smoke that dwarfs the Valley Parade floodlight pylons is genuinely shocking in another wide shot, as is the vivid orange of the flames. More and more supporters are dragged away from the inferno as a younger, lither fan collapses in exhaustion after making his escape. The most distressing image of the entire sequence follows, though, as an elderly man walks calmly from the stand, head to foot in flames. It's a surreal moment; his gait is such that he looks like he could be having a walk in the park on a summer's day were it not for the fact that fire licks from his entire body.

'Look at that!' shouts a disbelieving Helm. 'Oh, the poor man, this is awful,' he groans as the gentleman is bundled to the floor and people – too many people really – attempt to beat the flames from his clothing. 'He'd come to watch the football. This is human tragedy' is the commentator's sombre close as the counter reads 15:49:01. Sirens can be heard as ambulances and fire engines arrive at the scene, while outside the ground local residents, including many members of

Bradford's Asian subcontinental community in the city's Manningham district, were opening their doors to the shocked former members of the Valley Parade crowd. Fifty-six members of that crowd of 11,076 died as a result of the fire.

The timer at the bottom of the screen inspired the title of the definitive, indispensable account of the disaster. City fan Paul Firth was in the stand that afternoon, and later wrote *Four Minutes to Hell* in which he spoke to the ordinary people whose bravery saved countless other lives. It feels odd to say that the book is 'enjoyable' given its horrendous subject matter, but it was a necessary story to tell and Paul tells it in an extremely gripping way. The time that it took from the first wisps of smoke being spotted to the entire stand being engulfed is the key to the film's use as an instructional tool, too, in that it shows just how quickly a blaze spreads. Fire safety courses up and down the land include the footage, which Yorkshire TV only allows to be broadcast on television very rarely.

"We'd heard that there had been an incident and that there was no score in the Bradford game, but because of the reputation of football fans at the time, we thought it was because of hooliganism," remembers Malcolm Parr. "We went into the social club and heard that people had been killed, but even then we still thought it was a really extreme form of hooliganism, but someone said it was because of a fire and it all slowly started dawning on us how awful the events at Valley Parade were," he continues.

Bury's match day programme editor Peter Cullen had an inkling that something else was happening in the football world when he went back to the social club after the Peterborough game. "It had been disappointing to lose two of the last three and then draw the last match of the season, but we still had promotion to celebrate so we went to the club. I suddenly started feeling really ill and was doubled in pain in my seat, but after about half an hour I felt fine again. I can only think that I was having some kind of telepathic reaction to what was happening in Bradford because at the time I didn't know about what was going on at Valley Parade. It's my personal memory and I know it sounds daft, but it's what I think," he remembers.

Like his fellow City fan Paul Firth, James Mackenzie was in his usual place in the Main Stand that afternoon as a Bantam-mad nine-year-old. "There's no doubt in my mind that people like Stuart McCall grew closer to the club and its fans as a result of the fire. We still talk about it today because it's still important," he remembers.

"The city council took the decision to go back to Valley Parade after the fire even though we could have left and gone to a smaller newly-built ground that we'd have shared with the rugby club. Valley Parade was our home, we wanted to build on top of the memories and we went back there for the survivors. It wasn't like Hillsborough where someone was very clearly covering things up and the case has grown and developed because people lied. No one's lied about Bradford. We don't know who started the fire, and although we could have pressed for corporate manslaughter charges against the people who locked the gates, what purpose would that have served? It doesn't bring people back or change feelings. I don't recall anyone thinking anything other than that it was just a tragic accident, so we focused on helping survivors and helping the club rebuild.

"Margaret Thatcher visited the ground in the days after the disaster. She got a rough ride from the North in the 1980s, but she said the right things after the fire, namely that we must make sure that something like this never happens again. Leon Brittan, too, spoke about tearing down fences at grounds. Having fences at Valley Parade that afternoon would have been even more fatal than the disaster itself. If you think about Ken Bates's plan of electrifying perimeter fences, as he wanted to do at Stamford Bridge after Chelsea's League Cup game with Sunderland in March 1985, hundreds more would have died," he says.

"There's no bitterness or anger. In all probability, the person who dropped the cigarette which ignited the rubbish under the stand may have died in the fire. If they survived, how could you turn against one of your own for something like that which they may have done every week, only once, or which dozens of other people did?" he asks.

However, fellow Bradford fan John Dewhirst claims that the smoker has been identified. "The identity of the person who dropped the cigarette is known and he was identified [as a survivor] by the police – however his name was never released," he writes in an email sent in April 2015.

A BBC television programme called 'Missed Warnings: The Bradford City Fire' was broadcast on 12 May 2015. In it, a former detective inspector with West Yorkshire Police called Raymond Falconer named the person who dropped the cigarette which ignited the accumulated rubbish beneath the stand as Eric Bennett, who has since died naturally. He revealed that Mr Bennett emigrated to Australia from the UK in 1970 and was visiting relatives in Bradford when he decided to attend the game.

James Mackenzie remembers the afternoon of the disaster with an obvious clarity. "I was standing at the front of the stand by the perimeter wall. I was only about four foot ten inches, so I'd sit on the wall at games or rest my elbows on it. The first I knew of something happening was when the referee blew for half-time, and I saw an analogue clock that we used to have at Valley Parade showed the time as being 3.43pm, which I thought was odd.

"From then on, it was just pandemonium. I was in Block B and the fire had started in Block G so there was a commotion at the other end of the stand. I looked down the touchline, saw the flames and started to try and climb the wall. It was probably only for ten seconds but it felt like ten minutes, and eventually someone grabbed my hand and pulled me over the wall. As soon as I was on the pitch, I ran to the goal line in front of the away end and sat on the pitch there. I can still feel the heat on the left side of my face when I talk about it.

"The ground is built into a hillside, hence its name, and you could see the plume of smoke from everywhere. My mum was in Leeds that afternoon and she saw it from there. It was such an occasion for the club, in front of such a big crowd, that it felt like everyone in the city knew someone it had had an impact on, whether they were a spectator, a member of the emergency services, a member of staff at a hospital or a member of the council's social services. Because of that, the disaster helped forge friendships and build bridges which otherwise wouldn't have existed.

"I have a friend who's a doctor and he supports Brentford. He's married to another doctor and his wife didn't know that the Bradford sling, a way of treating burns in such a way that blood can circulate more freely, originated as a result of the fire. She thought that it was named after the person who discovered it. World advances in plastic surgery at the Bradford Burns Unit followed the fire and there are people around the world who owe the unit a debt because of what they discovered. And it all came from the horrific afternoon at Valley Parade," he says.

James remembers the reaction that followed the tragedy as being stoical and, as such, typically Yorkshire. "I couldn't get my nine-year-old head around what had happened when I looked at the remains of the stand at the memorial service.

"Leeds fans at school made jokes about the disaster. I don't think nine-year-olds would know to make jokes about barbeques so I'm sure there were a lot of parents and older siblings saying things, which upset me. A couple of other kids from my school were at the ground on the afternoon of the disaster too, but we didn't talk about it. In an assembly, the headmaster just made reference to supporting friends and supporting the city," he explains.

It took the Hillsborough disaster, four years after Bradford, for the psychological effects of the disaster to become really clear to James. "I was off school for days after it," he remembers. "We kept seeing footage of what happened on the news, again and again. Someone at school made a joke about it and linked it to Bradford and I just snapped. I sat in the school changing room with a PE teacher who had his arm around me, telling me to let it all out. I felt numb because in the immediate aftermath of the disaster, no one had asked me, or dared to ask me, how I felt. There were no counsellors or anything. I don't think it would have made much difference in hindsight because back then I don't think I really appreciated the enormity of what happened. I'm sure that teachers and classmates wanted to ask about it but didn't really understand, and I probably wasn't transmitting signals that I wanted to talk.

"That's changed now and I'll happily talk to anyone who wants to know about what happened. We saw it in the League Cup run of 2013 [when League Two Bradford reached the final] that a lot of opposition fans wanted to talk about it. I think it's immensely important that we did because it helps to keep the legend of oral history alive in the city.

"I go to games with six other people now and I'm the only one who was there that afternoon. When we talk about it, as we do relatively regularly, they're touched because understanding what happened is an important part of being a City fan. If a disaster like that had happened at a smaller club with a smaller community around it, like Bury for instance, it might have finished them off and destroyed their stability. We had a big city and corporation reach on our side," he notes.

James believes that witnessing the fire was one of two events which shaped him at such a young age. "When I was nine years old, I witnessed the fire and my parents split up. I think that these two events happening in the same year shaped me and influenced my feelings on collectivism versus individualism. The strength of the community's reaction formed my belief and directed my moral compass," he claims.

"There's a morbid curiosity about the fire that's driven by a feeling of 'What if it had been our ground?' Fans talk about their own grounds as part of the furniture, but to an away fan it's just a ground that you experience with the focus on your team. There are some grounds that everyone knows something about. Bury has a Cemetery End, Brentford has a pub on each corner. At Bradford, you know that fifty-six people died in a fire there.

"I've watched the Yorkshire TV footage of the fire because I think it's important to. Most people who go through tragedy can't replay it, and if you're given the opportunity to, why wouldn't you? It's not a pleasant experience to watch it, but I do it once a year at around the anniversary or if I feel I have to. It's important to, but it never changes any of my opinions," he concludes.

"The Bradford fire was horrifying, to see a stand that was the equivalent of one at your club being central to such terrible scenes," remembers Paul Greenlees. "You couldn't help thinking that it could have happened at Bury if you'd been in the old Main Stand as it was. If it had happened at Bury, you'd have known a lot of those people who died," he says.

With his *Red Riding* quartet and *The Damned United,* which told the story of Brian Clough's disastrous forty-four-day tenure in charge of Leeds, novelist David Peace is no stranger to the darker side of West Yorkshire. As a Huddersfield Town fan, he remembers casting envious glances in the direction of Valley Parade as the 1984/85 season progressed.

"It had been a very poor season for Town. We'd looked certain to go back down at one point, but finished mid-table in the Second Division (if I am not mistaken)," he writes by email from his desk in Tokyo, where he now lives.

"As you know, Bradford, along with Leeds, are Town's main rivals and throughout the eighties there had been quite a bit of trouble between some sets of supporters of both clubs. But that season, before the fire I think, Bradford had won the Third Division and would be promoted to the Second and so that didn't particularly gladden the hearts of many at Leeds Road. But that Bradford side had two ex-Town players in it: Trevor Cherry and Bobby Campbell. Later, Terry

Yorath would also coach at Town and Peter Jackson, of course, became a legend at the club.

"I was in a band at the time, the Paunchy Cowboys, and on the day itself we had gone into Pinderfields Hospital in Wakefield to be interviewed on their hospital radio. But while we were waiting to go on, reports started to come through of what was happening at Valley Parade and the hospital began to prepare to receive casualties. All I really remember now is going home as quickly as possible to find out what was going on. And then watching and listening in horror as the full extent of the tragedy became clear.

"And I do remember, as well as the grief you felt, there was also anger that such a thing had happened. Because I think, again, for anybody who was watching football at that time, you knew how unsafe many of the grounds were. And so it's not just with the benefit of hindsight, you knew at the time that something like that could always happen. So, as I say, at the time, the feeling I had was one of grief but also anger," he writes.

David goes on to disagree with James Mackenzie about the government's reaction to the tragedy. "I might be just speaking for myself here, but I found Thatcher's remarks and role in the aftermath as hollow and hypocritical as always. I mean, this was a woman who believed all football fans were animals and seemed to have nothing but contempt for the working class in general.'

"But I do also remember, I think, that there was a benefit match staged at Elland Road in the summer and there was also a cover version of *You'll Never Walk Alone* [by a cobbled-together supergroup christened 'The Crowd'] that was released to raise money, too. And again, and with that song in mind, when you think about what was still to come at Hillsborough, it's hard not to feel a great degree of anger that, even after something as terrible as what happened at Valley Parade, many more people would still lose their lives at a football match because the powers-that-be, for want-of-a-better-phrase, would still not make the safety of the ordinary supporters their priority," he concludes.

Football is a very close-knit world so it's no surprise that Bury's promotion squad was full of players who had former teammates involved with the game at Bradford. When he found out from ITV's *World of Sport* what had happened while he'd been playing out the draw with Peterborough, Leighton James would immediately have thought of his friend and former Wales teammate Terry Yorath who was on City's coaching staff. Winston White would have thought of his friend Don Goodman, whereas Wayne Entwistle would have hoped that John Hawley was OK after they'd travelled in opposite directions between Leeds and Sunderland in the late-seventies.

Bury's chairman Terry Robinson would also have been worried for a friend. "The Bury directors watched the footage of the disaster in what was then the old directors' lounge underneath the Main Stand," he remembers. "I had business connections in Bradford, and a friend called Dave Oddie was a massive City fan who I knew would be in the stand. It took me three days to call his wife to see if he was OK after I'd not seen his name in the reports of those who had died and I was frightened for him. He told me that he got his father out of the stand as well as himself," he says.

In April 2015, the month before the disaster's thirtieth anniversary, Martin Fletcher – who lost four members of his family in the tragedy which he himself survived – published a book which noted that Bradford's chairman at the time had previously owned eight other businesses as part of his dynasty which had gone up in flames. With an arched eyebrow, he asked 'Could any man be as unlucky as Stafford Heginbotham?' with the clear inference being that the fire was started deliberately as a way of fraudulently claiming an insurance payout.

Following the publication of Fletcher's book, there has been much talk on Internet football forums about these coincidences, all of which stopped short of accusing Heginbotham of ordering the blaze be started. Many column inches have been written about the new claims too, but John Dewhirst, who co-founded the Bradford City fanzine *The City Gent* in 1984, refutes them in this reply to several comments on the Bradford City fan website *Claret and Banter*.

"[There was] the accusation that The City Gent participated in a conspiracy of silence. The author, Brian Fox had both his parents badly injured in the fire. You are absolutely spot on in that during the period we were managing the magazine (through to 1988) we didn't mention the fire other than in passing. Why was that? A conspiracy? Were we in denial? During that period there was a judicial inquiry and a civic litigation against the club. I gave evidence to the former. Neither of us were arrogant enough to believe that we knew more or better than others who were writing about and investigating the fire. On my part I had no loss of confidence in the findings. But the reason why we didn't write about the fire is that for those of us who were living in Bradford at the time...we couldn't forget about the fire because we saw evidence of it every day, at work, in pubs and for some of us in our nightmares. Funnily enough we didn't want to write about it. We wanted to get back to normality," Dewhirst writes.

James Mackenzie takes a similar tack. "Having thought and pondered the news of the last week myself, I must concur that I still believe it was a terrible accident. As John says, to torch a stand at 3.45 with 3,000 people in it is such a heinous crime with no evidence to support this. Therefore despite Stafford's history I have to believe the facts and I'm struggling to see the difference between supposed new facts, PR to sell a book [and] grief for lost ones.

"My biggest concern now is that when other football fans engage with us and talk about my club and the fire they will say 'Wasn't it arson?' And that will now be the focus, not what a terrible loss of life. This has happened to me twice in the last week, from two Leeds fans no less," he writes by email after Fletcher's book was published.

As James pointed out in our original interview before Fletcher's book was completed, the official report that followed the disaster ruled that the fire was started by a discarded cigarette that ignited rubbish which had accumulated underneath the stand. In the BBC programme 'Missed Warnings: The Bradford City Fire', former West Yorkshire Police detective inspector Raymond Falconer described the emotion of Eric Bennett when the latter remembered how the fire started by accident because of his actions.

While the fire was officially ruled not to have been a malicious act, government papers from the time recently made public under the thirty-year rule have shown that Margaret Thatcher initially didn't hesitate to link the tragedy with the scourge of hooliganism. It was a view perhaps influenced by reports in the tabloid press the day after the disaster, of one person who allegedly saw smoke bombs being hurled inside the stadium. More of the once-secret papers that are now available to read show messages of condolence sent to the Prime Minister from around the world; Ghana, Swaziland, the League of Arab States and Chancellor Kohl of Germany all contacted Mrs Thatcher to express their sorrow.

While Terry Robinson felt the human tragedy as much as every other football fan in the immediate aftermath of the disaster, he would have known that it would present him with a huge headache. There was bound to be an inquiry into the disaster – what was to become the Popplewell Inquiry – and one of its key findings would almost certainly relate to stands made from timber, the material that made up all four enclosures at Gigg Lane. Five days after the disaster, Bury were due to play Manchester City, the first side they ever faced in a league fixture, in a match to celebrate the Shakers' centenary, but there was paranoia in the air after events at Valley Parade.

Tabloid newspapers went to town straight after the fire, picking up on which stadiums were at an immediate similar risk. Just three days after the disaster, the *Daily Express* wasted no time in naming Gigg Lane as a high-risk ground. The day after their report was published, Terry Robinson sought to reassure the people of Bury in the front page story of that week's *Bury Times Midweeker*. 'GIGG LANE GETS ALL CLEAR' reports that a fire prevention officer was satisfied that the club's stands had adequate exit facilities that would allow a rapid evacuation if it was needed.

The story also notes that £80,000 had been spent on ground safety work in recent years and that a previous inspection had been passed just three weeks before the disaster. Terry reportedly ordered the most recent investigation straight after Bradford. 'We are aware of the problems and we asked the fire service and the police to come to the ground. The main worry is the South Stand but the fire service stated that the exits there are quite adequate and that the stand would take two minutes to clear. The general opinion seems to be that under current legislation there are no areas for concern at Gigg Lane,' he told the reporter.

In the present day, Terry remembers things rather differently. "The fire chief and I walked into the middle of the pitch, to the centre spot," he says today. "He looked around the ground and he said to me 'You'll never play professional football here again.' I told him that we had the centenary game against City in a couple of days and he agreed to let the game go ahead but only if we had a fire engine in the car park. He said that we couldn't play any more games after that, so I rang David Dent at the Football League to tell him that we'd been told we couldn't play at Gigg Lane. He said something like, 'So you'll be out of the league next season then?' but I told him that if necessary we'd find somewhere else to play. It was the catalyst to make improvements to the ground," he remembers.

Paul Greenlees and Peter Cullen remember the risk too from when they ventured under the Main Stand before its wood was removed in the summer of 1992. "We were finding tram tickets from the 1920s that must have fallen down the cracks that had developed with the movement of the wood over the years. The debris was tinder dry and would have gone straight up if it was ignited," remembers Cullen.

The game against City went ahead with the cautionary fire

engine poised for action behind the Main Stand. The sports section of the issue of the *Midweeker* that has the safety report on the front page also claims, on the back page, that all of the pieces have fallen into place for the centenary match jigsaw as both Bury and City were celebrating promotion after the visitors sealed a return to the top flight with a 5–1 win over Charlton the previous Saturday. It's also breathless with excitement at the starter before the main course, as a match was pencilled in between Old Boys from both clubs. Harry Dowd, Tony Book, Glyn Pardoe, Mike Summerbee, Bobby Owen and Roy Cheetham are listed in the City side, while Bury were to line up with Ray Pointer, Derek Spence, John Forrest, Keith Kennedy, George Jones and Alec Lindsay.

The report for the main event, printed a week later, is fulsome in its praise of a well-received game enjoyed by everybody that followed such a dreadful season for the British game. 'All of the behind the scenes work received a handsome pay-off...It was a splendid family occasion and the whole operation ran smoothly in a relaxed and friendly atmosphere,' reads the intro to the report of the game that City won 2–0, with goals from David Phillips and Paul Power.

However, tabloid muckrakers didn't believe Terry Robinson's assertion of Gigg Lane's safety that had immediately followed the Bradford fire and had crept unnoticed into the 5,216 crowd for the match. 'CLUB SLAMS 'FIREBOMB' REPORT' is the front-page story of the *Midweeker* from 21 May which describes how a Sunday newspaper conducted a 'secret investigation' at the game which uncovered gas cylinders, fertiliser and pieces of timber kept in the groundsman's room underneath the Main Stand. The report also claimed that a fourteen foot exit gate was barred and impossible to open from the inside and that fire extinguishers kept around the ground were empty. With Terry away on holiday, it was left to director Ray Jacks to face the media. 'The report is derisory and substantially incomplete. We want the public, especially the people of Bury, to know the full facts,' he told the *Bury Times* reporter.

The report also covers the presence of the fire engine in the car park for the Manchester City game with an explanation from the local authority. 'The fire extinguishers in the ground had been set off previously by vandals and some of them had been sent for refilling. In view of this, we suggested a fire appliance and that several firemen should stand by during the match. [Terry Robinson] agreed and that is why we were on hand that night,' said Bob Graham, assistant fire chief of Greater Manchester Council.

The escape routes, which had been suggested in the refreshed inspection that came straight after Bradford, were installed in the summer of 1985. The Main Stand, already blighted by the cage that was erected following the rioting by Blackpool fans that March, took a further hit as emergency exits were carved into the front of it. These ugly steps rendered one of the most popular parts of the ground, the Main Stand Paddock where you could smell the liniment as players

The end of an era as the Boys' Stand is sacrificed in favour of an emergency exit.
Copyright: *Bolton Evening News*

235

jogged down the tunnel before kick-off, out of action and remain in place today, giving the stand a peculiarly top-heavy look when it appears on television.

Over in the South Stand–Cemetery End corner, generations of Bury fans looked on misty-eyed as the Boys' Stand, the place where so many, including the chairman, had begun their careers as Shakers, was demolished to make way for another emergency exit into Bury Cemetery. The demolition was to prove a handy development for those who didn't fancy paying to get in, though, as before the redeveloped Cemetery End filled in the corner in 1999 there would be a steady stream of local youngsters perching on the cemetery wall to watch for free games that, from their perspective at least, fanned out from the corner flag.

The Popplewell Inquiry that followed Bradford and the Taylor Report that followed Hillsborough would both have far-reaching implications for the ground that Bury had played at since 1885. Timber was stripped out to be replaced with concrete and plastic seating, and by the end of the 1999/2000 season – after Terry had played the system to claim every grant going for the stadium's redevelopment – the old girl was unrecognisable from the season when Leighton James was tearing up and down touchlines in front of cheering Bury fans.

Just seven days after Bradford, the FA Cup final was played between Manchester United and Everton at Wembley. The Toffees had won the First Division championship for the first time in fifteen years just over a week before the match, and on the Wednesday before the final had won the European Cup Winners Cup with a 3–1 win over Rapid Vienna in Rotterdam. Howard Kendall's squad was quite comfortably the greatest that a generation of Evertonians had ever seen and a treble was on, but their quest for the cup that they'd won the year before by beating Watford was unsuccessful. Despite having Kevin Moran sent off in the first ever instance of a player being given his marching orders in an FA Cup final, United clinched victory thanks to a tremendous curling shot from Norman Whiteside which beat Neville Southall.

"I don't remember a subdued atmosphere in the week that followed Bradford because we were excited about Rotterdam and then the FA Cup final," remembers Everton fan Greg Murphy today. "Maybe some fans felt sombre after Bradford, but I can honestly say for my part that it had slipped from my consciousness by the Tuesday with the Cup Winners Cup the next day and Wembley on the Saturday. Terrible to say, I know, but honest. Perhaps if there had been the kind of rolling news we have now, which would have kept the tragedy front and centre, it might have been different," he says.

"With what happened at St Andrews on the same day as Bradford, I think Evertonians felt that we would be under the microscope with the live screening of the game in Rotterdam and the game at Wembley, particularly because it was against United. That Rotterdam passed without incident, and that we were roundly applauded by the media and UEFA, was a massive relief to add to the joy. I'm not saying that Evertonians of that era were angels – in fact, it's implicit in what I'm saying that we were fearful we might shame ourselves because there was certainly potential for things to kick off. But we were known as lazy hooligans," he smiles.

"We had a minute's silence for Bradford before the cup final and it didn't occur to me that either us or United would ruin it," he continues. "It was pin-sharp, with added helicopter whirring, silence. I can still remember looking around and thinking that only football could do this: a wall of noise to deathly silence at the toot of a whistle before reversing the process and letting the sounds of the hounds of hell unleash themselves again just sixty seconds later. It was a very sombre, impeccably-observed moment, demonstrated for all to hear on TV at the height of the hooligan era. If I'm honest enough to say to any Bradford fan that, really, the fire tragedy didn't feature in our thinking that week, then I'd hope we at least brought some solace for them by participating in the silence which was a rarely-held observation then," he says.

Everton were obviously tired after their long season and were wilting in the baking North London heat. "I thought we were going to win it for about thirty seconds after Moran was sent off because we felt imperious," says Greg. "But the atmosphere was like a bear pit and that only intensified with every second it took him to leave the pitch. The sense of perceived injustice from the United end was palpable, their fans found an extra gear, as did their players, and straight from the restart it was clear that it was the worst thing that could have happened to us," he remembers.

Whiteside's beautiful effort in the one hundred and tenth minute denied Neville Southall a second consecutive FA Cup winners' medal, but following his side's heroics in the First Division, no one could take his league championship medal from him. The Welshman had risen from the very bottom of the Football League with Bury to the very top in less than five years. Plucked from non-league Winsford United in the summer of 1980, he made his debut for the Shakers in a 2-1 defeat at Wigan Athletic in September which saw Bury slump to rock bottom, ninety-second place in the league. His stock then rocketed as he made the number one jersey his own after wrestling it from John Forrest, and following the last of his thirty-nine appearances wearing the V-shaped badge, he signed for Everton for £150,000. Yet two years later, having already made forty appearances in the First Division for the Toffees, Howard Kendall 'rested' him in favour of Jim Arnold and sent him back down to the Fourth Division on loan, to Port Vale. While Neville must have been wondering where his career was heading, it was a masterstroke by his manager who ensured he got more and more experience in the Football League rather than the Central League and its reserve teams.

In 1985 he was voted the Football Writers' Player of the Year and considered the best goalkeeper in the world. "He was sheer football majesty," remembers Greg Murphy. "The best Everton team

I ever witnessed was that which took to the field for the European Cup Winners Cup final in Rotterdam in 1985, give or take a few minor tweaks or wider considerations over the years. But I won't budge on Southall because there's nowhere to budge to. The sheer breathtaking excellence of Southall defies any other description than that which records him as the best in the world at what he did for almost a decade. Starting at the top, it's a fact that Neville Southall is the most decorated Everton player of all, with two championships, two FA Cups and a European Cup Winners Cup. It's also a fact that he made the record number of appearances for Everton, with 751 turnouts being a comfortable 217 ahead of his nearest challenger Brian Labone.

"He joined Everton when I was fourteen and left when I was almost thirty-one," he continues. "During that time, the new back pass rule, which was brought in at the start of the 1992/93 season, represented the biggest sea-change in football during my time watching it, but to say he coped admirably is an understatement compared to the established 'keepers who faded rapidly in the face of it. I don't think Neville receives his due credit for managing such a monumental change.

"In fact," Greg concludes, "I think there's more than a touch of his achievements with Everton that we still take for granted, certainly within the club. I feel we're overdue in giving Neville Southall his true and justified recognition as an Evertonian. And I don't just mean a token nod either. You don't have to wait until someone's dead to erect a statue in their honour. That's the true status that Neville Southall should be occupying in the realms of Everton."

The good behaviour that the Everton fans were so rightly proud of would go on to count for nothing. Less than a week after the Toffees had ended their rivals' domestic season with a 1–0 win in the Merseyside derby at Goodison Park, Liverpool travelled to Belgium and the Heysel Stadium for the European Cup final against Juventus on 29 May. It was to be the night when hooliganism finally bubbled over and reached its nadir.

"We were hopeful of getting something because we were getting used to success," remembers Reds fan Phil Daniels who crossed the North Sea to the European mainland for the game. "It was just another European adventure for us, so we got the train to London, then the train to Harwich, then the boat to Amsterdam. We found a bar that was running a coach to the game so we didn't have to stay in Brussels itself.

"I went with five or six mates and I was the only one in our group who had a ticket. We got to Brussels in the middle of the afternoon and there was a good atmosphere. There were more Liverpool fans than Juventus milling around the place, but it was all very good natured. We did what fans do on afternoons like that and had a drink. A ball appeared and we had a bit of a kick-about.

"In the run-up to the game, though, we found that we'd only been allocated a small section of the ground. We had half of an end and one of the side stands which I thought was odd as we had at least two or three times more supporters there than Juventus. We went to the end and saw that we'd been given blocks X, Y and Z but that some tickets had the Block Z black-markered out, so we weren't getting our full allocation. There wasn't even a turnstile if you had a ticket, it was just a gate that was about ten foot wide with a bloke collecting tickets on either side of it. Imagine that, at a European Cup final. You can appreciate how many ticketless fans got in and the crush that was happening through the gate and on to the terracing, which was already crumbling underneath our feet," he says.

It comes as no surprise that the segregation at Heysel was as farcical as the entrance procedure. "We were standing near a dividing fence between us and Block Z, which was holding Juventus and neutral fans, which was made of chicken wire. It was only about four feet high, and as the ground started filling up, the Liverpool side more than the Juventus areas, people were moving across from the terracing over this 'no-mans' land'. Liverpool fans were spilling

240

over the fence and the Italians considered this a charge and fled to the bottom corner of the stand where the wall collapsed. It was total chaos as police in riot gear were soon on the scene and fans who were at the other end of the ground started running around the athletics track around the edge of the pitch to attack us before players came on to the pitch to plead for the trouble to stop," remembers Phil.

The collapsing wall which Phil remembers killed thirty-nine supporters in that same Block Z. The final was being televised by the BBC and their coverage, which had begun with Terry Wogan and Bruce Forsyth wearing football scarves on the former's chat show, was now showing Belgian police struggling to cope with what had been termed 'the English disease'.

Italian TV was also showing the game and their coverage was being watched by David Brown, former Bury goalkeeper John Platt, John Bramhall and former Bury striker Steve Johnson. The quartet had flown to Italy for the wedding of Brown and Vanna, who accompanied him to our interview for this publication, and on the night of the final they went to a local bar.

"It was horrendous," remembers Johnson. "We'd been to the bar already a couple of nights before so they invited us back for the game. They had the flags up and everything, and as we waited for the match to start because of the delay caused by the fighting, the atmosphere changed when it became clear that people had died."

"I didn't really understand Italian as well as I do today back then," remembers David Brown. "I was trying to ask them in my own way why the game hadn't started and what was happening. Then we saw why and it was just awful. The game shouldn't have been played, of course, and it was decided in such a ridiculous way with that penalty [scored by Juventus's Michel Platini] that was awarded for a foul committed outside the area," he says.

"We didn't know there had been deaths until we got back to the coach park," remembers Phil Daniels. "We thought it had been the usual kind of argy-bargy that you'd see up and down the country when you went to away games with Liverpool, which I used to do at the time. It all became apparent to us the next morning back in Amsterdam. I never felt before I set out to go to Belgium that it was a risk to go, even when you'd start to get people attaching themselves to the names of clubs when they weren't supporters and they just wanted to go for a scrap.

"It was an event that made me realise how UEFA put on showcase games with no regard for actual supporters. It was a game held in a crumbling stadium with no concept of the fan base which was going to arrive and was coldly corporate. Liverpool fans were by no means innocent, but we were made scapegoats and as we arrived back in London the police gave us a hard time, calling us murderers," he continues.

The day after the disaster, the Belgian government banned British clubs from playing in their country. The day after that, the FA banned its English clubs from playing in European competition for twelve months before, on 2 June, UEFA banned English clubs from all European games 'indefinitely'. It meant that the all-conquering Everton side were not going to get their tilt at the European Cup.

"It was like a runaway train," remembers Greg Murphy. "I can't remember who first suggested a ban but then it was almost like 'Yeah, that's a good idea, that's how we'll deal with it and be seen to be dealing with it – a ban.' And then someone else would nod. And before long it was like a self-fulfilling prophecy: English clubs could be banned, English clubs should be banned, English clubs will be banned.

"As late as 25 June, with the deadline for UEFA preliminary draws approaching, we teamed up with the PFA, Manchester United, Norwich and Southampton to take the whole thing to the High Court," he continues. "Mr Justice Vinelott threw out our case after Liverpool had mounted their own, and the day before Live Aid we announced that we wouldn't take it further and that we'd just eat our porridge. That was it. We'd genuinely, really, actually be banned. I couldn't believe it. By the time Freddie Mercury was on stage at Wembley the next day, I was ready to kick the telly in. '*We are the champions/We'd served our sentence/But committed no crime.'* It's just staggering that we accepted it. We rolled over, basically," he says.

"People were dying for no reason and the authorities had to be seen to be doing something, particularly as this was a problem that was no longer just confined to domestic football," remembers Bury fan Malcolm Parr. "One of the solutions that they came up with was the ID card scheme which I was against and which I marched in protest at. It was a little awkward because I was a civil servant so I was effectively marching against my employer, but I felt it was wrong. They had to do something, though, because this was affecting the UK's relationship with other countries," he says.

"Coming only two weeks after Bradford, I remember watching the scenes from Brussels with my dad and him switching off the television and saying he never wanted to watch another match again. Of course, he did. But I think many people felt like that at the time," remembers David Peace at the way that the 1984/85 season drew to a miserable close.

British football's worst season had ended in a way that had seemed grimly predictable as the campaign had worn on. Deaths had occurred at games in the past, most notably at Burnden Park in 1946 and Ibrox in 1971, but never in such garish technicolour. Ninety-six football fans had lost their lives at matches in May 1985, a month when Bury should have been sweeping up plaudits for an achievement that is unthinkable just thirty years later.

The recognition that Dobson, his coaching staff and his players so richly deserved did not come as the British game dwelt on its many troubles. The player-manager had achieved what had always been his stated aim of promotion at the first attempt, and it was a magnificent and unrepeatable achievement. Bury's rise to the third tier using just fifteen players all season remains a shining light in British football's darkest few months and in the club's history. It deserves so much more than to be filed as 'just another promotion'.

On Reflection

Martin Dobson was the mastermind behind the unlikeliest of promotions. When the elvation was confirmed, he had been in the Gigg Lane hot seat for just thirteen months, during which time he had revolutionised the club's infrastructure and playing style. A town and fan base that had grown weary of what could be termed 'typically Fourth Division football' had been treated to what is generally regarded as the most attractive brand of the game ever to be presented at Gigg Lane on a regular basis. He got the best from the players that he inherited, but he also had the wherewithal, astute-ness and connections to bring in men who fitted his ideals perfectly and who bought into his vision for a small club with big ideas. They were players that a Fourth Division squad had no right to include, but they were there because of a manager who refused to let convention get in his way.

Martin was another former player who I'd interviewed for the match day programme at some point between 2006 and 2009 when I only needed enough memories to fill a 500 word feature. We spoke on the phone for more than half an hour in a conversation which unknowingly planted the seed for the idea for this book, and once that idea had come to the forefront, I called Martin again and asked if he fancied a longer chat about his promotion-winning team. He agreed, and so I travelled to his home in Bolton to conduct the interview.

"I left Bolton Wanderers at nineteen-years-old on a free transfer. I'd not made an appearance for them and I joined Burnley, which meant going up a division and my salary going up from £14 a week to £20 a week which would rise to £24 with appearance and win bonuses on top of that. It was great to get the move and it's what I wanted to achieve at Bury. I wanted to bring young players in who I could make better," he remembers today.

"I had my ambitions when I was at Burnley, of course. I wanted to play in the cup final and things like that and I was able to play well under a great manager, Harry Potts, and great coaches who played the game simply, which suited my style," he adds.

Martin Dobson's 1984/85 season pen picture. (Copyright: Bury Football Club)

Martin took to his new role, inspired by the people who'd assisted in his career, instantly. "I'd given the chairman the list of players I wanted to keep from the end of the 1983/84 season and I'd signed Leighton, Trevor, Andy and Kevin. I also brought David Lee into the club as an apprentice and I feel that he deserves a special mention for his tremendous attitude," he remembers of the then-sixteen-year-old who left Bury for a then-record £400,000 in 1991.

"Leighton James was there for his class and the same can be said of Trevor Ross. I wanted them to be role models to the younger players. We had a lot of quality in the squad and a lot of credit for that must also go to John Heap, who was the secretary of the club at the time," he adds.

Gathering his squad together in the same summer as the Los Angeles Olympics, Dobson quickly forged a reputation bestowed

245

upon him by his players. "I asked them, 'What are your ambitions?' and they all said 'To play for you, Dobbo. I want to get in the Bury team.' I'd always encourage them to think more highly of themselves, though. I'd tell them to aim for the First Division so that they could go back to their old clubs at any time in the future as a great player, because that's what I did whenever I went back to Bolton," he says.

As well as telling his players to be their own men, Martin also lived by the same philosophy as a manager. "I was told that the way of getting out of the Fourth Division was to have two big centre-halves and two big lads up front. You'd pick up the bits and pieces at the back before launching the ball forward to the strikers, like Wimbledon had done. Playing like that was something I just didn't understand from the way I'd played in my career to that point, so I decided it wasn't for us. We'd play the right way. People laughed when I made it clear that I wanted us to play a passing game that the team would actively enjoy playing too. It also helped that I'd been to that Lilleshall seminar and learned the techniques from Wiel Coerver that we passed on to Enty," he smiles.

The most important player in terms of Dobson's vision that followed the Jim Iley era was undoubtedly Leighton James. His career in the upper echelons of the Football League had drawn admiring glances on newspaper back pages, but after a spell in the top flight with Sunderland, he was ready to call time on his playing days.

"Taffy had been released by Sunderland so I went to see him and explained that this was the next stage of his career," Martin laughs. "I had him in mind, from the start of my time as manager of Bury, to control the left side of the pitch and do a bit of coaching. Once I told him that Trevor Ross was on board too, he bought into the idea.

"I wanted Joe Jakub in the centre of midfield with Kevin Young as more of a touch player, and I wanted Winston White because he was great to have in the dressing room, as was Wilf. I moved Wilf to physiotherapist after Frank Casper joined as my assistant manager because there was no one like him on a Monday morning after a bad result at the weekend," he remembers.

Martin's memories were by now in full flow and I barely spoke as his philosophy for attractive football poured from him. "John Bramhall was six foot three inches and commanding at centre half because he was so strong in the air. I wanted me and him to play alongside each other and to pass the ball out from the back. It was going to be two-touch football in that I wanted the players to control the ball, pass it and move. I felt that when players were just asked to lump it up field, those players were being disrespected because playing that way wasn't going to help them get better.

"I'd tell David Brown to shout 'AWAY!' or 'KEEPER'S!' when he was coming for the ball. I always told him that if he shouted for it and dropped it, I wouldn't shout at him. The only thing I'd tell him off for would be if he didn't shout for it and he dropped it," he adds.

Despite being the manager of such a small squad compared to his contemporaries, Dobbo doesn't feel like it was a case of 'us against them'. "I never felt like that. On one occasion, we played Crewe at home and before the game I wasn't feeling well. I made a couple of mistakes and we ended up drawing. I told the players right from the start of the season that I wanted a seven-out-of-ten from them in each game, but that in some matches you'd get an eight- or nine-out-of-ten performance which would make up for some of the poorer performances. Being a player-manager with a small squad can be problematic if you need to criticise players when you've not done so well yourself, but at the end of the day it's about treating people as you would like to be treated yourself," he notes.

Martin also knew how to use the local press of a small town with a poorly-supported team to his advantage. "I used the *Bury Times*'s pre-season write-up ('ALL SYSTEMS GO FOR PROMOTION') to let the town know of my aims, and in the early games we really justified the plan that I'd laid out. Craig Madden and Wayne Entwistle were scoring regularly. They were two entirely different players: Wayne was big and had raw strength whereas Craig was what you'd now call a fox in the box. Pash [Terry Pashley] was the kind of player you could rely on because of his professional attitude and dedication to the cause, which was best shown by his refusal to have an Achilles operation. It was just a great time with a set of players that I trusted. I told them the kind of bookings that I wouldn't tolerate too, like for dissent and retaliation, and they accepted that," he says.

After assembling his promotion-winning side, Dobson continued to scout around the lower reaches of the Football League for more rough diamonds that he could polish. The most significant of all of these was the move for Lee Dixon, who signed for Bury in the summer of 1985.

"The club's joint highest outgoing transfer fee at that time was the £150,000 that we'd received from Everton for Neville Southall, matching the fee that Chesterfield paid for Danny Wilson," Martin explains.

"We signed Lee for minimal money [£3,500, which in 2006 Lee revealed he offered to pay himself] after John Bond had released him at Burnley and he'd spent time at Chester. He had a great single season with us, though we knew after six months that Stoke were sniffing around him. When we felt we had to sell him, we couldn't agree a fee with Stoke so it went to tribunal. The panel included Gordon Taylor [chief executive of the PFA] and Jimmy Sirrell [former Notts County manager] who'd both mocked me when I said I thought Lee was worth £100,000 and a 50 per cent sell-on clause. They said that his history didn't warrant that kind of deal and so we only got £40,000 with no sell-on.

"Some months later I got a call from George Graham asking what was 'wrong' with Lee because he'd had four clubs and he was still only twenty-one. I assured George that he was a great player and the rest is history. Gordon Taylor rang me later to apologise about the tribunal's decision too," he says with a wry smile.

Sell-on clauses were also a factor when Martin pulled another masterstroke as he persuaded a player of a more mature vintage to Gigg Lane in 1987. "I'd played with Mark Higgins at Everton and he was winding down his time at Manchester United, just after Alex Ferguson joined them. I persuaded him to sell Mark to me for £10,000, but Alex wanted 50 per cent of a sell-on fee. We gave Mark a bit of a new lease of life and Stoke came in for him too, like they had done with Lee, with an offer of £80,000. That would obviously have meant Bury would only have got £40,000 so I rang Fergie and told him the situation. He was brilliant and told me that he'd take a maximum of £50,000 from the deal. We persuaded Stoke to give us £150,000 which meant that we got a bit of a crumb of comfort from them after the Dixon deal in the shape of £100,000," he says.

"But going back to the promotion, if you look at the scores from the games we played against the other teams we were promoted with, we played six games and only conceded one goal," he concludes. "We won three and drew three which I reckon showed how organised we were. It was a satisfactory feeling, and even though we didn't win the championship as perhaps we should have done, we'd achieved our goal when we came off the pitch on the final day of the season.

"And then you see the pictures from Valley Parade that were all over the television. It was just shocking," he ends, recalling the images that would go on to define the entire season in the annals of the British game and which would cast a shadow over his side's achievements when thinking back to the state of British football in the mid-1980s.

Despite the praise that Bury received from all corners over the course of the season, recognition from the official bodies was rarely forthcoming. Dobson may have taken Bury to the summit of the division at Christmas and his team may have been the first in the country to hit fifty points, but he didn't win the manager of the month award at all throughout the course of the campaign. Managers of the other four clubs who made up the top five of the Fourth Division in 1985 all received the accolade at some point, but Dobson remained philosophical.

'I'm not too disappointed, although any kind of award shows that you are being appreciated for what you are doing,' he told the *Bury Times* promotion special. He also takes an obvious pride in his players and his right-hand man as he reviews the campaign just gone. 'They [the players] set high standards for themselves in terms of ability, attitude, determination and pride of performance and you need a mixture of these things. The really pleasing thing is that we gained promotion the right way by playing entertaining football. Frank's help has been invaluable and I have relied a lot on him, especially in spotting things about the team which are easy to miss when you're out there playing,' he continued.

While he never had to take home an over-sized bottle of Bells whisky, Dobson instead received the nod from his fellow pros when he, together with Joe Jakub, was named in the PFA's divisional team for the season. The cream of the fourth tier was named in a ceremony at the Hilton Hotel in London on 24 March, and in his programme notes for the home game which followed the do, the manager outlined his respect for his skipper while stepping out of the limelight himself.

'Ever since I have been at the club, Joe has been a tremendous player for me,' he wrote. 'He has a lot of qualities, is inspirational on the field and works for the team – not individual praise. His 100 per cent effort makes him a players' player who is well-respected. I look upon my selection as an award for the whole team – from David Brown up to Leighton James. It reflects how well we have played this season as individuals and as a team,' he continued.

Fans today remember Dobson as a visionary manager whose success in his first full season was richly deserved as they reminisce over a hugely enjoyable team to watch. "When Martin joined Bury in Easter 1984, the football changed. Previous Bury teams were boring, but Martin was a class act," remembers Steve Taylor who, as the club's reporter on BBC Radio Manchester in the 1980s and 1990s, has a voice that brings Proustian rushes coming thick and fast.

"He could pick out a pass and made everything look so effortless. He brought together a mix of quality players who had been around the block a bit, together with some good up-and-coming younger players. The tactics that he played were fairly basic in that they were simply to get the ball to the wingers who'd then get it in for Wayne or Craig to score, but it was a devastatingly effective plan," he continues.

Bury fan Malcolm Parr agrees. "Jim Iley had become a bit of a joke figure amongst the supporters, unfairly in my opinion. So to get Martin Dobson in as manager, someone who had been an England international, was a definite coup. The board took a bit of a gamble appointing him because the crowds had been dropping so low, as they did for that game against Northampton in 1984 [played in front of 1,096], that they needed to get people back. It could have gone two ways: we could either have had to end up applying for re-election or we could have got promoted, and though his tenure didn't start well we now know that he was sizing up his squad and the players he wanted for the next season when he could really have a go," he says.

Fellow supporters Peter Cullen and Paul Greenlees were similarly excited by the new manager. "Martin arrived at a time when he could write-off the end of the [1983/84] season. He started to plan who he was going to keep and then started making his other signings, but I still wasn't sure what to expect because of the previous season, which had been a disaster. But as his first full season went on, you really felt that the team was capable of achieving something," remembers Cullen.

Meanwhile, Greenlees remembers the prescient prediction in the *Bury Times* in the summer of 1984 as being typical of Dobson's immovable self-belief. "It was brave of him to say we were 'all systems go for promotion' after the season we'd had leading up to his arrival, but he was a cultured player and he wanted us to play in a similar kind of way," he says.

"It was great to watch and suddenly everyone wanted to come down to Gigg Lane. You started enjoying going to the match again, it was absolutely brilliant. We had something that people wanted to watch which you could see by how much crowds increased over the course of the first five home games of the season. He'd built the nucleus of the side by the end of the previous season and it was a classy team that wasn't at all defensive," he says.

Richard Beedie was only thirteen years old when the season kicked off, but even he could see how different things had become after Dobbo's influence on Lower Gigg and Goshen training sessions during the close season. "My first experience of the Dobson masterclass was the 3–0 win over Halifax in August 1984, because I wasn't allowed to go to the opening game up at Darlington. It was the same score as the game the season before but we played totally differently. We bamboozled them and it was a joy to watch. The drab, lifeless football of how we'd played under Iley had been replaced with a swift passing game which used genuine wingers who could beat a man, get to the by-line and ping a cross in for two hungry, willing strikers," he says.

"What stands out to me when I look at the results from the season is that we only lost three of our first twenty-three league games," says Malcolm Parr. "That's only three defeats in the league between August and January, and even then it wasn't until October that we lost our first match, at Stockport. People were sitting up and starting to take notice and thought that we could achieve something – and we were doing all of this while playing an attractive game that was a joy to watch," he continues.

Dobson may well have had his grand plan up his sleeve from the moment he was unveiled as manager, but he still needed the right players. Champions Chesterfield used twenty to clinch the title, while their runners-up Blackpool used twenty-two and third-placed Darlington used twenty-six. Every single man, therefore, was crucial to Bury's manager.

"Fifteen games in March and April with fifteen players really is a tribute not only to how fit they were but to how much they looked after each other and themselves," says Malcolm Parr. "Dobson was my favourite player from the season because of his class and the extra time he used to make for himself. He'd always find time for a pass and was pulling strings in midfield where he'd be in control. He's one of the best players I've seen play for Bury because he never seemed to exert himself. We ought to be grateful for what he gave us. He was a wonderful, wonderful player," he continues.

Every other fan who saw the team play has their own take on the strengths which made the squad. "Andy Hill was a tremendous signing, deceptively fast and very agile," remembers Steve Taylor. "Joe Jakub and Terry Pashley were honest pros, the kind of players that fans like, and John Bramhall was a good, steady centre-half who came into his own when playing with someone like Martin. Trevor had the strength to give the midfield the bite you need at that level and Craig was the poacher, whereas Wayne was more like your more traditional centre forward," he adds.

"Andy Hill was an inspired signing and his player of the season award, for which I voted for him, was well-deserved," says Paul Greenlees.

'Quiet man Hill…has hardly put a foot wrong since joining the Shakers on a free transfer from Manchester United – yet the bargain capture admitted the award came completely out of the blue,' says the *Bury Times* of 17 May. 'It was a total surprise but this has capped a great season. I've loved every minute of it here,' countered Andy in the same edition of the paper.

"Wayne Entwistle played the best football of his life and Kevin Young was a pleasure to watch too," Greenlees continues. "Even the lesser players used, like Gary Buckley, were vital to what Dobson wanted us to do. I don't remember much about Gary, I must admit, but I do remember that he was very combative when he played. It must have been difficult for him just being asked to fit into this team when the manager needed him to, because all of the others played so regularly that they would have known by instinct how their teammates played. I sometimes felt for Gary and Chris Cutler, solely because they were trying to get into a team that was so settled, especially Cutler trying to unseat Craig and Wayne," he reveals.

With the infectious enthusiasm that came with being a teenager at the time, Richard Beedie had four players that he considered his favourites when replicating matches from Gigg Lane on the fields at the Derby School. "David Brown, John Bramhall and Craig Madden were the ones for me," he says now, naming the three who come below his number one. "I'd thought that Brown was brilliant ever since the first game I went to, when he saved a penalty against Chester in 1983, and I fancied myself as something of a 'keeper at school so I always pretended to be him rather than Ray Clemence or Peter Shilton. In front of him you had the solid presence of John Bramhall, a proper defender who was hard but fair in contrast to the culture of his defensive partner, Dobson. Craig Madden was just the obvious hero for Bury fans at that time because of the goals he scored in his pomp thanks to the wing play. I went to an open day at the club that season where Winston White talked to our group on the pitch, in the six-yard box. He called it 'Craig Madden territory' and he couldn't have been more right," he says.

Richard's fourth player in his holy quartet is the player that's cited more than any other as the difference between the mid-table mediocrity that preceded his arrival and the promotion plaudits that followed his departure. "Leighton James was simply outstanding. Winston's pace on the other wing scared the living daylights out of many a left back that season, but Leighton shaded it as our best winger. Whatever pace he'd had in the past had now gone, but there wasn't a defender in the division who could cope with him. I may not have been watching football very long but I knew I was watching a football genius," he says.

Malcolm Parr remembers Winston White equally as fondly. "He chipped in with the odd goal and in my opinion was a very underrated player. We got him at his best and he could turn games for you. He was a lovely fella on the occasions I met him too," he remembers.

Back over on the left wing, Richard Beedie was stunned that Bury had attracted someone of Leighton's calibre. "I couldn't believe it when Bury signed him," he says. "I'm one of those men of a certain age who collected Panini stickers with the mindset that if you were on one, you were a big player. Here we were, lowly Bury, signing a player who'd been on a Panini sticker the season before when he was in the First Division with Sunderland. Trevor had been in the sticker album too, a few years before, when he was with Everton, so it was a really exciting time. Trevor was one of the players that I had as a 'swap' that kept appearing in new packets," he laughs.

The astonishment at signing Leighton was also echoed by Steve Taylor. "His signing was an indication that Martin was well-connected and could get a terrific standard of player to come to Gigg Lane," he recalls. But Taffy wasn't there to collect one final pay cheque as he played out his career; he started every single match of the season and played every minute of them but for fifteen minutes of the last game, when he was replaced by substitute Chris Grimshaw. Only goalkeeper David Brown played more minutes, which was quite the achievement when you imagine the frustrations that some of the Fourth Division's more physical players may have attempted to take out on his innate skill. "I've no idea what kind of salary he was on, but to accept it coming down from the First Division, it must have been impressive. I think he enjoyed himself at that level because he was just far too good for any full-back that came up against him," Taylor adds.

As well as the fans, talking to the players highlighted how much fun they had at Gigg Lane in the mid-eighties. There was a camaraderie that filtered down from the playing staff into every nook and cranny of life at the club while the British game's reputation lay battered and at its lowest ebb. "I'd covered Manchester United and Bolton earlier in my career," remembers Steve Taylor. "While Bolton is quite a homely club, and even Manchester United was friendlier than it is today, nowhere came close to how things were at Bury. It's a family club and they always allowed the press access to players and management. It may have been Wilf rather than Martin if it had been a bad result, but we always got a quote from someone, so from a media point of view they were great. You could find out whatever was going on around the place because everyone was on first name terms and we were relaxed with each other. In some ways it's still like that today. I took my daughter when she was seven years old and now I take my grandson. He calls himself a Manchester United fan but he's never seen them play – he's actually a Bury fan," he laughs.

Steve's dedication to indoctrinating new supporters chimes with Richard Beedie's attempts at getting schoolmates up Radcliffe Road from school to Gigg Lane. "I did my best to drum up support in my English presentation that year. It consisted of me giving a rundown of our history and using the six by four pictures of players that you could get from the club shop as visual aids. I'm not sure I got a good mark for it, especially after I spent a lot of time telling the class about Leighton James's career up to that point, but if it got a few more through the turnstiles then I felt it was worth it," he says.

Paul Greenlees was also doing his best to increase crowds as part of his role with the burgeoning supporters' club, members of which gave up their free time for nothing in the pursuit of making the Gigg Lane experience more enjoyable in the mid-eighties. As well as home games, they also sought to get more fans on the road with the Shakers too.

"We didn't have a home game for about six weeks after Christmas in the promotion season and there were only about forty or fifty people who used to travel to away games regularly, so I wanted to increase that number. I wanted us to be taking three or four coaches wherever we went because if you could get 200 or so supporters all standing together in a small away stand, you can get a good atmosphere going," remembers Paul.

"I understand that getting rid of terracing was necessary after the Taylor Report, but in crowds of 2,000 at places like Bury it creates an atmosphere. I feel that if someone's sitting down, they don't feel as capable of expressing themselves as they can when they're stood up. When people want to make a point, they stand up to do so. If I could bring anything back from that season, it'd be terracing," he claims.

When Paul took up the new role of producing video tapes of the Shakers' games, a position he only left in 2001, standing room only was sometimes the sole option when they were re-broadcast in the social club. "We'd show the full ninety minutes of away games again in the club on a Monday night, as it was a quiet night for the club and it helped them get a bit more cash behind the bar. It took off in a way we never imagined and we soon had between three and four hundred people coming to watch them," he says, shaking his head in disbelief.

While Greenlees was busy behind the camera, his friend Peter Cullen was busy sitting at his typewriter producing *Shakers Review*. "I took over editing the programme from John Waddington, who was former chairman Ron Clarke's son-in-law," he remembers. "I did it without being paid after Terry asked me to, but the access to players was limited. I'd ring Martin Dobson on a Sunday for his comment before typing it up and I'd have contributions from Tony Cunningham, who still writes for it to this day. I'd then drive to Blackpool at ten o'clock in the evening to the printers. I'd use my car, my petrol and I didn't get anything in the way of expenses, but I did it because I loved it," he laughs.

Dobson took his squad on a well-deserved break to Ibiza once the season had finished and the close bonding that had carried the team over the finish line of their domestic job of work was continued in the Balearics. Offering up more detail than the close counsel that Kevin Young kept on the subject when pressed in the interview with him for this publication, Terry Pashley reveals that Craig Madden's packing for the beano amounted to little more than the T-shirt and shorts that he rocked up at Ringway wearing, together with a toothbrush.

"We chucked the chairman into the sea and he had to lay his money out in the sun to dry," Pashley says, smiling at the memory. "We nicked Martin and Frank's hire car and parked it up a mountain too. We took it up there without any lights on and Joe Jakub did a U-turn in it. It was only in the daylight the next morning that we saw just how close he'd been to the edge of this cliff face and that he could easily have gone over it," he says, shaking his head in disbelief at the youthful exuberance.

Frank Casper remembers sharing a room with Terry Robinson. "I don't know if you know, but the chairman used to be a wrestler. We'd get back to the room after a few drinks and he'd be saying 'Come on, wrestle me!' at two in the morning before slam dunking me," he laughs. "It was a great break, though. It was a case of me, Martin and Terry walking one way down the beach, while the players walked in the other direction. I'm sure they had a great time," he smiles.

Relaxed, refreshed and pledging that what happened in Ibiza stayed in Ibiza, the squad returned with further progress on the management and directors' collective minds. The *Bury Times* promotion special's poignantly-titled story 'NOW FOR DIVISION TWO' describes how Terry Robinson feels that the second tier is Bury's natural home, but doesn't quote the chairman on his thoughts.

'Consolidation in Division Three is far from the chairman's mind and he feels with the same commitment from players, management and the like and with the support of the town, that the Shakers' 101st year could be equally as successful as their centenary year,' concludes the piece.

Bury would have to wait twelve years for a tilt at the second tier, by which time much had changed in football and Dobson had left Gigg Lane. Stan Ternent's side won the 1997 Second Division championship, following the divisional reorganisation of 1992, at a time when match day squads were made up of the starting XI and three substitutes. Television cameras were also present at each game on the road to the title meaning that every goal, save and incident could be replayed again and again, thus avoiding the frustration that footage from only one game, the fixture at Swindon Town in March 1985, shows the Forgotten Fifteen in action.

Dobson left Gigg Lane in March 1989, just four years after he pulled the ultimate miracle from up his sleeve. The *Bury Times* of 4 April 1989 describes his sacking and how the manager had felt under strain when he was not allowed to appoint a new assistant after Frank Casper left to join Burnley as manager.

The paper then goes on to say: 'Lately, there had been more unrest after the appearance of a series of articles in the national press which seemingly advertised the availability of the Bury boss. Some members of the board were known to be upset that the stories should appear at a time when the team was pushing hard for promotion. Even so, the decision to sack Dobson was not taken lightly,' reads the article before a long justification from Terry Robinson for the course of action taken.

In the same way as he always appeared in newspaper reports during the promotion season, Dobson was philosophical about his dismissal. 'I said I would be considering my future over the next couple of months but I suppose I'll have to do it a lot sooner. I haven't got anything planned but I feel the board here have already got someone in mind to bring in to replace me.'

Dobson's last act was apparently to say goodbye to his players, of whom only Terry Pashley and Andy Hill remained from the 1985 promotion season. 'They seemed genuinely upset by the news but

I told them to put it out of their minds and go for everything over the next few games,' he ends.

The memories of the promotion team he assembled remain strong, though. "For me, that was, and still is, the best Bury team I've ever seen," says Richard Beedie. "I compare each team that's come since and none have come close. Stan Ternent's team of the late-nineties had much more success, but Dobson's team couldn't be beaten for the joyful, beautifully attacking football it produced that season," he says.

Paul Greenlees agrees. "The transformation of playing so badly just twelve months previously to the total football that we played across the promotion season was brilliant. I was young, I went to every game and I enjoyed every minute of it. It was a very good season!" he beams.

Appendix:
Results, Appearances and Final League Table

Canon League Division Four, 1984/85: Bury's results

25 August 1984
Darlington 1 Bury 1 (Madden)
Brown, Hill, Pashley, Ross, Bramhall, Dobson, White, Madden, Entwistle,
Jakub, James
Sub: Young (for Entwistle)
Attendance: 1,441

1 September 1984
Bury 3 (Bramhall, Ross, Young) Halifax Town 0
Brown, Hill, Young, Ross, Bramhall, Dobson, White, Madden, Entwistle,
Jakub, James
Sub: Buckley (not used)
Attendance: 1,717

8 September 1984
Chester City 2 Bury 3 (Jakub 2, Madden)
Brown, Hill, Young, Ross, Bramhall, Dobson, White, Madden, Entwistle,
Jakub, James
Sub: Buckley (not used)
Attendance: 2,030

15 September 1984
Bury 4 (Entwistle, Madden 2, White) Colchester United 3
Brown, Hill, Young, Ross, Bramhall, Dobson, White, Madden, Entwistle,
Jakub, James
Sub: Pashley (not used)
Attendance: 2,145

18 September 1984
Bury 2 (Madden, Entwistle) Swindon Town 0
Brown, Hill, Young, Ross, Bramhall, Dobson, White, Madden, Entwistle,
Jakub, James
Sub: Pashley (not used)
Attendance: 2,769

22 September 1984
Exeter City 0 Bury 2 (Entwistle 2)
Brown, Hill, Pashley, Ross, Bramhall, Dobson, White, Madden, Entwistle,
Jakub, James
Sub: Buckley (for Pashley)
Attendance: 2,830

29 September 1984
Bury 0 Chesterfleld 0
Brown, Hill, Buckley, Ross, Bramhall, Dobson, White, Madden, Entwistle,
Jakub, James
Sub: Welsh (not used)
Attendance: 4,079

1 October 1984
Stockport County 2 Bury 0
Brown, Hill, Young, Ross, Bramhall, Dobson, White, Madden, Entwistle,
Jakub, James
Sub: Buckley (not used)
Attendance: 3,546

6 October 1984
Bury 2 (Hill, Entwistle) Southend United 0
Brown, Hill, Young, Ross, Bramhall, Dobson, White, Madden, Entwistle,

Jakub, James
Sub: Buckley (not used)
Attendance: 2,647

13 October 1984
Aldershot 0 Bury 1 (Entwistle)
Brown, Hill, Young, Ross, Bramhall, Dobson, White, Madden, Entwistle,
Jakub, James
Sub: Buckley (not used)
Attendance: 2,426

20 October 1984
Blackpool 0 Bury 0
Brown, Hill, Young, Ross, Bramhall, Dobson, White, Madden, Entwistle,
Jakub, James
Sub: Buckley (not used)
Attendance: 5,100

23 October 1984
Bury 2 (Madden, James) Hereford United 1
Brown, Hill, Young, Ross, Bramhall, Dobson, White, Madden, Entwistle,
Jakub, James
Sub: Buckley (not used)
Attendance: 4,147

27 October 1984
Bury 0 Scunthorpe United 1
Brown, Hill, Young, Ross, Bramhall, Dobson, White, Madden, Entwistle,
Jakub, James
Sub: Pashley (for Hill)
Attendance: 3,324

3 November 1984
Northampton Town 0 Bury 1 (Young)
Brown, Hill, Young, Ross, Bramhall, Pashley, White, Madden, Entwistle,
Jakub, James
Sub: Buckley (not used)
Attendance: 2,240

6 November 1984
Rochdale 1 Bury 1 (Madden)
Brown, Hill, Young, Ross, Bramhall, Pashley, White, Madden, Entwistle,
Jakub, James
Sub: Buckley (for White)
Attendance: 3,380

10 November 1984
Bury 2 (Entwistle, Jakub) Crewe Alexandra 2
Brown, Hill, Young, Ross, Bramhall, Pashley, White, Madden, Entwistle,
Jakub, James
Sub: Buckley (for Young)
Attendance: 3,459

24 November 1984
Mansfleld Town 0 Bury 2 (Madden, Entwistle)
Brown, Hill, Young, Ross, Bramhall, Dobson, White, Madden, Entwistle,
Jakub, James
Sub: Pashley (not used)
Attendance: 2,575

1 December 1984
Bury 3 (Bramhall, Entwistle, James) Torquay United 1
Brown, Hill, Young, Ross, Bramhall, Dobson, White, Madden, Entwistle,
Jakub, James
Sub: Buckley (not used)
Attendance: 2,682

15 December 1984
Wrexham 3 Bury 0
Brown, Hill, Young, Ross, Bramhall, Dobson, White, Madden, Cutler, Jakub,
James
Sub: Buckley (for Cutler)
Attendance: 1,450

19 December 1984
Peterborough United 1 Bury 4 (Hill, Madden 2, James)

Brown, Hill, Buckley, Ross, Bramhall, Dobson, White, Madden, Entwistle, Jakub, James
Sub: Pashley (not used)
Attendance: 3,836

26 December 1984
Bury 4 (Bramhall, Madden, Entwistle 2) Port Vale 0
Brown, Hill, Buckley, Ross, Bramhall, Dobson, White, Madden, Entwistle, Jakub, James
Sub: Pashley (for Hill)
Attendance: 4,664

29 December 1984
Bury 3 (Madden, Entwistle 2) Tranmere Rovers 0
Brown, Pashley, Buckley, Ross, Bramhall, Dobson, White, Madden, Entwistle, Jakub, James
Sub: Young (not used)
Attendance: 4,065

2 January 1985
Hartlepool United 0 Bury 1 (White)
Brown, Hill, Buckley, Ross, Bramhall, Dobson, White, Madden, Entwistle, Jakub, James
Sub: Pashley (not used)
Attendance: 3,199

12 January 1985
Halifax Town 4 Bury 1 (Madden)
Brown, Hill, Buckley, Ross, Bramhall, Dobson, White, Madden, Entwistle, Jakub, James
Sub: Pashley (not used)
Attendance: 2,854

26 January 1985
Colchester United 1 Bury 0
Brown, Hill, Buckley, Ross, Bramhall, Dobson, White, Madden, Entwistle, Jakub, James

Sub: Pashley (for Entwistle)
Attendance: 2,028

2 February 1985
Chesterfleld 0 Bury 1 (Entwistle)
Brown, Hill, Buckley, Ross, Bramhall, Dobson, White, Madden, Entwistle,
Jakub, James
Sub: Pashley (for Hill)
Attendance: 5,416

9 February 1985
Bury 2 (James, Cutler) Exeter City 2
Brown, Pashley, Buckley, Young, Bramhall, Dobson, White, Madden,
Entwistle, Jakub, James
Sub: Cutler (for Jakub)
Attendance: 2,726

23 February 1985
Bury 3 (Buckley, White, Madden) Northampton Town 1
Brown, Pashley, Buckley, Ross, Bramhall, Hill, White, Madden, Entwistle,
Young, James
Sub: Cutler (for Pashley)
Attendance: 2,938

2 March 1985
Scunthorpe United 2 Bury 2 (Madden, Entwistle)
Brown, Hill, Buckley, Ross, Bramhall, Dobson, White, Madden, Entwistle,
Young, James
Sub: Cutler (not used)
Attendance: 2,710

6 March 1985
Hereford United 5 Bury 3 (Ross, White, Young)
Brown, Hill, Buckley, Ross, Bramhall, Dobson, White, Madden, Entwistle,
Young, James
Sub: Pashley (for Hill)
Attendance: 4,600

9 March 1985
Bury 1 (Ross) Blackpool 0
Brown, Hill, Buckley, Ross, Bramhall, Dobson, White, Madden, Entwistle,
Young, James
Sub: Pashley (for White)
Attendance: 7,978

12 March 1985
Swindon Town 1 Bury 0
Brown, Hill, Buckley, Ross, Bramhall, Pashley, White, Madden, Entwistle,
Young, James
Sub: Cutler (for Buckley)
Attendance: 3,147

19 March 1985
Bury 1 (Hill) Darlington 0
Brown, Hill, Pashley, Ross, Bramhall, Dobson, White, Madden, Entwistle,
Young, James
Sub: Cutler (not used)
Attendance: 4,926

23 March 1985
Southend United 3 Bury 3 (Madden, Entwistle, Young)
Brown, Hill, Pashley, Ross, Bramhall, Dobson, White, Madden, Entwistle,
Young, James
Sub: Jakub (for Bramhall)
Attendance: 1,984

26 March 1985
Bury 2 (Madden 2) Stockport County 1
Brown, Hill, Pashley, Ross, Dobson, Young, White, Madden, Entwistle,
Jakub, James
Sub: Grimshaw (not used)
Attendance: 3,740

29 March 1985
Bury 2 (Madden, Entwistle) Rochdale 2

Brown, Hill, Pashley, Ross, Dobson, Young, White, Madden, Entwistle, Jakub, James
Sub: Kerr (for Madden)
Attendance: 4,559

6 April 1985
Port Vale 0 Bury 0
Brown, Hill, Pashley, Ross, Bramhall, Young, White, Madden, Entwistle, Jakub, James
Sub: Kerr (for White)
Attendance: 3,544

8 April 1985
Bury 1 (Entwistle) Hartlepool United 0
Brown, Hill, Pashley, Ross, Bramhall, Dobson, White, Madden, Entwistle, Jakub, James
Sub: Kerr (for Bramhall)
Attendance: 3,726

13 April 1985
Crewe Alexandra 1 Bury 0
Brown, Hill, Pashley, Ross, Dobson, Kerr, White, Madden, Entwistle, Jakub, James
Sub: Grimshaw (not used)
Attendance: 2,826

20 April 1985
Bury 0 Mansfleld Town 0
Brown, Hill, Pashley, Ross, Dobson, Young, White, Madden, Entwistle, Jakub, James
Sub: Kerr (for Young)
Attendance: 3,298

23 April 1985
Bury 4 (Pashley, Ross, White, James) Chester City 1
Brown, Hill, Pashley, Ross, Bramhall, Dobson, White, Madden, Entwistle, Jakub, James
Sub: Kerr (for Hill)
Attendance: 2,703

27 April 1985
Torquay United 0 Bury 2 (Bramhall, Madden)
Brown, Hill, Pashley, Ross, Bramhall, Dobson, White, Madden, Entwistle, Jakub, James
Sub: Kerr (not used)
Attendance 1,532

30 April 1985
Bury 2 (Madden, Entwistle) Aldershot 1
Brown, Hill, Pashley, Ross, Bramhall, Dobson, White, Madden, Entwistle, Jakub, James
Sub: Kerr (not used)
Attendance: 3,252

4 May 1985
Bury 2 (Ross, Madden) Wrexham 3
Brown, Hill, Pashley, Ross, Bramhall, Dobson, White, Madden, Entwistle, Jakub, James
Sub: Young (for Dobson)
Attendance: 4,155

6 May 1985
Tranmere Rovers 3 Bury 2 (Entwistle 2)
Brown, Hill, Pashley, Ross, Bramhall, Young, White, Madden, Entwistle, Jakub, James
Sub: Kerr (for Hill)
Attendance: 2,439

11 May 1985
Bury 1 (Ross) Peterborough United 1
Brown, Young, Pashley, Ross, Bramhall, Kerr, White, Madden, Entwistle, Jakub, James
Sub: Grimshaw (for James)
Attendance: 2,986

Canon League Division Four, 1984/85:
Bury appearances

Player	Appearances (Substitute)	Goals
David Brown	46	0
Andy Hill	43	3
Terry Pashley	23 (6)	1
Trevor Ross	45	6
John Bramhall	42	4
Martin Dobson	38	0
Winston White	46	5
Craig Madden	46	22
Wayne Entwistle	45	21
Joe Jakub	39 (1)	3
Leighton James	46	5
Kevin Young	30 (2)	4
Gary Buckley	14 (4)	1
Chris Cutler	1 (3)	1
John Kerr	2 (6)	0
Chris Grimshaw	(1)	0
Andy Welsh	(0)	0

Canon League Division Four, 1984/85: Final Table

	P	W	D	L	F	A	GD	Pts
Chesterfield (C)	46	26	13	7	64	35	+29	91
Blackpool (P)	46	24	14	8	73	39	+34	86
Darlington (P)	46	24	15	9	66	49	+17	85
Bury (P)	**46**	**24**	**12**	**10**	**76**	**50**	**+26**	**84**
Hereford United	46	22	11	13	65	47	+18	77
Tranmere Rovers	46	24	3	19	83	66	+17	75
Colchester United	46	20	14	12	87	65	+22	74
Swindon Town	46	21	9	16	62	58	+4	72
Scunthorpe United	46	19	14	13	83	62	+21	71
Crewe Alexandra	46	18	12	16	65	69	-4	66
Peterborough United	46	16	14	16	54	53	+1	62
Port Vale	46	14	18	14	61	59	+2	60
Aldershot	46	17	8	21	56	63	-7	59
Mansfield Town	46	13	18	15	41	38	+3	57
Wrexham	46	15	9	22	67	70	-3	54
Chester City	46	15	9	22	60	72	-12	54
Rochdale	46	13	14	19	55	69	-14	53
Exeter City	46	13	14	19	57	79	-22	53
Hartlepool United	46	14	10	22	54	67	-13	52
Southend United	46	13	11	22	58	83	-25	50
Halifax Town*	46	15	5	26	42	69	-27	50
Stockport County*	46	13	8	25	58	79	-21	47
Northampton Town*	46	14	5	27	53	74	-21	47
Torquay United*	46	9	14	23	38	63	-25	41

Halifax Town, Stockport County, Northampton Town and Torquay United all had to apply for re-election to the Football League. All were successful in their bids.

Acknowledgements

If Bury hadn't used just fifteen players to get promoted from Division Four in the 1984/85 season, there wouldn't be a story to tell. So thanks are due to David Brown, Andy Hill, Terry Pashley, Trevor Ross, John Bramhall, Martin Dobson, Winston White, Craig Madden, Wayne Entwistle, Joe Jakub, Leighton James, Kevin Young, Gary Buckley and Chris Cutler not only for getting the job done, but for kindly taking the time to talk to me about the season in such depth. I hope, too, that John Kerr's family are aware of the important role he played in the achievement.

It wasn't always easy to find these former footballers, so thanks to Gordon Sorfleet, Veronica Simpson, Scott Hill, Chris Joslin, James Clarke, Chris Long, Jemma James, Matthew Clarke, Rob Leach and Neil Fissler for help in tracking them down.

I spoke to an awful lot of people about their memories of British football's worst year. I haven't been able to include every conversation but thank you again for taking the time to speak to me if you did. I've tried to refer to other authors' works using their names and the title of what they've written if I've quoted them.

If the book was just made up of text it would double as a very handy doorstop. Pictures have helped the project come to life and for those I'm indebted to Peter Cullen, John Labrow and Ian McPherson for providing them and Chris Tofalos, Ian Lunn, Simon Egan, Bob Lilliman, Vince Taylor and Johnny Meynell for taking them.

Thanks are also due to those who've been there with keen eyes for detail and to offer encouragement: to Carol Lowe for helping me through the entire process; to Graham Bentley and Collette Dickson for transcribing interviews; to Jamie Hoyle for creating the website;

to Robin Maryon at Sundog for the cover design; to Dave Yates for providing insight into publishing; to Mike Brooks, Alan Horrocks and Steve Welch for their frequent reviews; to Dave Parker and Nigel Bentley for proof-reading.

Lastly, extra special thanks to Craig Clarkson for making me want to write something about the club in the first place and for guiding me throughout the process of getting this down on paper, and Phil Young for believing in the project to the extent that he has. Thanks, lads.